9/30/99

"... *Investing in Latin America* is a much needed book in an increasingly important, and still largely unknown market in global finance. It provides an in-depth review of the major markets and instruments... It's **A SELF-CONTAINED PRIMER ABOUT INVESTING IN LATIN AMERICA THE RIGHT WAY. THIS BOOK WILL BE THE STANDARD REFERENCE AND HELPFUL COMPANION TO CHECK ON WHAT THE EXPERTS ARE DOING WITH OUR MONEY.**"

PAULO VIEIRA DA CUNHA
Senior Vice President & Senior Latin American Economist
Lehman Brothers Inc.

Investing In
Latin
America

Also available from
BLOOMBERG PRESS

Investing in REITs:
Real Estate Investment Trusts
by Ralph L. Block

Investing With Your Values:
Making Money and Making a Difference
by Hal Brill, Jack A. Brill, and Cliff Feigenbaum

The Latino Guide to Personal Money Management
by Laura Castañeda and Laura Castellanos

The Winning Portfolio:
Choosing Your 10 Best Mutual Funds
by Paul B. Farrell, Ph.D., J.D.

Investing in Small-Cap Stocks
by Christopher Graja and Elizabeth Ungar, Ph.D.

Investing in Hedge Funds:
Strategies for the New Marketplace
by Joseph G. Nicholas

The New Commonsense Guide to Mutual Funds
by Mary Rowland

Investing in IPOs
New Paths to Profit with Initial Public Offerings
by Tom Taulli

BLOOMBERG PERSONAL BOOKSHELF

Investing In
Latin
America

Best Stocks ◆ Best Funds

MICHAEL MOLINSKI

BLOOMBERG PRESS

PRINCETON

Books are available for bulk purchases at special discounts. Special editions or book excerpts can also be created to specifications. For information, please write: Special Markets Department, Bloomberg Press.

This publication contains the author's opinions and is designed to provide accurate and authoritative information. It is sold with the understanding that the author, publisher, and Bloomberg L.P. are not engaged in rendering legal, accounting, investment-planning, or other professional advice. The reader should seek the services of a qualified professional for such advice; the author, publisher, and Bloomberg L.P. cannot be held responsible for any loss incurred as a result of specific investments or planning decisions made by the reader.

First edition published 1999
1 3 5 7 9 10 8 6 4 2

Molinski, Michael, 1963—
        Investing in Latin America / Michael Molinski.
              p.   cm. - -   (Bloomberg personal bookshelf)
        ISBN 1-57660-065-3
        1. Investments–Latin America. 2. Investments, American–Latin America.   I. Title.   II. Series
        HG5160.5.A5M64   1999
        332.67'3'098–dc21   99-17934
                                                                      CIP

Acquired and edited by Jared Kieling
Book design by Don Morris Design

For Nicholas and Nathan

ACKNOWLEDGMENTS

IT WOULD BE IMPOSSIBLE to thank everyone whose advice, expertise, and knowledge I used in putting this book together. Nonetheless, I want to try to acknowledge those who were either particularly helpful in my efforts to collect and analyze data or whose expertise and resources I relied upon heavily. First and foremost, I want to thank Bloomberg Press for giving me the opportunity to write this book, and my editor, Jared Kieling, for his advice, expertise, and, most of all, his patience. I also want to thank Mike Bloomberg, who had the foresight to recognize Latin America's potential several years ago and the wisdom not to pull back when the economies and the market went sour. The Bloomberg Terminal was a crucial tool in conducting the research for this book.

I can't express enough thanks to the staff of Bloomberg News, especially Matt Winkler, who gave me the time and the latitude to write this book, and the gang at Bloomberg News in Latin America, whose articles were an essential resource. Some of you might recognize a quote or a tidbit of information in this book that I pulled from one of your stories. I wish I could have mentioned the reporter's name in each case, but for practical reasons we decided to just say "Bloomberg News." Nonetheless, I do want to mention five people who had a more direct hand in helping me gather information and in fact-checking for accuracy: Eduardo García in Mexico City; Mike Smith in Santiago, Chile; Peter Wilson in Caracas, Venezuela; Richard Jarvie in Buenos Aires; and Tim Wilkins in New York.

A special thanks is also due to Columbia University and the Columbia School of Business, whose library, faculty, and students were invaluable resources. The Business School faculty whose research and input I used most were Douglas Lindgren, Michael Pettis, Michael Adler, David Beim, Ann Harrison, Matthew Eichner, and Gur Huberman.

I also want to thank the many asset managers, company analysts, economists, and others whose expertise on investments, on emerging markets and on Latin America I used throughout this book, especially: Paul Rogers and the rest of the Latin America staff at Scudder Kemper Investments; James Barrineau, formerly at Salomon Smith Barney and now at Alliance Capital; the public relations staff and research department at Salomon Smith Barney; Burton Malkiel of Princeton University; Eduardo Cabrera and the Latin America research team at Merrill Lynch; John Welch at Paribas Securities; the Latin America credit ratings staffs at Standard & Poor's and Moody's Investor Services; Luiz Carvalho at Morgan Stanley Dean Witter and the research staff at Morgan Stanley Capital International; Ian Wilson at Micropal; Thomas Herzfeld of Herzfeld Funds; Robert Gordon of 21st Century Securities; the staff at the Council of the Americas in New York; Pedro-Pablo Kuczinsky of the Latin America Enterprise Fund; Bob Willens of Lehman Bros. and the Latin American research team at Lehman Bros.; Shaun Roache and Matthew Merritt of ING Barings; Tulio Vera of ABN Amro; Arturo Tapia of Wall Street Securities in Panama; Sonia Olinto of CLSA; and Joe MacHatton of Banque Nationale de Paris.

The companies that I profiled in this book also deserve thanks. Most of them were extremely helpful in putting me in touch with top executives and providing me with important company information. If some of the information is vague or out of date, I apologize, but let me know if it is, so I can change it if this book has a second edition.

Thank you also to the rest of those at Bloomberg Press who helped make this book possible: Bill Inman, Barbara Diez, Melissa Hafner, Rameen Soltani, John Crutcher, Lisa Goetz, Priscilla Treadwell, Christina Palumbo, Michelle Roth, Maris Williams, Laurie Lohne, Ana Castañeda, and Christopher Floersch.

And finally, thank you to my parents, Ralph and Eileen Molinski, who are responsible for instilling in me the value of a good education and introducing me to Latin America on my first trip across the border to Puerto Peñasco, Mexico, when I was eight years old.

INTRODUCTION

OU'VE PROBABLY HEARD about the tremendous profits that some people have been getting by investing in Latin America. For example, the major stock indices of Brazil, Chile, and Mexico posted more than double the average annual returns of the U.S. stock market between 1987 and 1997. What you may not have heard is that investing overseas can not only bring you higher returns but can actually reduce the overall risk of your investment portfolio.

Among the Americans who have bought huge stakes in Latin America are billionaire hedge fund manager George Soros and the Walton family, owners of Wal-Mart. Companhia Vale do Rio Doce might not ring a bell, but the Brazilian company is the world's largest exporter of iron ore and recently uncovered some of the biggest gold mines outside South Africa. Soros owns 7 percent of it. If you've visited Mexico

City or Acapulco, you might recognize the name of Mexico's largest retail chain, Cifra SA. Wal-Mart owns a majority stake in it.

What they and thousands of others who own shares in Latin American companies are betting on is economic growth. Latin America is poised to be the fastest-growing region in the world over the next decade. Latin American stocks over the past five years have easily outperformed the other two major emerging markets, Asia and Eastern Europe. The turmoil in Asia and Russia in 1997 and 1998, which for a while panicked investors into pulling money out of Latin America, too, has since boosted Latin America's image and led smart investors to allocate more of their investments there, not less. From Mexico to Argentina, it's not the same region it was ten years ago. Companies are more transparent. Governments are more democratic. Markets are more efficient. Economies are more open. In short, the ride isn't as bumpy as it used to be.

That's not to say that Latin America is without its risks. In 1995, all seven of the major Latin American stock markets plunged by an average of 15 percent, and during its worst 30-day period in 1998 (August 10 to September 10), Latin American stocks dropped an astounding 38.5 percent, according to the Morgan Stanley Latin American index—a benchmark used by investors to measure the performance of the region's stocks. Investing in Latin America is not for the weak of heart, and it's not for those who are in it to make a quick buck and leave. However, if you're looking to diversify, if you're in it for the long run, and if you can weather an occasional downturn, Latin America is for you, and so is this book.

If you've ever traveled through Latin America, you might have taken note that the cuisine differs from country to country. Most Bolivians have never heard of the Brazilian dish *moqueca,* most Chileans would be surprised to discover that *boda* is not a wedding but a Nicaraguan vegetable stew, and you'd be hard-pressed to find an *enchilada* in Bogota or an *arepa* in Buenos Aires. Yet, across all their diversity there are two dishes that are staples of any Latin American diet—rice and beans. From the fanciest feast to the simplest fare of a backwoods eating hole, *arroz con frijoles* (or *arroz com feijão* in Portuguese) is served virtually everywhere from the Río Grande to Tierra del Fuego.

Investing in Latin America is kind of like eating there. There are differences from country to country in the way economies are run, the way companies are managed, and the way stock markets perform. However, there are also some similarities—the rice and beans—that are consistent across borders and that differentiate Latin America from the other regions of the world. Among them are high price volatility, strong growth potential, low correlation of price movements with developed-country stocks, and a tendency for the region's stock markets to move together during times of crisis. In this book, you'll learn about both the familiarities and the surprises that await anyone investing in Latin American countries.

This book is not intended to present complex analytical tools for weighing investment decisions; nor is it meant to give you everything you need to know about Latin America and its publicly traded companies. What it will do is give you the basics of buying Latin American stocks and mutual funds, and show you how to build them into a portfolio that suits your individual finances and investment goals. It will also describe thirty-five companies in the region and tell you what you most need to know about the countries themselves—things like which governments place restrictions on selling stocks, and which nations have the best growth prospects. Even if you plan to buy only mutual funds, knowing something about the individual companies the funds invest in is important, and these thirty-five companies profiled in Part Two of this book represent most of the holdings of major Latin American mutual funds. The appendix gives you a list of the most actively traded Latin American companies, complete with phone numbers of their depository institutions where you can call to get financial reports, and a list of resources where you can find current information on

Latin America and Latin American companies.

One thing to know about investing in Latin America is that it's not just for the guys with deep pockets, nor is it just for experts. Even an investor with as little as $5,000 in his portfolio should begin to invest some of it overseas. By using the tools in this book and keeping an eye on current events, small investors can gain an advantage over big, institutional investors who often don't have the time needed to research Latin American companies and who must follow strict rules about where they can put their assets and how much they can concentrate in one holding.

Unlike most books about investing, this is written by a financial journalist rather than a finance professor, portfolio manager, or investment banker. As a result, you'll find a balanced assessment of leading strategies and an easy-to-follow approach to investing based on dozens of interviews that I conducted with investment experts and the top managers of the companies profiled here. As a journalist, I avoid buying stocks in companies that I write about, but you can benefit from the knowledge I've gathered.

WHY NOT STICK TO U.S. STOCKS?

RESEARCH HAS PROVEN that investing a portion of your portfolio in foreign stocks reduces the overall risk of the portfolio, even if the individual foreign stocks you buy are riskier than the domestic stocks you own. Up to a point, the more you invest overseas, the lower your overall risk becomes. The reason is that owning foreign stocks removes you somewhat from the risk of a downturn in the U.S. stock market. Buying even one Latin American stock can lower the risk of a domestic portfolio.

Therefore, if you've avoided emerging markets until now because they're too risky, then that's the wrong reason. In fact, the best way to truly diversify an investment portfolio internationally is to put between 3 and 20 percent of it into emerging markets stocks. Putting that portion of your holdings into European or Japanese stocks doesn't provide a high level of risk reduction because their stock markets are too closely correlated with those of the United States. Why leave all your money in the United States—or in Europe—

when by allocating a portion to Latin America you can get higher returns and lower overall volatility?

This book will show you how to minimize the risk of big losses without giving up returns.

WHY LATIN AMERICA?

THE ATTRACTION OF Latin America these days can be summarized in four points: high returns, cheap stocks, lower risk relative to a decade ago, and good economic growth prospects. We'll look at each of these points in detail. For now, suffice it to say that Latin American companies have among the world's highest rates of return on capital. Their price-to-earnings ratios and price-to-book values are lower than in most other regions, meaning the stocks are bargains relative to the value of the companies. The price volatility of Latin American equities has been declining over time, and sovereign country ratings, a measure of a nation's fiscal stability and creditworthiness, have been climbing. Finally, and most importantly, economic growth is increasing and is expected to speed up.

STEP BY STEP

CHAPTER ONE TAKES a deeper look at these Latin American growth prospects and shows you some companies that have already made big strides. Chapter One also compares Latin America's economic expansion to the outlook for Asia, and shows you why the 1997–98 Asian financial crisis has been a blessing for investments in Latin America. Why spend so much time talking about future economic growth? Because over time, economic growth is the only thing that will drive earnings growth; and earnings growth, over time, is the most important factor in stock prices. A company can beef up its books in the short run by cutting costs or by any of several measures that allow it to steal market share from competitors, but if the economy isn't advancing, a company's earnings can rise only up to a point. The trick is to pick a company whose market share is growing in a country whose economy is growing.

Chapters Two and Three explain the two main vehicles for putting money to work in Latin

America—mutual funds and American Depository Receipts. Latin American mutual funds are similar to U.S. mutual funds. They are managed by professionals whose aim is to seek the best returns possible, given a certain level of risk. Some funds are much riskier than others. A fund that invests all of its assets in Mexico in companies that were picked for their value, for example, is sure to be a more volatile holding than a fund that spreads its assets over both value and growth companies and is diversified throughout Latin America. Funds can invest directly on Latin American stock exchanges, or they can buy American Depository Receipts. ADRs are stocks in foreign companies that are traded in the United States. Some of them are listed directly on the New York Stock Exchange, while others are traded over the counter. The popularity of Latin American ADRs has soared so fast that they may soon surpass European shares as the most heavily traded foreign equities on the New York Stock Exchange. For the seven months ending July 31, 1998, $79 billion worth of Latin American ADRs were traded in New York, just shy of the $82.5 billion in European

ADRs and far greater than the next highest region, Asia, at $8.4 billion.

Chapter Four presents some investment strategies from people who manage billions of dollars in funds and who know Latin America. It will tell you how to best divide your portfolio between mutual funds and ADRs. Mutual funds have the advantage of being less risky than individual stocks, and because these funds can buy stocks directly on local stock markets, they have access to hundreds of stocks that individual U.S. and European investors can't trade. Latin America mutual funds, however, carry administrative costs that average about 2 percent of the fund's value, and their returns are often far below those of specific individual stocks. The advantages of ADRs are most evident when you can afford to buy at least three or four, thus reducing the risk of any one company's doing poorly. I recommend—and I'll show you why—that you put as much as 20 percent of your total portfolio in Latin America, depending on your individual finances and investment goals.

Chapter Five discusses other types of Latin

American investments—Brady Bonds, Eurobonds, other fixed-income instruments, and derivatives. It also looks at investments in countries that aren't yet considered safe by most investors, from reasonably stable ones such as Panama to the ultra-risky, like Cuba. These are recommended only for more sophisticated investors, and are not as readily available to small investors. If you're a beginner, you might want to skip this chapter.

MAKING YOUR PICKS

THE SECOND HALF of the book gets you started on what to buy. There are only some 217 Latin American companies that sell ADRs, and only 84 of them are listed on U.S. exchanges, so the choices for U.S. investors are limited. I've tried to narrow those choices even more by picking 35 companies that, according to a number of experts, are good long-term stock picks. But there are plenty of bargains among the other 133 ADRs. The Resources section in the appendix will help you look up those companies, too.

HOW CAN I GET STARTED?

READ THIS BOOK. Develop a short list of mutual funds and Latin American stocks you might want to buy. Then, check the business section of your local paper or call your broker if the securities aren't listed, and note the current share prices. Compare them to its 52-week highs and lows. Then follow the movements of each price for a few weeks. If it's an ADR you're looking at, gather current news about the company. The list of resources in the back of this book will help. Finally, find some news about the country the company is based in, watching for signs of something that might either drag the entire stock market down or give it a boost, such as an upcoming election, a new corporate tax law, or a jump in interest rates. When you're ready to invest, buy for the long term, three to ten years. If your newly acquired stock falls, don't panic and sell. If the company you picked is a strong one, the share price will rebound once circumstances change.

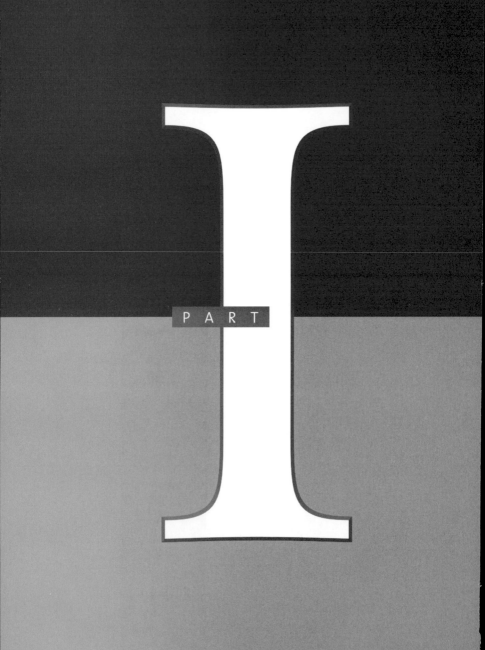

PART

I

SINCE YOU'RE READING this book, you've probably already decided there's at least a chance you'll invest in Latin America. The first half of this book will give you some good reasons to do so, tempered with important cautions. This groundwork is vital. Knowing why you invest in a region, a country, or a specific company will help you in the long run as you formulate your portfolio and manage it.

◆ Recognizing the names of the "best companies" isn't enough to lead you to sound investment decisions, though, especially in a region as complex and changeable as Latin America. So, Part One will give you some key strategies used by emerging markets experts and will also teach you the mechanics of investing there, from how to buy an ADR or a Brady Bond to how to report the purchase on your taxes. ◆ These first five chapters set you up for Part Two, which gets you started on picking the actual stocks.

CHAPTER

1

THE
Background
YOU NEED

THIS BOOK PRESENTS advice from some of the best investment minds in the world and some of the foremost experts on Latin America. Often their investment philosophies differ. One may recommend that investors focus on specific companies, while another will suggest choosing investments from a particular country, and still another may prefer to concentrate on regions of the world. Some experts will tell you to put all your money into mutual funds, although others say investing in individual stocks is better. You've probably already heard much of this conflicting advice. You may have read somewhere that investing in one emerging market is the same as investing in another, whether it be Asia, Africa, or Latin America. You may have heard from some people that the 1997–98 Asia crisis was bad for Latin America, or that Asia is a better investment than Latin America now because stock prices have fallen and shares are cheap.

This chapter gives the background you need in order to weigh the risks and rewards of having a portion of your investments in Latin America. It expands on the introduction with information about where Latin America has been and where it is going. It will quote experts on why they invest in the region. Fidelity's Peter Lynch, the world's most successful fund manager, likes to remind investors that it's important to know exactly why you buy a particular stock or mutual fund. It's no less important that you be able to define why you invest in a particular region or country.

This first chapter will also give you examples of Latin American corporations that are benefiting from their countries' economic situation and explore their opportunities for global expansion. Later, when you read from one expert that betting on a country is the best method, and from another that concentrating on a particular sector or company is preferable, you'll be equipped to make your own decision. You'll probably find that combining their strategies, tempered with your own common sense, is the best method.

THE EVIDENCE

UNTIL 1994 LATIN AMERICA was considered exceptionally risky by most fund managers, not to mention individual U.S. investors. The debt crisis of 1982, followed by periods of hyperinflation and debt moratoriums in the late 1980s, scared away all but the strong-hearted. But spectacular returns in 1993 and the first half of 1994 caused investors to take a second look: what they saw was a region that was on an irreversible path toward free-market economies, democracy, and widespread acceptance of foreign investment. Gone are the days when foreign companies were nationalized and armies took control of the central bank.

Latin America stock prices, as measured by the widely watched Morgan Stanley Latin America Equity index, increased on average 27.8 percent a year from 1987 to 1997. That compares to average annual increases of 17.7 percent by the Standard and Poor's 500 index. If on December 31, 1987, you had invested $1,000 in the stocks that comprise those indices and kept it there, your Latin American investments would have been worth $10,647 on December 31, 1997, whereas your U.S. investments would have been worth $2,928. The Morgan Stanley index also beat the S&P 500 in two of the five years between 1992 and 1997, including 1993, when it outperformed the S&P by 40 percent.

What's more, Latin America easily outperformed the other two major emerging markets, Asia and Eastern Europe. Between 1992 and 1997, Latin American stocks doubled in price on average, while Asian stocks declined about 25 percent. Eastern European stocks, which have only been tracked since September 1996, declined 11 percent.

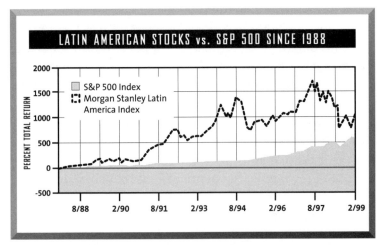

LATIN AMERICAN STOCKS vs. S&P 500 SINCE 1988

S&P 500 Index
Morgan Stanley Latin America Index

PERCENT TOTAL RETURN

8/88   2/90   8/91   2/93   8/94   2/96   8/97   2/99

WHY SMALL INVESTORS CAN BEAT THE BIG GUYS

THE BENEFITS OF diversifying into emerging markets haven't been lost on big institutional investors. Most have portions of their portfolios invested in Latin America or other emerging markets. However, most institutional investors lump all "emerging markets" companies together with the rest of the "high-risk" section of their portfolios. Those who do are overlooking the fact that some Latin American stocks, such as Cemex in Mexico or Telebrás in Brazil, are less risky than many U.S. stocks, based on historical price volatility.

Managers of big mutual funds or pension funds often are given a set percentage of their assets to allocate to a specific region. Thus, they can't shift money around when prospects improve in any area. Likewise, if a region is going downhill—Asia in 1997, for example—fund managers still leave significant percentages of their portfolios invested there, dragging down their overall returns.

What's more, most Latin American companies would be classified in the United States as *small-cap* stocks, which basically means that the market value of their common shares is less than $1 billion. Most institutional investors don't have the time or the money to spend researching companies that small, so they stay clear of them. For individuals, that creates an opportunity to do your own research and discover bargains.

Another advantage small investors have in Latin America is that it is easier for an individual to buy or sell shares than it is for an institutional investor, who is buying or selling a much larger stake. Selling large numbers of shares of a company in any Latin American country can be tricky. The volume of trading is often so light that big investors can't find buyers fast enough when they decide they want to sell down their positions. This often forces them to hold onto the shares for longer than they would have liked, and to settle for lower prices. This gives you, the small investor, an advantage, because you have so many fewer shares to sell than does a company like J.P. Morgan or an investor like George Soros, and finding buyers is easier.

Despite these attractions, 90 percent of U.S. investment dollars stays in the United States. It's what the experts call "home country bias," and what you and I know as "fear of the unknown."

"There is something about human nature that leads us to invest in the familiar," says Gur Huberman, a finance professor at Columbia University, who recently completed a study on home country bias.

Huberman points to U.S. stock ownership statistics. The median value of equities held by U.S. individuals is $13,500 ($21,300 for the segment who make between $50,000 and $100,000 a year). Yet, the median (most common) number of stocks owned by U.S. individuals is just two. So much for a diversified portfolio! What's more, about 37 percent of U.S. 401(k) funds are invested in the fund holders' companies, in spite of overwhelming evidence that such concentration is a terrible investment strategy.

REASONS TO INVEST

LET'S EXPAND ON the four principal reasons to invest in Latin America:

1 Returns. Returns. Returns. The impressive profits that U.S. investors have achieved in Latin American stocks are partly a result of the high returns on invested capital that Latin American companies have been able to get.

2 Economic growth rates in Latin America are already double those of the United States and Europe, while in Asia growth rates are actually going down. The 1998 emerging markets crisis was a temporary setback to Latin America's pattern of increasing long-term growth rates. As Latin American countries expand their economies, companies will continue to experience sharp increases in earnings.

3 Latin American stocks are cheap. Based on almost any method of measurement, it's hard to top the bargains. The following table shows a comparison of the average *price-to-book values* (P/BV) and *price-to-earnings ratios* (P/E) of Latin American, emerging market, and U.S. stocks as of December 31, 1998. P/BV is a company's market capitalization divided by the value of its total assets, net of liabilities. P/E is the price of a stock divided by the company's annual earnings per share.

LATIN AMERICA, EMERGING MARKETS, & U.S. STOCKS

REGION	PRICE-TO-EARNINGS (P/E)	PRICE-TO-BOOK VALUE (P/BV)
Latin America (EMF)	10.58	0.87
Emerging Markets (EMF)	17.70	1.21
S&P 500	32.27	5.86

4 The riskiness of Latin America (expressed by the magnitude of the standard deviation of stock prices there) has been getting gradually lower since the early 1990s and is expected to continue declining. It is no longer the white-knuckle ride it once was. Democracy, modern economic structures, and foreign investment are now so widely embraced by the people of Latin America that even the unlikely event of a coup would probably not significantly alter economic policy in the seven major countries. With the possible exception of Venezuela, big Latin American countries are financially well managed. And with a new president in 1999, perhaps Venezuela, too, will improve. Mexico recovered quickly from its 1994 crisis. In spite of all the pressure put on Brazil in 1998 by the Asian and Russian crises, Brazil managed to avoid what critics feared would be a calamitous devaluation and a return to hyper-inflation. Also, the risk of an investment asset being frozen or even seized by a government is virtually nonexistent in Latin America, while that can happen—and has happened—in other fast-growing places like China and Russia. Risk is also lessened by Latin America's interdependence on the United States in trade and politics. Latin America is a huge market for U.S. goods and services, so big that the United States could not afford to let any major Latin American country founder. While the United States consistently posts large trade deficits with Asia, the U.S. actually had a $3.9 billion trade surplus with Brazil in 1996. U.S. exports to South America are growing twice as fast as those to any other area, and by 2010 U.S. exports to Latin America and Canada are expected to be greater than those to Europe and Japan combined.

We'll get back to three of those reasons—high returns, cheap stocks, and lower risk—in later chapters. The remainder of this one will discuss what I believe to be the most important Latin American investment rationale: sharp economic growth.

GROWTH

TO GET A CLEARER picture of Latin America's prospects, let's compare the region to Asia. For years, Asia was a dar-ling of investors—both those playing the Asian stock markets and those investing directly by setting up facto-ries, banks, and condominiums. What attracted all of them to Asia was its astoundingly high growth rates. The four tigers—South Korea, Singapore, Hong Kong, and Taiwan—posted average growth rates of 20 to 30 percent during the 1970s and 1980s; Indonesia, Malaysia, and the Philippines eventually caught up, too. Many investors believed that Asian countries had found a formula that allowed them to avoid the boom-and-bust cycles that Western economies habitually pass through. The longer the double-digit growth continued, the more investors wanted in.

Meanwhile, Latin American countries lagged behind, with growth rates that averaged between 0 and 10 percent. Often the explanation offered for the difference between the two regions was that Asians work harder, and Latin Americans are lazy. Visions of Asians doing morning calisthenics at auto plants before starting work contrasted with pictures of Latin Americans taking afternoon *siestas* before ambling back to their posts.

Then came 1997. Foreign investors lost billions as one Asian country after another skidded into financial crisis. When the dust settled, what investors saw was a region shattered by poor economic planning, overly confident investors, and inefficient industries. The debacle was bigger by far than the Mexican peso crisis of 1994–95, and in many ways worse than even the foreign debt crisis that rocked Latin America in 1982. However, just months before the Asia bubble burst, even the usually cautious International Monetary Fund was praising the economic fundamentals of the region.

If they had looked more closely, they would have seen that although these countries had laudably high domestic savings rates, piles of foreign reserves, and little or no budget deficits, they had carelessly allowed investment to run amok. The total amount of investment dollars being plunged into Thailand, Malaysia, Indonesia, and other Asian countries—from both foreign and domestic sources—was so high that no amount of savings could finance it. As a result, companies borrowed billions in local currencies from banks, who turned around and borrowed billions of dollars on world markets. These investments were not only creating overcapacity—factories sitting idle without orders, vacant office buildings, etc.—but they weren't earning steady returns. Those factories that were producing were not doing so at high operating margins.

Only after the markets imploded did those involved take a deeper look. What they found was that even Korea, arguably the second most robust country in Asia, was showing returns on investment that were about half of those in some Latin American countries, such as Brazil. Capital had been flowing into Asia at such high rates that people thought the bonanza would never stop, and they got careless.

In August 1998 the Russian government allowed the ruble to devalue and at the same time defaulted on some of its foreign and local debt. Coming as it did on the heels of the Asia crisis, the pressure was more than many foreign investors could bear. People started pulling their money out of all emerging markets, regardless of how strong the economies were, and putting it in safer investments such as U.S. Treasury bills. The first victims were the countries whose currencies were deemed the most overvalued, and thus the most susceptible to a devaluation: Brazil and Venezuela. More than $40 billion was pulled out of Brazil in a two-month period between mid-August and mid-October.

That Brazil's economy didn't collapse and the government went on a massive budget-cutting campaign is a testament to the government's desire to maintain economic stability at almost any cost. It also says a lot about how important stability is to the Brazilian people, who re-elected President Fernando Henrique Cardoso in the midst of the crisis, knowing that it meant they would probably have to endure a recession. During the crisis, stock prices tumbled, not just in Brazil but across Latin America. It's a good lesson for investors: that stock prices can plummet even though the economic fundamentals of a country or a company might be strong. Investor panic is something that is hard to predict and even harder to stop once it gets rolling. In Brazil's case, what finally stopped the panic was a joint effort by the Brazilian government, which cut fiscal spending and increased tax revenue, and by foreign governments and multinational institutions, who chipped in with a $41 billion rescue loan package. Eventually, defending the *real* became too costly, and Brazil devalued the currency in early 1999. At the time this book went to press, it was too early to predict the level at which the *real* would settle and how the devaluation would affect the economy and the stock market. Still the devaluation did remove what had been the single biggest worry of foreign investors for more than a year.

Looking forward, the 1998 crisis has not damaged Latin America's potential. On the contrary, it might have strengthened it, and it created opportunities for investors who are brave enough to buy when prices were low.

"These crises in the end prove healthy," says John Welch, chief Latin America economist at the French bank, Paribas. "It ensures that the governments don't go backward on reforms."

Adds Thomas Trebat, head of emerging markets research at CitiGroup's Salomon Smith Barney, "The time to go into volatile markets is when most people don't want to look at them."

PINCHING PENNIES

WHEN YOU'RE ACCUSTOMED to pinching pennies, you make every penny count. That's what's happening now in Latin America. Foreign money has flowed into Latin America in recent years—about $12 billion in net foreign direct and indirect investment a year during the 1990s. And Latin American companies have borrowed billions more on world debt markets. In most cases, that money is put to good use. Companies that had fallen more than a decade behind in technology have been busy catching up.

Consider Brazil's Pão de Açúcar supermarket chain. The company was in bankruptcy in 1991 and was forced to shutter two-thirds of its stores, but with the help of some outside capital, chairman Abílio Diniz spent heavily on computers that keep track of inventory and cash flows. Now the company is one of the hottest growth stories in the region. Pão de Açúcar is opening new stores and buying out smaller chains, and even tough foreign competitors like Carrefour of France and Wal-Mart of the United States haven't been able to steal market share.

"All of our investments have allowed us to maintain lower prices while at the same time providing more variety to our customers," Ricardo Florens, chief operations officer of the supermarket chain, told me in an interview. "It prepares us for the growth of Pão de Açúcar."

In many cases, the inflows of foreign investment brought transfers of new technology that led to substantial improvements in companies' performance. Another Brazilian company, Cemig, is a good example. New minority owners Southern Electric and AES Corp. brought in new money and new operational talent that helped the regional electric utility improve its technology and its operations. In just one year after the two U.S. companies bought a 33 percent voting stake in Cemig, the company boosted its return on capital to 15 percent from 10 percent, brought down the amount of energy that it loses, and signed up 226,000 new customers—a company record.

REDUCING DEBT, INCREASING PRODUCTIVITY

IN MEXICO, COMPANIES with high foreign debt loads were caught in a precarious situation during the 1994–95 peso crisis, but because their foreign bank loans and international bond issues were invested smartly and companies kept their cost ratios to a minimum, most big Mexican concerns have returned to their pre-crisis profitability levels.

Vitro is one such survivor. The Mexican glassmaker was caught with massive dollar debt when the peso was devalued, and it had just sold its unprofitable Anchor glass subsidiary in the United States, so it had virtually no dollar revenue to pay back the debt. Through a combination of cost-cutting, strategic refinancing, and growth in Mexican consumption, the company was able to bring things around by reducing its total debt load—especially its worrisome short-term debt, and cutting its cost of debt to a manageable 10.9 percent in 1998.

For anyone who has been to São Paulo on a weekday or to Lima, Caracas, Monterrey, or any of a number of industrialized Latin American cities, it's obvious that the only people napping in hammocks are tourists.

Look at Argentina. The country's industrial production index hit an all-time high of 205.9 in May 1998, and the labor activity rate has increased from 40.8 percent in 1994 to 42.6 percent in May 1998. What that means for companies is that they are producing more per employee. Telecom Argentina, for example, flush with cash from foreign owners Stet of Italy and France Telecom, has invested heavily in expanding its number of lines, and the productivity of the company's average employee has shot up dramatically. In the fourth quarter of 1998, Telecom Argentina boosted its number of lines by 8.5 percent while at the same time cutting the number of employees by 4 percent. The average number of phone lines per worker has soared from less than 100 a decade ago to more than 300 now.

INCREASED TRADE

WHEN LATIN AMERICA began opening its markets to free trade in the early 1990s, critics predicted Latin America could never compete with the rest of the world. Now, it is the rest of the world that is fearing competition from Latin America. The products coming out of Latin America these days are sleek, sophisticated, and of high quality. However, prices can remain low since labor costs reflect an average annual per capita income of only $1,000 to $3,400 in the seven largest countries.

As free trade increases under the proposed Free Trade Zone of the Americas, so will Latin America's competitiveness. Even if the United States or other countries balk on commitments to free trade, Latin America is unlikely to be deterred. Already, the Mercosur common market (a grouping of South American countries with reduced tariff barriers among each other and common external tariffs for most products) is adding countries to its membership. If the United States won't buy Chilean steel, Argentina will.

One company that has benefited from increased trade is Cemex, the world's third largest cement company. Based in Mexico, Cemex has used the North American Free Trade Agreement (NAFTA) to boost commerce with the United States, which now accounts for 11 percent of the company's revenue. Mexican operations now account for only 43 percent of total revenue, with Spain, Venezuela, and other countries making up the rest. Indeed, Mexico's free-trade agreements with other Latin American countries have helped the country's expansion, and construction activity all over Latin America has boosted cement sales. By diversifying its revenue base, Cemex can make sure its growth is steady and not dependent on construction activity in only one country. Receiving export earnings in currencies other than the Mexican peso also guards against devaluations and protects Cemex's ability to repay its dollar-denominated debt.

GROWTH IN THE LONG TERM

FROM AN ECONOMIST'S perspective, too, Latin America's prospects for long-term economic growth look good. According to classical economic theory, apart from a windfall, such as discovering oil, the only ways to speed up per-capita economic growth over the long run are by increasing a nation's savings rate, which allows a country to invest more, or by improving technology, which allows the average worker to be more productive. Latin America for decades was caught in what economists like to call a "low-level economic trap," in which individual countries could never get together enough investment capital to lift their economies to the next level. Every time their economies picked up steam, they were dragged back down by precarious fiscal situations, hyperinflation, and unmanageable trade gaps.

In Asia, high savings rates and technological progress allowed countries to achieve high growth rates. Those growth rates hit their long-term peaks in 1995 for two reasons: Savings rates were as high as they could get (you can only save so much of your income without starving), and after twenty years of rapid improvements in technology, Asian countries had reached a technological plateau. By contrast, Latin America's savings rates are abysmally low but are increasing. Every increase in national savings rates creates capital that can be used for investment. Add to that the big inflows of foreign capital recently—a record $56 billion in foreign direct investment streamed into Latin America in 1997 alone, up 28 percent over 1996. Increased capital has finally pushed most of Latin America over the hump, into that group of industrialized countries that are getting richer rather than poorer, moving toward what economists call a "steady state" economy. The 1998 global liquidity crisis delayed the march toward steady progress, but didn't stop it.

The increase in savings rates also has implications for the strength of the stock market. One reason more money isn't invested in Latin American stocks is that individual Latin Americans haven't had the money to do so.

"As savings rates develop, these markets will become much more domestic," says Paul Rogers, co-portfolio manager for several of the Scudder Kemper Investments Inc. Latin American funds. Increases in both the number of stocks listed on Latin American exchanges and the prices of existing stocks will be fed more by additional local investing than by foreign investment.

The icing on the cake is technology. Latin America is far from its potential. Years of protectionist trade resulted in most Latin American countries lagging behind in manufacturing and information technology. They are now catching up, but they probably have another ten years before they approach a plateau on a par with the rest of the world.

Skeptics may ask why Latin America fell into technological ruin because of protectionism, while countries such as Japan and Korea used protectionism to improve technology. One answer is that Japan and Korea fostered domestic competition, whereas Latin America never did.

Latin American companies, many of them state-run and many of them corrupt, enjoyed monopolies and profit margins that often exceeded 50 percent. They had no one to compete against, and as a result their technologies fell further and further behind. Now, domestic competition is thriving in Latin America. As economies have opened up, companies are facing foreign competition for the first time, which necessitates more efficient operations.

Look at the Peruvian financial firm Credicorp. For decades it and other Peruvian banks had the advantage of no foreign competition. Few Peruvians even used banks, and Credicorp's flagship holding, Banco de Crédito del Perú, did little to try to change that. In the mid-1990s, however, Peru relaxed its laws on foreign ownership, and foreign banks began to enter the scene. Most notably were the two big Spanish banks, Banco Santander and Banco Bilbao Vizcaya. Since then, Credicorp has lost about 3 percent of its market share, which in 1998 was at 25 percent, not because Credicorp has done poorly but because the banking sector as a whole has expanded into new areas of the population and new areas of services. Although a few years ago automated teller machines didn't exist, they are now prevalent, and a country in which only 10 percent of the people ever use banks is quickly becoming a nation where even the Incas of Machupicchu have access to teller machines. Banco de Crédito's loans and deposits, meanwhile, have been growing at a rate of about 15 percent a year, and 33 percent of transactions are now conducted electronically, through ATM machines, the telephone, or the Internet.

NOW WHAT?

WE'VE SAID THAT over time, a portfolio with 10 to 20 percent of its assets invested in Latin America or another strong region outside the United States will post a higher return and carry a lower level of risk than a portfolio invested solely in U.S. stocks, or in the stocks of any one country for that matter. Economic growth is the primary fuel for growth in stock markets and in stock prices over the next several years.

Understanding the background material in this chapter is important because:

♦ It will help you weigh the importance of Latin America in your own investment portfolio.

♦ It will give you a basis for comparing Latin America with either emerging or developed markets, which is important for dividing up and diversifying your portfolio.

♦ If at some point you feel that the situation in Latin America has changed enough to warrant a reevaluation of your investments, knowing why you invested in the first place will make it easier to decide whether you should sell.

Already in the first half of 1999, Latin markets were recovering. That recovery is due to not just what's happening inside Latin America, but what's happening outside as well, said Denis Parisien, an economist and former Latin American equity strategist at Dresdner Kleinwort Benson. "Externally, you have a set of very positive circumstances—interest rate cuts globally, the first signs of a recovery in Asia, higher energy and metals prices—that are conducive to asset price appreciation in all emerging markets."

It's true that you as an individual investor have as much chance of making a good profit in Latin America as does the manager of a corporate pension fund or mutual fund. It's also true that small investors have more flexibility and fewer restrictions placed on them than big institutional investors, and small investments are often easier to buy and sell in low-liquidity markets like most of those in Latin America. But the easiest way to get started in Latin America is to invest in a couple of mutual funds that will give your money some exposure there and give you the benefit of professional management. That strategy is the subject of the next chapter.

CHAPTER

Mutual
FUNDS

PICKING THE RIGHT stocks can be difficult. Probably the best way to start investing in Latin America is to buy a Latin American mutual fund. Funds are generally less risky than individual stocks, and if you're just starting out, it's better to trust your money to professionals than to invest it on your own. If you own a mutual fund or two, you can get a better idea how stock markets in the region move by watching the performance of your fund and comparing its ups and downs to news events and economic swings in Latin America and the rest of the world. You can also get to know specific countries better and start to follow leading companies by finding out what stocks the fund holds and where. (I'll show you how to keep track of changes in the fund's holdings.) Later, if you want to buy individual stocks, you'll have a better idea of how the experts do it. One of the best ways to pick stocks for the long term is to buy what the experts buy, and successful mutual fund managers are some of the most knowledgeable around.

But even buying mutual funds isn't always easy, especially if you plan to buy one outside your home country. This chapter will help you decide if Latin American mutual funds are best for you, and it will help you choose among them. For a more complete look at domestic mutual funds and how to invest in them, check out Mary Rowland's book *The New Commonsense Guide to Mutual Funds* (Bloomberg Press, 1998).

WHAT'S DIFFERENT ABOUT LATIN AMERICAN FUNDS

LATIN AMERICAN MUTUAL FUNDS resemble mainstream U.S. mutual funds, but there are some key differences. For one thing, they cost more. A fund company's cost of operating a U.S. mutual fund includes transaction fees for buying the stocks, the salaries of the fund managers, marketing expenses, and other administrative outlays. For a Latin American fund, costs include all of those plus the added expenses of researching Latin American companies, setting up offices in Latin American countries and/or paying a local broker for services, hiring a local custodian, setting up bank accounts in the countries, and numerous other costs involved with doing business internationally. On average, the costs of Latin American mutual funds amount to about 2.28 percent of the fund's value, compared with about 1.44 percent for all equity mutual funds and around 1 percent for most good U.S. mutual funds.

Another key difference is that about half of the popular Latin America funds are closed-end funds, while most U.S. funds are open-ended. A *closed-end fund* has a fixed number of shareholders and is closed to new investors, meaning the only way a new investor can put money into the fund is to buy existing shares through a securities exchange or directly from another fund shareholder, just as you would buy a stock. The advantage of closed-end funds is that many trade at a discount to their net asset values. It's like buying a bunch of stocks for less than what they trade for on the stock exchange. *Open-end funds* are constantly adding (and losing) customers. With each new inflow of cash, the total value of the fund's holdings increases. Open-end funds will redeem for cash the shares of investors who want out, making it easier for investors to sell their shares when they want to, but making it harder for the managers to execute their strategies because they are often forced to sell assets when investors start redeeming shares. At the beginning of 1998, there were about thirty open-end Latin America funds and another thirty or so closed-end Latin America funds traded in the United States and available to individual investors.

Probably the biggest difference between U.S. and Latin American funds is that Latin funds are more volatile. During the Mexican peso crisis in 1994–95 and again in the emerging markets crisis of 1998, Latin American funds saw big drops in the value of their holdings, both because of decreases in the price of the stocks they held and because of redemptions by jittery investors. That volatility shows up in the short term, too. For example, the biggest U.S. mutual fund, the Fidelity Magellan Fund, had a volatility level (measured as the standard deviation) of 20.7 over the 100 days ending April 9, 1999, as compared to a volatility of 34.8 for the Scudder Latin American Fund, one of the biggest in the region.

Volatile currencies—something U.S funds aren't exposed to—is one of the key parts of the added risk faced by Latin funds. The Emerging Mexico Fund, at the time one of the largest Latin American funds in terms of assets, lost more than half its market value when the Mexican peso was devalued in 1994. That's an extreme example, but even regional funds are routinely hurt or helped by swings in the value of Latin American currencies. For a more complete explanation of how currency movements can affect your investments in Latin America and whether or not you should do something about it, see Chapter 3 under the section on currency hedging.

BUY A MIX OF REGIONAL AND COUNTRY-SPECIFIC FUNDS
FOR ALLOCATION OF ASSETS, there are two general types of Latin America equity mutual funds. *Regional funds* spread their assets across stock markets of at least four Latin American countries. Examples are the Morgan Stanley Latin America Fund, the Fidelity Latin America fund, and the T. Rowe Price International-Latin America fund. *Country-specific funds* invest solely in the stocks of one nation. Examples are the Emerging Mexico Fund and Scudder Kemper's Brazil Fund. Most regional funds are open-end funds, while most country-specific funds tend to be closed-end.

There are advantages to each. Regional funds generally carry less risk, since their assets are spread across a number of economies. A devaluation of the Mexican peso would hurt a fund that was 100 percent invested in Mexico much more than it would hurt a fund that was 20 or 30 percent invested there.

As of August 1998 the average weightings for major regional Latin American mutual funds, according to an index compiled by the International Finance Corp., was 31.1 percent in Brazil, 31.8 percent in Mexico, 12.6 percent in Argentina, 16.2 percent in Chile, 1.6 percent in Venezuela, 3.7 percent in Peru, and 3.0 percent in Colombia.

Country-specific funds can post higher returns than regional funds, but they can also post bigger losses. In the year ending April 1998, for example, the four best-performing Latin America funds were all country-specific Mexico funds, out of a list of more than sixty open-end and closed-end funds that are registered for sale to U.S. investors, according to the London-based research company Micropal. In that same year, however, the four worst performing Latin America funds were also country-specific funds, targeted to Brazil and Chile (*see page 52 in this chapter for a list of closed-end Latin America funds and page 53 for a list of open-end funds*).

Most money managers interviewed for this book advise that if you're a first-time investor and can afford only one fund, buy a regional Latin American fund. Among the best in terms of high returns and low fees are the Latin American Discovery Fund (a closed-end fund managed by Morgan Stanley), and three no-load mutual funds—the Scudder Latin American Fund, the TCW Galileo Latin American Fund, and the T. Rowe Price Latin American Fund. A *load* is a one-time commission charged to fund purchasers, on top of the administrative and other ongoing costs that are built into the price of the fund's shares. These four funds have relatively low expense ratios, and their returns over time have been impressive. They are also well managed and widely available to small investors. There are also several load funds which, while they tend to be more expensive initially, sometimes post returns that can make up for their higher fees. Among them are the Fidelity Latin American Fund, the Kemper Latin America Fund, and the Rembrandt Latin American Equities Fund.

Deciding between regional and country-specific funds is a little like choosing between funds and individual stocks. If you think you have enough information on a company to give you an advantage over other investors, then you probably want to buy that stock rather than spread your money out by buying a fund. Following this analogy, if you think you know enough about a country to give you an advantage over other investors—and if what you know is positive information—then you might want to buy a fund that invests only in that country rather than a regional fund that spreads your money over several countries.

The best bet, of course, is to buy more than one fund and to select a combination of regional and country-specific funds. Two or three funds are all you need for the Latin American portion of your portfolio—perhaps one regional fund and two country-specific funds, or vice-versa.

WEIGH A FUND'S EXPENSE RATIO AGAINST ITS RETURNS

I MENTIONED ABOVE that costs can be charged to investors in the form of a sales load or they can come in the form of higher share prices for the funds themselves. The assets that a fund holds might be worth $13 a share, but the price of the fund might be listed as $13.03, the extra three cents being the fund company's costs of buying the assets, selling the shares, marketing, and paying fund managers. But lower costs don't necessarily mean better funds. Some funds have higher costs yet deliver higher returns. It might be that they spend more money on research in order to improve their returns. Or they may buy more stocks in small companies and small countries that have higher transaction costs. This is especially true of some Latin American funds.

Some big Latin American funds keep their costs low by buying mostly American Depository Receipts instead of buying stocks locally. (ADRs, discussed in the next chapter, are foreign stocks that are traded in the United States.) ADRs, however, offer less variety; consequently, the funds may be passing up some good buys on high-growth stocks. Until recently, for example, purchasing the ADRs of Mexico's big tortilla company, Grupo Maseca, was easier and cheaper than buying the local shares of Grupo Maseca's parent company, Gruma SA. However, Grupo Maseca shares represent only the Mexican operations of the company, which suffered in recent years due to fears of corn subsidy reductions and a slow Mexican economy, while Gruma shares represent the company's worldwide operations, which are booming as tortilla sales expand internationally. Happily for investors, Gruma S.A. (GMK) was listed on the New York Stock Exchange in November 1998.

Finally, a fund might have higher costs because the fund's managers are highly regarded and the fund has posted high returns consistently. Buying a fund is like buying any service. Your yardstick should be total return, and your aim is to get what you pay for.

For many funds, though, you get less than what you pay for. That's where a little research comes in handy. When deciding on a fund, look at its three-year or five-year average returns, not just its return in the past year, and review its expense ratio—the ratio of the fund's costs to its price. Compare historical returns for a Latin American regional fund to those of other funds and then compare them all to the returns of a major Latin American composite index, such as the Morgan Stanley Emerging Markets Latin America Index. Next, look at its expense ratio: A higher expense ratio means the fund has to do better than the composite index to make investing in it worthwhile. You can get a fund's historical returns and its cost ratio from the fund prospectus or annual report, Morningstar, or the Bloomberg Web site, www.bloomberg.com, which also has the Morgan Stanley index.

One common mistake that people make in selecting Latin American funds is buying the name rather than the performance. Several major U.S. and worldwide fund companies have Latin American mutual funds, but just because a fund family has a good performance record in U.S. or global funds doesn't mean it does well in emerging markets. For example, Franklin Templeton's Latin America funds have posted returns far below those of many of its competitors, and yet the Latin America funds of Scudder Kemper Investments, which isn't nearly as well-known for U.S. funds, routinely lead the pack in Latin America. And the tiny Wright Equities-Mexico fund beat out all other Latin American open-end funds in 1997, with an annual return of 42.36 percent, according to Micropal. Some big fund companies don't spend the money necessary to improve their returns in Latin America, while others simply don't have enough experience in the region to be able to beat the companies whose fund managers have been there for a long time, like Scudder's. That's why it's important to look beyond returns and cost to find out who manages the fund you are considering. If the manager has been there for five years during which the fund has consistently posted high returns, the person probably knows how to continue making good decisions. But if the fund has posted high annual returns and the fund manager is new, find out where he came from and what his investment record was before the fund hired him. Fund companies are usually quick to respond to a request for a fund manager biography.

One way of keeping costs really low is by buying *index funds*. Index funds are still a novelty among Latin American funds, and as of the date this book went to press, there were none registered for sale to U.S. investors. However, there are several available to offshore investors, and it's inevitable that an inventive fund company will come up with one soon. The first U.S. index fund was sold in 1976 by the Vanguard Group, and since then funds have popped up that are indexed to everything from the Russell 2000 small-capitalization stock index to the Morgan Stanley EAFE index (Europe, Asia, and the Far East).

Index funds usually have low cost ratios because they

don't pay anyone to do research or manage the asset allocation. The portfolio simply tracks a major index such as the International Finance Corp.'s Latin America index or the Morgan Stanley Latin America Index, both of which are weighted baskets of stocks from throughout the region that are designed to mimic the overall combined stock markets of Latin America, as the Standard and Poor's 500 index does for U.S. stocks. Or, in the case of country-specific index funds, they can track a local stock exchange index such as the Bolsa index in Mexico or the Bovespa in São Paulo. There are, however, some costs involved in these funds, in part because the fund company tracks changes in the make-up of the index it follows and must buy and sell shares accordingly.

All of this information, including historical returns, cost ratios, descriptions of holdings, and managers' backgrounds, can be obtained by calling the fund companies. You can also check in *Morningstar Mutual Funds,* a collection of reports of 1,600 funds, or in several Web sites, which are listed at the back of this book.

MAKE SURE THE RISK FITS

A COMMON MISPERCEPTION is that funds are usually low-risk investment vehicles, and that risk doesn't differ much from one fund to another. In general, funds are less risky than stocks, but some funds can be extremely volatile. In many cases managers will take on added risk if under pressure to boost returns. That's fine if the risk pays off, but make sure you know what you're getting into.

For comparing market risk, the best measure is something called *beta.* Beta measures the volatility of a stock or a fund by plotting its price movements in relation to those of the rest of the market, usually represented by the Standard and Poor's 500 index. The S&P is assigned a beta of 1.0. The exact formula used to get beta is complicated, but you can get historical betas from the fund company or from your broker. A beta of 2 would mean that a stock is highly volatile, swinging twice as much as the S&P in either direction. A beta of 0.5 would mean it is more stable than the market—if the S&P went down by 20 percent, the stock would go down by 10 percent. The lower the beta, the less the volatility. Higher betas generally mean higher risk. U.S. mutual fund managers generally try to keep the beta of their funds below 1.0, meaning they are more stable than the market. Most Latin America funds, which are inherently more risky, have betas above 1.0. They can go slightly above that, perhaps as high as 1.2, and still be attractive. *Standard deviation,* another measure of risk, expresses how much and how often the price of the fund varies from its own average price.

When analyzing risk, don't rely on just the numbers and the recommendations of others, but also on your own common sense and knowledge of the market. For example, even if a fund you are looking at has low historical betas, is logging fairly good returns, and comes highly recommended by a newsletter, the fund may be heavily invested in a country that is in the midst of political upheaval, or perhaps it owns a big stake in a company whose chief executive officer is in the hospital with heart problems. Researching mutual funds can be as important as researching stocks.

Size also matters when buying a fund, though not so much as it does in buying a U.S. fund. In the United States, some mammoth funds are so large that their size cramps their ability to improve returns. The Fidelity Magellan Fund, for example, had $72 billion in assets as of late 1998. The more assets a fund has, the further it must look for places to put that money. We noted in the previous chapter that most funds have limitations on the percentage of the fund that can be invested in one company, and in the percentage of ownership that the fund can hold in a single company. Among Latin America funds, those restrictions aren't yet as important because even the largest Latin America funds are small enough that they have plenty of places to put their money. Nonetheless, size can play a role in performance. During periods of large inflows, fund managers can be saddled with large chunks of money that dwarf the amount of stock available on small and medium-sized Latin American companies.

Likewise, "If you have a large position in a company, by the time you sell it down again, the company could be out of favor," says Paul Rogers, comanager of the Scudder and Kemper Latin America funds.

DIVERSIFY

DIVERSIFICATION DOESN'T JUST mean having non-U.S. stocks. It means diversifying within Latin America itself, too. If too many of your Latin America investments are in one country, you may not be well diversified.

Mexico, Chile, and Argentina, for example, have historically tracked the U.S. market much more closely than Peru and Venezuela. There are reasons for that: Mexico borders the United States, Argentina's currency is pegged to the dollar, and Chile has been a favorite U.S. trading partner for decades. Peru, on the other hand, is more closely tied in trade and other aspects to its own South American neighbors than it is to the United States. Peru's trade relations with Japan are as close as its ties with the United States. Venezuela's stock market is even less correlated with U.S. markets, depending as it does on the price of oil for most of its economic growth.

Mutual fund diversification can be measured in the same way that diversification is measured for stocks: by looking at the correlation coefficient. The *correlation coefficient* is the result of a mathematical formula that measures how closely a stock or a fund is correlated with another stock, fund, or index, most commonly the Standard and Poor's 500 index *(see Chapter 4 for a more detailed explanation)*. The second half of this book lists the correlation coefficients for each of the thirty-five companies profiled.

You should avoid concentrating your investments in one type of industry. If you are heavily invested in telecommunications in the United States and don't want to take on more risk in that sector, avoid Latin American funds that invest heavily in that sector.

Also, if you own either a global mutual fund or an international mutual fund, you may already own shares in Latin America companies. Global funds and international funds may sound like the same thing, but they're not. Global funds invest the bulk of their holdings in either foreign companies or domestic companies with large foreign operations, whereas international funds are focused specifically on foreign companies. If you have decided to put 20 percent of your portfolio in Latin America, check the other mutual funds you own first; you may find that 3 or 4 percent of your portfolio is already there.

GROWTH VS. VALUE; SMALL CAP VS. LARGE CAP

WHEN CHOOSING A Latin America mutual fund, approach the decision as if you were picking which type of U.S. fund to invest in. Do I invest in a blue-chip fund or a small-cap fund? Should I put my money in a "growth" fund, or a fund slanted toward "value" companies?

Growth funds, by definition, invest in companies whose earnings are increasing and are expected to continue increasing. Typically that means companies in their early stages that have not yet reached maturity. Their profit margins are generally high, and their sales and profits are on the upswing. Often the price-to-earnings ratios of growth companies are higher than an investor might otherwise accept.

Value funds invest in companies whose price-to-earnings ratios or price-to-book values are low and are thus considered to be undervalued by the market. It is possible for a company to be considered a growth company and a value investment at the same time. Some telecommunications companies in Latin America are good examples.

Which style of investing is better? Both approaches can be effective, but in Latin America it's sometimes possible to have your cake and eat it, too. Because Latin American economies are likely to experience faster economic growth over the next decade, company earnings are also likely to improve. Emerging market investing, in fact, is usually viewed as an investment in growth. Latin American companies on average are good values compared with the rest of the world. You can, therefore, find companies that offer both reasonable value *and* growth potential.

There are some exceptions. For example, Panamerican Beverages, a Mexico-based bottler of Coca-Cola and other drinks, would by most standards be considered a growth investment but not a value investment. It has operations throughout Latin America and is poised to take advantage of high growth in consumer buying power regionwide. Its earnings have grown sharply and are expected to continue doing so. However, the company is not a bargain from either the price-to-earnings or price-to-book perspective. In late 1998, it had a P/E of 18 times estimated 1998 earnings and a price-to-book-value of 1.24 (the average price-to-book value in Latin America is about 0.87).

A good example of a value company, on the other hand, is Vitro SA, Mexico's biggest glass manufacturer. It had one of the lowest PE ratios in Latin America in late 1998, dipping at times below 4.0. But because it makes glass, which is gradually losing market share to plastics, Vitro isn't considered by many investors to have good growth prospects.

You can also buy both *small-cap* and *large-cap* Latin America funds. Capitalization simply means the total market value of a company's common stock. Small cap is shorthand for small capitalization and in most cases is synonymous with "small companies." In the United States, large cap usually refers to companies with capitalizations of $3.5 billion or more, while small cap refers to anything less than $1 billion. Anything that lies in the middle is a midcap.

In Latin America, however, a large-cap stock is usually considered any company with a market capitalization of $1 billion or more, while a market capitalization of $300 million or less is considered small-cap. Thus, most large-cap stocks in Latin America would be considered midcap in the United States, and small-cap stocks in Latin America wouldn't even make it into any of those categories. They would be considered *microcap* stocks in the United States. Most major Latin American mutual funds are large-cap funds (using the Latin American definition of *large cap*). Indeed, six prominent large-cap companies are among the top ten or fifteen investments of most major Latin American regional funds. But there are a growing number of small-cap Latin American funds, too. Among the mutual fund companies offering small-cap funds are Gartmore Capital Management Ltd., Global Asset Management Ltd., and Edinburgh Fund Managers Plc.

CLOSED-END VS. OPEN-END FUNDS

AS I MENTIONED at the beginning of this chapter, closed-end funds dominate the Latin America mutual fund business. Some investors are put off by closed-end funds; others like them for the flexibility they give to management. Especially in emerging markets like Latin America, a closed-end fund has an advantage over an open-end in that the fund manager is not obligated to redeem shares for investors who want to cash out, and so is not forced to buy or sell stocks or bonds to keep up with inflows and outflows of cash. Closed-end funds don't allow new investors, so the value of the fund is always determined by the price changes in the assets it holds. As a result, closed-end fund managers can buy stocks when their prices are low, hold them, and sell when they are high.

Thomas Herzfeld, who wrote a book on closed-end funds and manages a few of his own, says closed-end funds have many advantages over open-end funds, including their flexibility, their lower costs, their frequent discounts, and the fact that many of them have high trading volume and are listed on the New York Stock Exchange.

"The closed-end fund is much better suited for a bear market than an open-end fund, because the portfolio manager of an open-end mutual fund is most likely in a position where he is receiving redemptions and has to sell securities in declining markets," Herzfeld says. "The closed-end manager, on the other hand, can use his cash reserves to buy in these markets. They also don't have to be kept off balance by receiving new money during market tops."

Critics of closed-end funds point out that many of their shareholders have been waiting for years for the share price of the funds to catch up to the value of the holdings. And in times of panic, such as immediately following the Russia devaluation in August 1998, the discounts on closed-end funds can widen significantly. Some Latin American funds, such as the Brazil Fund and the now-defunct Emerging Mexico Fund, were trading at prices more than 25 percent below their net asset values. That's in part what prompted Santander Investments, managers of the Emerging Mexico Fund, to liquidate it and return the assets to shareholders.

LATIN AMERICA CLOSED-END FUNDS

REGIONAL FUNDS	SYMBOL	3-YEAR AVERAGE ANNUAL RETURN	DISCOUNT
Aberdeen Latin America	ABL	-9.57	24.9%
Edinburgh Inca Trust	EBI	-11.18	20.5%
Latin America Discovery Fund	LDF	16.95	12.7%
Latin America Equity Fund	LAQ	-8.54	23.0%
Templeton Latin America	TLA	-3.71	20.9%

COUNTRY-SPECIFIC FUNDS	SYMBOL	3-YEAR AVERAGE ANNUAL RETURN	DISCOUNT
Argentina Fund	AF	-2.65	23.6%
Brazil Fund	BZF	1.32	16.6%
Brazilian Equity Fund	BZL	-15.47	14.3%
Chile Fund	CH	-7.99	25.1%
Mexico Equity Income	MXE	10.04	17.7%
Mexico Fund	MXF	6.27	23.7%

At left is a short list of Latin America closed-end funds traded in New York and London as of April 8, 1999, showing 3-year average annual return and discount to net asset value.

Many open-end funds can be bought directly through the fund company, avoiding the transaction fees normally paid to a broker. Some discount brokers even allow clients to buy open-end funds through them without transaction fees. The chart below is a list of open-end funds in existence for at least three years and registered for sale in the United States as of April 4, 1999.

For information such as net asset values, discounts, and cost ratios, look to Morningstar's Web site (www.morningstar.com) or to the books and reports it publishes, all of which have information on both closed-end and open-end funds.

LATIN AMERICA OPEN-END FUNDS

FUND NAME	3-YEAR AVERAGE ANNUAL RETURN	TELEPHONE NUMBER
AIM Latin America Growth Fund	-5.7	800-824-1580
BT Investment Latin America Fund	10.0	800-730-1313
Evergreen Latin America Fund	-0.1	800-343-2898
Excelsior Latin America Fund	-6.0	800-446-1012
Fidelity Latin America Fund	4.4	800-544-8888
Invesco Specialty Latin America Fund	-5.5	800-525-8085
Merrill Lynch Latin America Fund	2.1	609-282-2800
Morgan Stanley Latin America Fund	12.7	800-869-6397
Scudder Latin America Fund	6.8	800-225-2470
T. Rowe Price Latin America Fund	3.4	800-231-8432
TCW Galileo Latin America Equity Fund	1.4	800-386-3829
Van Kampen Latin America Fund	12.2	800-282-4404
Wright Equifund Mexico National	8.1	800-888-8471

SOURCE: BLOOMBERG L.P. (MICHAEL MOLINSKI)

EMERGING MARKET FUNDS VS. LATIN AMERICA FUNDS

IF YOU HAVEN'T already done so, consider buying emerging markets funds in addition to Latin America funds. This book makes the point that Latin America will be a good investment over the next decade. There are, however, other regions whose prospects are also good—Eastern Europe for example, and perhaps India, and parts of Africa. Emerging markets funds invest in those regions, too. They also invest in Asia. Although I have argued that Asia's prospects aren't as good as Latin America's, Asia is certainly not going to experience zero growth rates in the years ahead. And even if it did, there are plenty of good Asian companies who will find a way to boost earnings regardless of the external economic environment. A good fund manager will pick the best companies from each of the regions and will overweight the regions with the most promise.

If you do buy an emerging markets fund, pay careful attention to these weightings—the percentage of the fund's assets directed to each region—and make sure the fund manager's investment choices are in line with your own. Buying an emerging markets fund can reduce the risk that I am completely wrong and that Latin America will fall into a ten-year decline. If you believe in Latin America but also believe in emerging markets as a whole, buy some exposure to each type. Chapter 4 will show you how to balance the two so that you are as invested in Latin America as you want to be *and* well diversified from the rest of your portfolio.

At right is a short list of some of the better emerging markets funds, ranked by three-year average annual return as of April 9, 1999.

FUND STRATEGIES

FOLLOWING ARE SOME approaches used by mutual fund managers and some additional tips on buying mutual funds:

PAUL ROGERS of Scudder Kemper Funds says, "We just look to buy the best companies in the region at the best

EMERGING MARKETS EQUITY FUNDS

FUND NAME	3-YEAR AVERAGE ANNUAL RETURN	TELEPHONE NUMBER
Evergreen Emerging Markets Growth	-2.38	800-343-2898
Federated Emerging Markets A	-1.53	800-341-7400
Glenmede Emerging Markets Portfolio	-9.72	800-442-8299
Ivy Developing Nation Fund	-10.22	800-456-5111
JP Morgan Emerging Markets Equity Fund	-11.10	800-766-7722
Merrill Lynch Developing Cap Markets	-9.45	609-282-2800
Morgan Stanley Emerging Markets	-7.90	800-869-3863
Nicholas Applegate Emerging Countries A	3.19	800-334-3444
PaineWebber Emerging Markets A	-7.43	800-647-1568
Pilgrim Emerging Countries A	2.33	800-334-3444
PIMCO Emerging Markets	-7.56	800-800-0952
Pioneer Emerging Markets	-3.93	800-225-6292
Schroder Capital Emerging Markets	-6.51	207-879-1900
SIT Developing Markets Growth	-6.73	800-332-5580
SSGA Emerging Markets	-2.69	800-647-7327
Templeton Developing Markets Trust	-2.46	800-292-9293
Van Kampen Emerging Markets	-6.68	800-225-2222

prices. It's very much a value approach. We focus on the long term. If we buy a company, we expect it to be in our portfolio for three to five years." Rogers says he tries to buy companies with low price-to-earnings ratios as well as high growth potential.

TARA KENNEY, who comanages the Scudder Latin America Investment fund with Rogers, said they also look for companies with low debt and high cash flows.

"It's something we've learned not to deviate from," she told Bloomberg News in a May 1998 interview. "If they have to use all their cash flow to pay off the debt, there's nothing to reinvest in the company or to benefit shareholders." The result is that the Scudder fund is heavily invested in telecommunications companies, utilities, and beverage companies.

CHRIS EDWARDS, a fund manager at London-based National Provident Institution, says their NPI Latin American Fund favors stocks that benefit from a rise in consumer spending on small-ticket items.

"Low end consumption is a key variable," Edwards told Bloomberg News in an interview. Consumers in Latin America "are going to buy Cokes and fake designer sunglasses. They are not going to buy cars first."

The fund invests in the four most developed countries in the region: Brazil, Mexico, Chile, and Argentina. Like Scudder, it focuses on telecommunications, utilities, and beverage companies, but also has large stakes in Grupo Televisa, the Mexican broadcasting company, and in some banks.

MARY ROWLAND, a columnist and author of *The New Commonsense Guide to Mutual Funds*, lists seventy-five "Dos and Don'ts" of mutual fund investing in her book. Among the ones that apply particularly to emerging markets are:

◆ Do build your overall portfolio with at least three core mutual funds. Consider three areas: stocks with a large market capitalization, small-company stocks, and international stocks.

◆ Do start with just one fund if that's all you can afford.

◆ Do invest in different asset classes. Asset allocation—selecting the right mix of asset classes, such as international stocks, small-company stocks, and large-company stocks—determines an astounding 90 percent of your return, while selecting the right stock or mutual fund accounts for just 10 percent, according to many studies.

◆ Don't try to time the market. The market goes up and down in sudden spurts. But the long term direction is up. (This applies to Latin America, too.)

◆ Don't buy and sell with your emotions. (Especially applicable to Latin America.)

◆ Do look under the hood. Make sure any funds you're considering (and the ones you already own) follow chosen investment objectives.

◆ Don't buy (or sell) a fund based on recent performance alone.

◆ And finally, Don't ignore expenses.

COMPARING

WHEN YOU PICK a mutual fund, the average annual return is probably the first thing you'll look at, but don't stop there. Look at the cost ratio of the fund and whether or not it has a load fee. If it's a closed-end fund, look at the discount to net asset value. Check the manager's reputation and track record. Determine where the fund is invested, and see how diversified it is, both within Latin America and in relation to the U.S. stock market.

For most investors, a regional fund such as the Scudder Latin America Fund that combines both value and growth approaches is probably best. That way you're not betting the farm on either increasing growth rates or on recovering the price of an undervalued stock. If you're just getting started in Latin America, stick to funds that invest in large-cap stocks. Most big funds do, including those I've just mentioned.

Knowing which stocks your fund holds gives you a head start on the next step in building your portfolio: picking individual stocks. Owning Latin American mutual funds is fine if you're new to investing, or if you have $5,000 or less to invest. But if you have the time, energy, and motivation for researching, selecting, and maintaining your own portfolio of Latin American stocks, you can take fullest advantage of the diversification benefits of investing overseas and shoot for the highest return you can get by investing in stocks via American Depository Receipts.

CHAPTER

ADRs

HAPTER 2 SHOWED you how to invest in Latin America the easy way, by letting professionals do the groundwork for you and paying them fees for their services. This chapter will explain how to do it yourself—how to select and buy Latin American stocks.

Since this is a book for individual investors, I'm not going to talk about the myriad of stocks that are sold only on local exchanges in Latin America, because there's little reason for foreigners to buy them. Foreigners can buy shares legally, but most countries require minimum investments of $100,000 or more. Even then, brokers charge higher transaction fees for buying foreign securities than for buying U.S. stocks, and there's the additional hassle of converting them from the local currency into dollars and worrying about how to report them on your U.S. tax returns. Buying stocks on local exchanges is therefore usually reserved for institutional investors who qualify with local securities and exchange commissions and have the budgets for intensive research.

However, there are 217 Latin American stocks that U.S. and other foreign investors can buy quickly and easily. In the United States, these stocks are called *American Depository Receipts,* or ADRs, and you can buy them over the counter or on an exchange, almost as you would any other U.S. stock. They are denoted in U.S. dollars, and dividend payments are automatically passed on to shareholders in U.S. dollars.

I say, "almost as you would any other U.S. stock," because certain properties of ADRs make them unique investment vehicles and in some cases make trading mechanics a little tricky. This chapter will unravel those small mysteries, so you can feel almost as comfortable acquiring stock in Banco de Crédito de Perú as you would in buying shares at Chase Manhattan Corp.

Before you buy stocks, you have to select them. This chapter will help you sort through the Latin American ADRs and pick the ones most likely to give you the best returns over the long run. Techniques will be explained, building on familiar methods used by investors analyzing U.S. stocks. But I'll also explain the nuances of Latin American stocks and show you why evaluating them as you would a typical U.S. stock could cost you lots of money.

WHAT'S AN ADR?

SOME DAY, PROBABLY well within our lifetimes, the globalization of capital markets will make it possible for any individual to quickly and cheaply buy any stock in any company in any country in the world. Until then, individual U.S. investors have to live with high transaction fees, minimum investment requirements, and sometimes, government restrictions on direct sale of shares to nonresidents and noncitizens on local exchanges. Part of the rationale for such laws is that governments have a hard time taxing foreigners for capital gains, and in spite of all the recent hullabaloo about free trade, most governments are still protectionist at heart. Heavy restrictions on foreign ownership of companies are still in place in most of the countries of the world.

European investors have an easier time of it than U.S. investors. Not only can they buy shares in each others' countries directly, and often on their own home-country exchanges; they can also buy shares listed in offshore centers such as Ireland, Luxembourg, and the Channel Islands, where they have access to hundreds of closed-end Latin American funds. These funds often have returns that far exceed U.S.-based funds, mainly because they avoid U.S. tax laws and aren't subject to the asset restrictions imposed by the Securities and Exchange Commission. Nevertheless, European investors, too, face high transaction fees and minimum investment requirements when buying Latin American stocks directly on Latin American exchanges.

To get around these difficulties, Latin American companies reach individual foreign investors by selling ADRs,
or Global Depository Receipts (GDRs) and listing them on
overseas exchanges, such as the New York Stock Exchange
or the Tokyo Stock Exchange. When this book went to
press, there were 76 Latin American companies whose
shares were listed on the New York Stock Exchange, 4 on
the NASDAQ, 4 on the American Stock Exchange, and
another 133 trading over the counter in the United States.

It might seem that small investors are at a disadvantage
because their choices are so limited, but in many ways the
opposite is true. For most people, ADRs provide more
than enough opportunities for diversification, and buying
them eliminates most of the headaches you would have
buying stocks directly: tax questions, currency exchange,
and repatriation of assets.

"The advantage of depository receipts is that they
enable investors in America and Europe to invest in an
emerging market company without leaving their home
market," writes Mark Mobius in his book *Emerging Markets*.
Mobius, who manages the Templeton Emerging Markets
Funds and is one of the deans of emerging market investing, adds, "In many instances, the home market brokerage
and other costs associated with purchasing and holding
shares are lower in the investor's market. By not going into
the emerging markets directly, considerable administrative and other complications are avoided."

An important thing to remember about ADRs is that
the companies issuing them are usually the cream of Latin
America. They are the blue-chip corporations that dominate trading in their local markets.

However, it's important to know that in special cases
investors might want to purchase shares directly on local
exchanges, principally when they have decided that they
must own stock in a particular company, and that company doesn't have shares listed in their home country. Most
investors would simply choose another stock that does
have an ADR, rather than go through the hassles of buying

shares overseas. Nonetheless, let's look at Gruma, the Mexican tortilla company mentioned in the previous chapter, as an example of an exception to the rule. ADRs are available in Maseca, the Mexican subsidiary of Gruma, but until November 1998 the parent company didn't have an ADR. Many North Americans were interested in Gruma, because they were familiar with the company through its tortillas in U.S. and Canadian supermarkets; the company's growth prospects are tied to the popularity of Mexican food outside of Mexico itself. But most North Americans have little interest in owning stock in Maseca: it sells tortillas only in Mexico and isn't considered a good growth prospect because tortillas are such a staple of the Mexican diet and a decline in government corn subsidies could hurt company earnings. Before the Gruma ADR, North Americans were calling their brokers and buying Gruma shares directly in Mexico, rather than settling for the Maseca ADR. A good broker will convert the shares into U.S. dollars and even explain Mexican taxes, so you can ask Uncle Sam for a discount (tax questions are explained later in this chapter). A really good broker won't charge a higher transaction fee.

ADRs were invented in the 1960s to allow trading European equities in U.S. markets. For twenty years, no region's ADRs came close to those of Europe in either trading volume or number of listings on U.S. exchanges. Beginning in 1990, however, Latin America has not only overtaken Europe but is far ahead of any other region, including Asia, in both average daily trading and cumulative dollar trading. In the number of ADRs listed on the NYSE, Latin America is still second to Europe, which has 135. But Latin America has more than twice as many companies listed as Asia does at 34. What makes this number especially remarkable is that the first Latin America ADR to be listed in New York was the Telephone Company of Chile in 1991. Through 1997, trading in Latin American ADRs was dominated by companies from Mexico and Chile, but in 1997 and 1998 Brazil's Telebrás easily led trading of all ADRs from all countries. Mexico and Chile still lead Latin America with the number of ADRs listed, at 28 and 23 respectively, but new listings from Brazil and Argentina and to a lesser extent Colombia, Peru, and Venezuela are surfacing all the time. The split up of Telebrás into twelve "baby bras" companies in November 1998 boosted the number of Brazilian ADRs to 17.

BUYING ADRS

U.S. INVESTORS CAN buy and sell NYSE-listed ADRs as easily as they can trade shares in U.S. companies. Usually they trade at a small premium, meaning they're worth slightly less than shares in the same company traded back in Mexico, or Colombia, or wherever the company is based. But that means little to an individual investor because whatever premium you lose when you buy the ADR you will almost always regain when you sell it. I say "almost always" because sometimes the difference—known as the *spread*—between the local price and the ADR price will narrow.

Another way that ADRs differ from shares in domestic companies is that most ADRs are not traded on a one-for-one basis with the local shares. For example, one ADR might be worth 100 local shares. But this also makes little or no difference to U.S. investors. What matters is that when you buy or sell an ADR, that share is worth what global investors have decided it is worth considering the percentage of the company each share represents and the market value of the company at that point in time.

TYPES OF ADRS

THE SEC PUTS ADRs into four general categories: Level One, Level Two, Level Three, and Rule 144A. Level One ADRs are the simplest way for foreign companies to sell shares in the United States. These shares are sold on the *over-the-counter* (OTC) market, either in the *pink sheets* or on the NASD's electronic Bulletin Board system. These systems are explained later.

Level One ADRs are sold mostly to institutional

investors in large blocks, but some are available to small investors. The main difference between Level One ADRs and other types is that Level One ADRs do not require the issuing company to meet SEC reporting requirements. They must only meet some minimum requirements related to size and other characteristics and disclose English versions of the same annual financial documents required in their home countries.

Level Two ADRs are intended for companies listing their shares on a U.S. exchange; their reporting requirements are similar to those of U.S. companies. They also must follow U.S. accounting standards.

Level Three ADRs are similar to Level Two ADRs but are reserved for companies raising new capital in the United States, rather than just listing their existing shares on U.S. exchanges. Both Level Two and Level Three ADRs must also meet the requirements of the exchanges on which they are listed.

A fourth type of ADR, created by the SEC in the early 1990s, is referred to as a Rule 144A ADR. These are private placements that companies arrange with their depository institutions in the United States in order to judge the demand for their shares among institutional investors.

Level One ADRs are generally considered riskier than other types, because they do not adhere to U.S. standards and reporting requirements. On the other hand, ADRs that come in as Level One or as a 144A are frequently from companies that plan to upgrade to Level Two or Level Three later. Buying a Level One ADR before its upgrade can often give an investor a head start on the rest of the public. It's similar to buying a stock before its initial public offering. A higher level usually brings higher trading volume, and higher trading volume can often boost stock price.

For Level Two and Level Three ADRs, however, disclosure is not only complete, but in some cases it is much more thorough than the information available on many publicly traded U.S. companies. Companies with Level Two or Three ADRs have passed the muster of both their local exchange authorities and the U.S. SEC. Having so much information available to shareholders means that corruption is probably kept to a minimum, and enough information on the company is available to make large, unexpected shocks to its balance sheet extremely unlikely. Also, as we discussed in the previous chapter, a large majority of the holdings of U.S.-based Latin America mutual funds is invested in companies with ADRs.

Note, however, that although financial statements are required for Level Two and Level Three ADRs, they are often more difficult to obtain than those of U.S. companies. *(See the Resources section for an explanation of where to find them.)*

Leo Guzmán, whose company Guzmán & Co. researches ADRs, explained during an interview that bookkeeping practices among Latin American companies are still far from being as forthcoming and accurate as those of U.S. companies.

"I know a lot of people in senior positions at Latin American companies, and sometimes I am taken aback by the kind of things that go on," Guzmán says. "Disclosure is never as good as it is in the United States, not just in Latin America but in other countries." Regulations attempting to apply U.S. standards to the financial reporting practices of Latin American companies is sometimes awkward. "There are things you would think should be an easy disclosure issue, but are not," Guzmán says. "However, the trend is toward greater disclosure, and listings in the U.S. market have given them a big push. So has the expansion of the Internet."

Not all Level One, Two, and Three ADRs are available to small investors, but most are. Sometimes small investors are kept out by high per-share prices. For example, Venezuela's national telephone company, CANTV, sets its share price above $2,000. Small investors are also kept out by minimum share purchase requirements, although a good broker can get around this rule by buying lots for several investors at a time. For example, Charles Schwab allows investors to buy 50-lot shares in the Brazilian electric utility Cemig, although the minimum is reported to be 100. And apparently Schwab's demand for the stock is fairly large, because the transaction can take only minutes to complete.

One final distinction on the types of ADRs is the difference between a sponsored ADR and an unsponsored ADR. All of the ADRs discussed so far are sponsored ADRs. Before the SEC established all of the above rules about the various levels of ADRs, a bank or other institution could establish trading of the shares of a foreign company without that company's permission. They essentially bought the shares in the foreign country and made them available to investors in the United States or elsewhere. But unsponsored ADRs have since become obsolete, and no Latin American companies I know of trade unsponsored ADRs in the United States.

FINDING THE BARGAINS

THE LOWER-LEVEL ADRs often present the best bargains. Such stocks are usually more volatile than heavily traded ADRs such as Cemex or Telesp Participações, but because lower-level ADRS are lightly traded and not as much information is available on them, a savvy investor can sometimes beat the market. Lower-level ADRs have disadvantages, though. Because trading is so light, prices are often quoted only once a day at the end of trading by stock information services such as Dow Jones, Bloomberg, and Reuters.

The prices of ADRs are normally quoted in one of four different ways, depending on how they are traded. If the ADR is listed on the New York Stock Exchange or the American Stock Exchange, or the National Association of Securities Dealers Automated Quotations system (NASDAQ), the price is updated whenever a trade takes place. NYSE, Amex, and Nasdaq listings are readily available electronically, and almost every stockbroker has access to them.

Level One ADRs, however, are not listed either on the
NYSE, the Amex, or with NASDAQ. The prices of such
stocks are available in one of two places: the OTC Bulletin
Board or the Pink Sheets. The OTC Bulletin Board provides continuously updated prices on some stocks and
twice-a-day updates on others that do not meet the minimum net worth or other requirements of the NASDAQ.
In the case of ADRs, the minimum net worth requirement
is usually not a problem. Latin American companies may
choose to list on the Bulletin Board because financial
reporting procedures in their home countries is different
from that in the United States. Likewise, the Pink Sheets is
a similar system of stock listings that do not meet the
reporting requirements of NASDAQ or of the SEC. Prices
for Pink Sheet stocks are quoted once a day by an organi-
zation called the National Quotation Bureau.

Investors who are unfamiliar with Latin American financial reporting standards often criticize Pink Sheet stocks
and Bulletin Board stocks, claiming that companies listing
their shares there are not providing enough information
to the public and thus must be hiding something. In some
rare cases they are, but it is a gross generalization to put
all Latin American companies whose stocks are on the
Pink Sheets or the Bulletin Board into that category. In
many cases, the financial reporting standards of those
companies are just as strict as those of NYSE-listed U.S.
companies, but their methods are different, and they
don't want to go through the expense of revamping their
entire accounting procedures to bring them in line with
U.S. standards. In any case, to list on the Pink Sheets or
the Bulletin Board they must meet some minimum reporting requirements with the SEC. Also, they must provide
more extensive financial information to the securities
commissions of their home countries in order to list on
local exchanges.

What all this means in terms of actually purchasing
Level One shares is that it is difficult to know what the
going price is when you buy them and sell them. You

might, therefore, place an order to buy 100 shares of Company A immediately. The most recent price you can find on the stock is the closing price from the day before, when it was at 50 a share, but after you buy it you might discover you paid 55. Or, you might also have bagged them at 45. For that reason, it is usually better to purchase lightly traded ADRs with limit instead of as market orders. For those unfamiliar with these terms, a *market order* is an order to buy or sell a stock at whatever the going price is on the market. A *limit order* is an order to buy or sell a specific number of shares at a specific price or better. In the example above, if you had put in a limit order to buy at 50 or less, the broker would not have executed the order with the stock at 55, but would have if the stock was at 45. The same is true of selling lightly traded ADRs: use limit orders, not market orders. You may sell at a point or two below the day's high, but at least you know you're getting your asking price for the shares.

As with any investment, a good piece of advice is to avoid selling when you need the money. Too many investors sell at the market price when a stock starts to fall because they need the money fast, and as a result lose 5 or 10 percent of their profit. Buy low, sell high, and keep whatever rainy day cash you might need in your money market account.

Another good tip about buying ADRs is to find access to a source that lists the real-time price of the company's stock on its local exchange. I use the Bloomberg system, which can simultaneously show you both the ADR price and the price on the local exchange. Most small investors don't have access to something like Bloomberg, but there are several other ways to access ADR quotes, such as the Bloomberg Web site (www.bloomberg.com) and Yahoo! If the Pink Sheets or Bulletin Board stocks you are looking for aren't listed, you can call your broker. Most brokers have some way of accessing financial data systems. There are some local sites with real-time data for foreign stock quotes in several Latin American countries, but they are costly, and you might want to rely on a broker. Finding the price on the local exchange is especially helpful for ADRs that are priced only once a day.

Sometimes the spread between the ADR price and the local price is larger or smaller than normal. This is usually because of liquidity differences. Local shares typically trade more frequently than ADRs, so the prices that are quoted on them are usually more up-to-date. That means you can sometimes buy an ADR at more or less than what that ADR is actually worth in terms of the number of local shares it represents. You can monitor the daily ADR price in the newspaper until it gets close to a price you've targeted; then start following the real-time price on the local exchange, and issue your buy order when the spread between the ADR price and the local price widens. This is a form of arbitrage, and you don't have to be a Wall Street guru to make money at it.

"There are differences in the price when both the local market and the ADR market are open at the same time," says Robert Gordon, an arbitrage expert and president of 21st Century Securities. "If the ADR is lower, we would buy that and break it apart into local shares. If the local shares are lower, we would buy those and assemble them into ADRs."

Gordon says it's harder to arbitrage with Latin American ADRs than with ADRs of European companies because executing and clearing the trades can sometimes run into delays, which could alter the price difference.

"We don't do it unless there's a large enough gap to make it worthwhile," he said. "The best opportunities are when the currency is more volatile than the stock."

Some ADRs can be purchased directly from the company. Since 1996, U.S. banking companies that act as the U.S. agents for foreign firms have begun to offer shares directly to individual investors, allowing them to avoid going through a broker. It's similar to buying mutual funds directly from the fund company. The advantage is that you avoid what can often amount to huge transaction fees charged by brokers. It's especially advantageous for investors who want to buy only a few shares at a time, which is hard to do at many brokerages due to minimum investment requirements and high per-transaction costs. To find out whether or not the company you're interested in has such a program, call their U.S. depository *(see phone numbers in the Resources section, or visit the Bank of New York's Web site at www.bankofny.com/adr).*

SELECTING STOCKS— THE FUNDAMENTALS

BEFORE YOU BUY ADRs, you have to sift through more than two hundred Latin American companies whose stock is available to you. The thirty-five companies listed in the second half of this book have ADRs that are traded in the United States on a regular basis, and most are listed on the New York Stock Exchange. Each of them was recommended by at least one if not several of the experts interviewed during research for this book. Because they were chosen for long-term investments, all thirty-five companies meet some, if not all, of the following criteria: large market capitalization, stability of earnings and sales growth, strong growth potential, competitive market advantage, consistently high operating margins, and strong management. But attention was also paid to the price and liquidity of each of the company's ADRs. Companies with excessively high price-to-earnings ratios or price-to-book values were not included, and companies whose ADRs are lightly traded were also ignored.

These thirty-five aren't the only attractive ADRs out there, and indeed some of these might no longer be attractive if you're reading this book a few years after its publication. There are new ADRs coming on the market all the time. This list is intended to give investors a good starting point for picking Latin American ADRs. Adding any four or five companies from this list to your domestic portfolio is intended to reduce the overall risk of your portfolio while—providing you buy and sell at the right time—significantly boosting your overall returns.

Analysts and traders use a wide array of data and measurements to predict how a stock will perform in the future—unfortunately, none of them always works. Some measurements work in some cases, though, and by looking at a few of the more important analytical tools, you can get a fairly good picture of where a company and its share price are headed. In no particular order, here they are:

PRICE-TO-BOOK RATIO

THE *PRICE-TO-BOOK RATIO,* sometimes written as P/BV (for price-to-book value), is the price of a stock relative to the percentage that share represents of the book value of all the company's tangible and intangible assets. An intangible asset is something that isn't concrete, such as a trademark or a patent. If you can buy a stock at lower than its book value, you're doing well, although there are lots of good stocks that trade at many times their book values. Microsoft is one example. It has traded at many times the company's book value for more than a decade. P/BV works better as a measure of share price in some industries than it does in others. In high tech, it usually doesn't mean much, but in mining or real estate it's important. Latin American companies traded on average at prices between 0.5 and 1.0 times their book values in 1998, which compares to between 5 and 6 times for U.S. stocks.

PRICE-TO-EARNINGS RATIO

PROBABLY THE MOST important measure of the value of a stock is not its share price but rather its *price-to-earnings ratio,* or P/E, which measures the share price divided by the yearly net income. Is a stock priced at $50 a better buy than a stock priced at $10? If the $50 stock has earnings of $5 per share and the $10 stock has earnings of $1 per share, the answer is that both have the same value to investors, all other things excluded. Be careful to look at more than just one year's P/E, as companies often have distorted earnings in one or another year due to major investments, legal losses, a down cycle in their industry, or other factors that have little to do with the company's long-term performance. Most Latin American companies trade at anywhere from 5 to 15 P/E ratios, which is far below the average 25 to 35 P/E ratios the Standard and Poor's 500 traded at in 1997 and 1998. Although you should try to buy stocks with P/E ratios of 10 or below, there are some exceptions. Mexico's Panamerican Beverages, for example, had a P/E ratio of 21 in mid-1998, but because of other factors explained later in this book, the share price may still represent a bargain.

Also, keep in mind that just because a stock has a low P/E or low P/BV ratio, it isn't necessarily undervalued. The company may be considered extremely risky by other investors, or for some reason its potential for future earnings growth may be considered low. That's why it's always important to get updated on the current news of a company before buying its stock. The Mexican glassmaker Vitro SA, for example, had a P/E below 4.0 in late 1998. Some investors might consider that a bargain, but others look at the fact that glass is gradually losing market share to plastics and other materials, and for that reason have not awarded the company a higher share price.

OPERATING MARGINS

THE *OPERATING MARGIN,* or *profit margin,* of a company is simply the profit during the year after taxes divided by annual sales revenue. It's important to find a pattern over time in the company's margins. Ideally, you want to see the margins going up, but that may not be the case for some good companies in Latin America. Many Latin American countries, especially Brazil, were accustomed to giddy profit margins of around 50 percent or more during their decades of protectionist trade rules. Those trade rules have since been eliminated or significantly reduced in Brazil and elsewhere, and margins have dropped to become more in line with those of other countries—in the 30 percent range or less—as a result of competition from outside Latin America. However, in most countries, the worst is behind them and good companies are now seeing their margins creeping up again, although they are unlikely to reach the high levels of the past. At the very least, you should be looking for a slower reduction in profit margins and some signs that margins will begin increasing again in the future. You should also compare the profit margins to the industry average. Some industries, such as supermarkets, typically have lower profit margins than other industries.

RETURN-ON-EQUITY AND RETURN-ON-INVESTED-CAPITAL

THESE ARE TWO separate but similar measurements that, like operating margins, tell you how well a company makes use of its money. *Return on equity* (ROE) is the company's profits after tax divided by the outstanding common equity. Although ROE is the more widely published figure and the easier to research, it is not as telling as *return on invested capital*, ROIC. Return on invested capital is simply the company's *earnings before interest and taxes*, or EBIT, divided by the sum of all capital on which a return must be earned. Some companies with high ROEs might gain those high returns on borrowed money rather than on equity. ROIC, on the other hand, looks at the total amount of money the company invests. But again, ROIC is harder to come by, so if you must use ROE, then you might also want to look at the company's return on assets in its annual report to make sure they aren't leveraging earnings.

DEBT-TO-EQUITY AND CURRENT RATIO

INVESTORS IN ANY STOCK should be aware of whether or not a company has borrowed more money than it can afford to pay back. Investors in Latin American stocks should be doubly concerned because of the effect a devaluation or a sudden rise in domestic interest rates can have on a company's balance sheet *(see Chapter 4 for a more detailed discussion of currency risk)*.

Two items shown on most company's annual reports will illustrate whether the company is carrying too much debt. The *debt-to-equity ratio* compares the amount of debt it has to the amount of equity on its books. Different industries have different ideal debt-to-equity ratios, and companies can often exceed those limits during periods of production capacity expansion or for other strategic reasons. Finding comparative numbers for ideal debt-to-equity ratios can be difficult, so it's helpful to look at reports of analysts who follow the company. You can usually get analyst reports from your broker; some large houses, such as Merrill Lynch, provide some of their research on the Web site. If the company isn't well covered by analysts, you can at least compare its debt-to-equity ratio to those of its competitors.

The other measure of debt is called the *current ratio,* which tells you the company's ability to pay its bills in the short term. Current ratio is simply the company's current assets divided by its current liabilities, a number you can compare to the average in its industry.

When looking at debt, be careful to distinguish between debt denominated in dollars and debt denominated in local currency. A company might have a reasonable debt-to-equity ratio and a reasonable current ratio, but if all its debt is in dollars and all its revenue is in local currency, a sudden devaluation could sharply increase the company's total debt load. Conversely, though, the company should have a portion of its debt in dollars, or at least access to dollar debt, to avoid being prisoner to sharp increases in local interest rates.

STRATEGIES FOR BUYING STOCKS

JAMES BARRINEAU, FORMERLY the chief Latin American strategist for Salomon Smith Barney and now emerging markets strategist of Alliance Capital, is a big proponent of ADR investing.

"First of all, you want to be diversified throughout the region," Barrineau says. "There are differences—and they're always changing—in the growth prospects, risk, and economic policies of the various countries.

"Next, you want to be exposed to the safer sectors like telecommunications and beverages, which are the long-term growth plays. Bank stocks are the most volatile, but if you're betting on interest rates, you buy them when you think that rates have peaked. Consumer stocks are more the [medium term] economic growth stocks."

Barrineau thinks some oil and construction stocks can also be good buys. Also, "In the telecommunications sector, buy Latin American companies that are backed by big international firms. Just like in the United States, low P/E stocks tend to outperform in the region."

John Welch, chief Latin America economist at the French bank Paribas, said in late 1998 that the best sectors for Latin American investments were telecommunications and electric utilities. Latin America was likely to be in a recession in 1999, he said then. Telecommunications and utilities are the industries most able to weather a recession. They're also good investments for the long term.

FORMULAS FOR VALUING STOCKS

I PROMISED I wouldn't introduce complex analytical tools. However, for those who like to have an equation in front of them, there are some simple formulas that can help you evaluate a company's stock price. These formulas are meant to appraise a stock by forecasting how the stock will do in the future based on some historical information. They are useful only in that they can tell you if the current stock price is above or below what the stock should be trading at based on the numbers. It doesn't tell you what other information—such as a recent management change, a downturn in the economy, or a new law opening up the company to competition—might already be factored into the stock price. As we've said, investing in Latin America emphasizes growth much more than it does income. Some Latin American companies don't even pay dividends, and others pay them irregularly.

To get an estimate for the value of a stock, you'll need

three things: the dividend (D), the growth rate of the stock (g), and the expected return (r). The first is easy. You can find the dividend from most financial Web sites, including Bloomberg, Yahoo!, or Intuit, on the stock's description page.

The growth rate is a little more complicated. You need to multiply the return on equity by the retention ratio. Return on equity is available on some financial Web sites and in the annual reports of some Latin American companies, and I list ROE for many of the thirty-five companies profiled in Chapters 6 through 10. The retention ratio is the percentage of after-tax earnings credited to retained earnings. Retained earnings can be gathered from the company's annual report.

The final component of the valuation equation, expected return, you can calculate by using the famous *Capital Asset Pricing Model,* or CAPM. Over the years, much debate has been stirred about whether or not CAPM is an effective model for predicting returns on assets, but it is still the most widely used method on Wall Street. For a more detailed explanation of this and other pricing models, see Burton Malkiel's *A Random Walk Down Wall Street* (W.W. Norton; 1996) or an investing textbook, such as *Investments* by Bodie, Kane, and Marcus (Irwin; 1998).

The basics of the CAPM are these:

$$R = R_f + [E(R_m) - R_f]B$$

where **R** is the expected return of the stock

R_f is the risk-free rate (usually the current rate on Treasury bills)

$E(R_m)$ is the expected return of the market (from an average of past years) and **B** is the beta of the stock versus the market.

"The market" is usually defined as the Standard and Poor's 500. In Latin America, one could use local indices instead, but because we are referring here to ADRs and we're balancing them within U.S. portfolios, the S&P 500 is the benchmark to use.

What the formula says, then, is that the expected return on an asset is the risk-free rate plus a risk premium. It is based on the theory that investors demand higher returns for higher risks.

For example, if a particular stock you are considering buying has a beta of 0.5 versus the S&P 500, the going T-bill rate is 4 percent, and the expected return of the S&P 500 is 12 percent a year, the expected return on your stock, providing it is fairly priced, is:

R = 4 + (12-4)0.5 or R = 8 PERCENT

The beta of a stock is a way of comparing the risk of a stock to the risk of the market. Specifically, it measures the sensitivity of the asset's return to the market return.

Now that you have the three components of calculating valuation, here's the formula:

$$P = \frac{D}{r - g}$$

Here's an example: Let's say the expected return on Telmex stock is 15 percent. Its most recent dividend was $1.63 a year, and its growth rate is 12 percent. The value of the stock, then, is:

P = D/r-g = 1.63/(.15-.12) = $54.33

You look at the newspaper and find that the current stock price is $49 a share, so based on your valuation, the stock is a bargain.

You could get more technical than the above formula if you wanted to. It assumes that growth is constant, for example. There are ways of calculating value based on varied growth rates. And there are other ways of coming up with estimates of expected return. There's a plethora of theories, called *factor models,* that attempt to predict expected returns based on such factors as the growth rate of industrial production, changes in inflation, and the size of the firm. For most investors, the CAPM is a good enough basis for getting a round estimate of the expected return of an individual stock.

IMAGINING THE FUTURE

MOST OF THE stock-selection methods I've discussed so far look at the past and recent state of the company, and try to guess its future based on the numbers. Often, however, a company's future has nothing to do with today's numbers. Look at the Chilean electric company Enersis, for example. Two years ago, Enersis was considered the best-run, most profitable electric company in Latin America, and investors heralded the announcement that it would be sold to Endesa, a Spanish electric company. But behind the good numbers was a team of corrupt managers that was secretly orchestrating the details of the sale so that a huge part of the proceeds would go straight into their pockets, rather than to shareholders. The result was that the sale was bungled, the company and shareholders lost millions, all of the managers were fired, and some of them were sent to jail.

Predicting instances like that is impossible, but by looking behind the numbers of a company or at a different set of criteria, you can minimize the frequency of surprises. Below I have reprinted a list of nine points from Douglas Lindgren, who manages $250 million in venture capital funds for U.S. Trust and teaches at the Columbia Business School. Venture capitalists are people who invest directly and significantly in a company and may even have a hand in managing it. There are several other lists that have been published by other investment authorities, but most of the good ones don't vary much from Lindgren's. The fact that his recommendations were written for venture capital investments doesn't matter. They apply just as well for small equity investors. In fact, that they come from a venture capitalist makes them even more credible because no one looks at a company in more depth and detail than a venture capitalist who is about to plop down $10 million or $20 million.

LINDGREN'S LIST OF STOCK SELECTION METHODS:

◆ **Superior management.** Probably the most important of the nine points. A superior management team usually can bring to the company any of the other eight factors that it might be lacking. Experience and a successful track record in the same or similar industries are important characteristics of good managers.

◆ **Large, growing markets.** A rising tide raises all ships. Companies whose business serves large, growing markets are better able to withstand occasional mishaps and setbacks. In good times, a growing market also provides more opportunities to expand and diversify a business.

◆ **Defensible competitive advantage.** For fast growth, companies need some sort of advantage in the marketplace that tilts the competitive playing field in their favor. It could be a proprietary technology, a new product, or a novel operating or marketing strategy.

◆ **Compelling business economics.** Good economics means more than just competitive prices. It means a competitive cost structure and high, sustainable margins.

◆ **Intelligent business strategy.** A sound and well-articulated business plan that leverages the company's core competencies, takes maximum advantage of its competitive advantages, and addresses the various business risks confronting it.

◆ **Attractive valuation and structure.** Look at the numbers for both price-to-earnings and price-to-book-value, and make sure you're not paying too much for your investment. Also, try to come up with a reasonable estimate of where the company's annual revenue and earnings will be ten years from now, and estimate the current stock price based on that data (as we did in the previous section).

◆ **Identifiable exit opportunities.** This is useful for venture capitalists, but it can apply to many ADR and mutual fund investments as well. You should be able to sell your investment when you want to, at an attractive price. Give preference to stocks with high trading volume and low spreads between their bid and ask prices. These numbers can be obtained from your broker or through the financial information Web sites listed in the appendix of this book.

◆ **Strong coinvestors and board.** Get a copy of the annual report and look at those who have invested in this company. Do some mutual funds whose managers you respect have big stakes in it? Who are the minority owners of the company? Does the company have a strong board of directors who, in the event of a breakdown in management, could come in and patch things up?

◆ **Manageable risks.** Every business has its risks. Understanding what they are makes it easier to know when they get too high. You can break risk into five categories:

TECHNOLOGY RISK refers to the risk that the company's technology won't work well or will become obsolete.

MARKET RISK is the risk that the market for the company's products or services will evaporate.

EXECUTIVE RISK is the risk that the company, for whatever reason, won't be able to implement its business plan.

REGULATORY RISK is the risk that government or courts will intervene in some negative way.

FINANCIAL RISK is the risk of the company's financial structure falling apart, such as, not being able to make debt payments.

Make sure you understand the risks in each of those five categories. You can analyze these risks by getting a copy of the company's annual report and by checking news stories about the company. We'll show you in the resources section of the appendix how to find company news. (Note: Lindgren's list is designed for U.S. investments, so he doesn't include two other types of risk that are important to look at in analyzing Latin American stocks: currency risk and political risk. We'll cover those later in this chapter and again in Chapter 4.)

Lindgren rates a company from one to five, worst to best, on each of those nine points. He has no set minimum for how many total points a company should have, but he says rating them helps give him a better idea of what he is investing in and why.

Many of the items on Lindgren's list reinforce something already mentioned, and that is to read the news. Follow articles about the company from Bloomberg, Reuters, *The Wall Street Journal, the Financial Times,* or *Latin Finance* and *Latin Trade* magazines. Most of these reports are available from the various Web sites listed in the back of this book. Here are a few of the issues you should be looking for:

Has there been a change of management lately? If so, why?

Was the company recently privatized, and are there any remaining shares that the government still holds and may sell at a later date?

What are competitors doing?

Is there any legislation in the works that is directly related to the company's industry?

Have tariffs and other trade measures been reduced lately within the industry? If so, how will this affect the company?

Are there any legal proceedings such as corruption investigations, patent cases, or consumer litigation against the company?

Does the company plan any new bond or equity issues in the near future?

Does the company plan to invest in any capacity expansion or acquire other companies?

Does it plan to sell any divisions or close down any production lines?

Did its most recent earnings beat the street's expectations?

SHARES LISTED IN EUROPE

MOST OF THE DISCUSSIONS in this chapter apply just as well to Latin American shares listed in Europe as they do to shares listed in the United States. There are, however, some unique differences about buying and selling Latin American stocks in Europe that should be mentioned. First, when a Latin American company sells shares in Europe, its shares are usually referred to as Global Depository Receipts, or GDRs. There are far fewer GDRs sold in Europe than there are ADRs sold in the United States, but that is mostly because there is little need for them. Many European stock exchanges, including the London Stock Exchange, allow direct trading of the shares listed on most major stock markets around the world, including those of Latin American countries. European citizens can therefore buy and sell shares in Latin America much more easily than U.S. citizens can. The transaction fees that brokers charge to complete the trades are often higher than the added expense a U.S. citizen would have in buying ADRs.

As mentioned earlier in this chapter, most Europeans are also free to buy shares listed on each other's exchanges, which makes it easier for Latin American companies that want to sell GDRs to reach all of Europe by listing shares on a single exchange. The added attraction of being able to buy shares and funds listed on offshore exchanges such as those of Luxembourg, Dublin, and the Channel Islands is another advantage Europeans have over U.S. citizens. (Chapter Five gives more information about offshore investing.)

IPOS

WHEN A COMPANY first decides to sell shares to the public, it does so through an *initial public offering,* or IPO. In the past, when a Latin American company did an IPO, the offering was done exclusively in its home stock market. Years later the company might issue an ADR. Today more

Latin American companies are seeing the benefits of reaching shareholders by launching their new shares simultaneously in several markets worldwide. Given all the publicity that recent initial public offerings in the United States have generated, many investors in Europe and North America are curious about the Latin American IPO market. It's neither as big nor as exciting as the U.S. IPO market, but it's growing. Probably the most visible recent offering, and the one that opened the door to future Latin American IPOs, was TV Azteca. Mexico's up-and-coming, number two television broadcaster sold $526.2 million in a global offering in August 1997.

Eduardo Ramos, head of investment banking at Casa de Bolsa Banorte in Mexico City, says he expects more Latin American companies to go public over the next few years. "The TV Azteca sale really encouraged other companies that were thinking about going public," he told Bloomberg News in an interview.

In early 1998, several Latin American companies were preparing to launch IPOs. Unfortunately, the Asia crisis and then the Russia crisis postponed everyone's plans, but they'll be resurrected once the markets stabilize.

Another good sign that more IPOs are imminent is the huge increase in private equity investing in Latin America. Private equity encompasses venture capital and other forms of direct purchase of minority or majority stakes in companies. Until the early 1990s, private equity investing was almost nonexistent in Latin America. Since then, dozens of financial companies both inside and outside Latin America have started private equity funds. One common trait of most private equity funds is that they don't invest anywhere unless they see a good chance of pulling that investment out again in its entirety within five or ten years. In many cases, that chance comes when the company they invested in does its IPO.

In an interview in October 1998 Pedro-Pablo Kuczinsky, president of one of the oldest private equity funds in the region, the Latin America Enterprise Fund, said, "Right now, IPOs in Latin America are like palm trees in Greenland. This year and next year are going to be slow years, no question about it. But the prospects for getting out of this crisis are very, very good." For that reason, private equity investors were looking to do more deals, not fewer, to take advantage of low prices during the economic downturn, he said.

You can find out about Latin American IPOs well in advance of the stock sale through your broker or by looking up one of the Web sites or publications listed in the back of this book, such as, Yahoo!, Intuit, or Bloomberg.

A note of caution: As in the United States, Latin American IPOs can sometimes be overly hyped. Unsuspecting investors can be led to believe that a hot new company is going to list its shares on the Nasdaq and that its shares will immediately shoot through the roof; but in reality what happens is that the big institutional investors who get in early take all the profits, and the small investor who puts in a "buy" order on the stock doesn't see the order filled until the price has already shot up.

Another warning: In many cases, what is described as an IPO of a Latin American company in the United States doesn't necessarily mean the shares aren't already listed in the home country. Latin American companies often refer to their first launch of equity outside their home country as an IPO. That said, even these are often good investment opportunities, because they represent the first time that shares are being offered to individual foreign investors, and the added demand can drive up the price of the shares.

TAX IMPLICATIONS OF ADRS

IF YOU'RE LIKE me, just the idea of any new taxes or any additional complications on your IRS 1040 form is enough to cause you to flinch. Fortunately, buying and selling ADRs creates little pain at tax time, and the only added expense you might incur is an extra $20 to your tax accountant for filling out an extra form.

"The major impact of owning stock in a foreign company is the fact that when dividends are paid, a withholding tax is assessed at the source, and that applies whether you have ADRs or local shares. But you will usually get an equal credit against your U.S. taxes," says Bob Willens, a noted tax and accounting analyst at Lehman Brothers in New York City.

As in the United States, most foreign countries charge taxes on dividend payments. When that happens with ADRs you own, most good stockbrokers will let you know in a little box that appears on your year-end tax statement. Show that to whomever prepares your taxes, and you should be able to get a credit for the same amount on your U.S. tax return.

What about capital gains taxes?

"No country I know of assesses a capital gains tax on foreign investors," says Willens.

Some countries from time to time establish temporary transaction taxes on stock purchases, but those usually don't apply to foreigners either. Brazil, for example, started charging transaction taxes in 1998 to help it weather an economic downturn, but foreigners were exempt.

CURRENCY RISK AND HEDGING

ALL FOREIGN INVESTMENTS, whether they're mutual funds, ADRs, or fixed-income securities, entail some currency risk. Currency risk is simply the chance that the currency in the country you are invested in will suffer a devaluation relative to the U.S. dollar. In Latin America, the biggest recent examples of this were the 1994 Mexican peso crisis and Brazil's devaluation of the *real* in January 1999. On one day, December 20, 1994, the peso lost about half its value. Mexican stocks trading locally fell only slightly, because their prices were quoted in pesos, but their dollar values dropped 50 percent. Likewise, Mexican ADR prices also dropped about 50 percent. And mutual funds that invest in Mexico lost heavily on the day of the devaluation and then continued to slide as the crisis affected the Mexican economy and corporate earnings.

In Brazil, the *real* slid 69.66 percent versus the U.S. dollar in January 1999. However, stock prices didn't take much of a beating since the devaluation was widely anticipated.

Currency risk also has an upside. If a currency is strengthening against the dollar, the value of ADRs will rise.

Most experts I talked to about currency hedging said that it isn't wise for individual investors to even think about trying to hedge their Latin American investments. The risk of currencies plunging is just part of the whole game of investing in Latin America. Besides, investing in Latin America is in itself a form of hedge against the risks of your U.S. portfolio. Hedging means buying one investment to offset the risk of another. Hedging costs money, and it also requires much more time and effort than most individuals are willing to put in. For example, you could buy peso futures on the Chicago Mercantile exchange as a hedge against your stock investments in Mexico, but you would have to keep a constant watch on the peso rate to buy continuously and to sell peso futures as they expired in order to keep up the hedge. The transaction fees would be enormous.

BE COMFORTABLE

IN THIS CHAPTER, you've seen what American Depository Receipts are and how to buy them. You've seen how the fundamentals of companies can be used to size up Latin American ADRs. You'll want to go beyond the numbers to look at the more subjective characteristics of a company and to get a picture of how the company will do in the future. And you'll want to think about whether other investors are going to buy the stock, too. Investors don't always act rationally and can sometimes buy a specific stock for no apparent reason other than the fact that it's "hot"—what Burton Malkiel calls the "castles in the air" theory. Also in this chapter, you've seen that, depending on how you invest, you might want to know about hedging, tax implications, investing in IPOs, and investing from Europe and Asia, before you start buying shares.

But before you buy anything, let me reiterate one extremely important fact: investing in Latin America can be risky. Studies have shown that the stock market investments of most U.S. individuals routinely return less than the market average. In Latin America, beating the market can be even harder.

When deciding which ADRs to buy or even whether to buy ADRs at all, the best question to ask yourself is "Do I feel comfortable making this investment?" Investing in ADRs is like investing in U.S. stocks to the extent that the more you know about the company, the better your chance of a high return on your investment. You don't have to be a Latin American scholar or an investment genius, and you don't have to know the companies from top to bottom. If you do your homework and follow the advice in this book, you may or may not be able to beat the market, but you'll have the knowledge to become a confident player.

With these first three chapters under your belt, you're ready to start planning your investment portfolio.

CHAPTER 4

Strategy

NOW THAT YOU understand the characteristics of ADRs and mutual funds and how to buy them, you're ready to build your investment portfolio. Before you start picking stocks and funds, however, you need to map out your financial goals, then look for the right combination of securities to match these objectives. This chapter presents the basic strategies that can make a world of difference to the total value of your portfolio—and to your ability to get at your money when you need it. After your investment expectations are established, you'll need to keep watch over your holdings so they don't move away from the balance of risk and expected return that you chose for yourself. Conversely, you'll also be rearranging your holdings as your goals and risk tolerance change. The investments you choose when you're a thirty-year-old single renting a downtown apartment won't be the same as when you're a forty-year-old spouse and parent living in a suburban house that you own.

Some strategies you'll use for Latin America are similar to those you might use for other investments. Your company's 401(k) manager may have recommended how best to divide up your retirement assets depending on your financial goals. Your stockbroker or financial adviser may have offered some advice on following the market: that stocks tend to go up in January, for example, or that you should keep track of interest rates and business cycles. In addition to these, there are some strategies peculiar to Latin America that you'll read about in this chapter.

WHO ARE YOU, AND WHAT DO YOU WANT FROM YOUR INVESTMENTS?

ON PAGE 95 THERE'S A LIST of questions that an adviser, such as a stockbroker or financial planner, typically asks new clients during a first interview. These questions were taken from the Charles Schwab Web site, but you can use any similar test that your broker may have to give you a rough estimate of your investment style. Although Schwab has its own scale, we'll use your answers to the questions to measure something called your A: a number that measures how much you dislike risk, or more specifically, how much you dislike variance in your investments. The larger your A, the more averse you are to risk. The average A for American investors is about 2.46, so if you are below that, you're willing to tolerate more risk than the average investor; if you're above it, you're more risk averse. This number will be used in a formula to determine your investment allocations. Most investors fall between 2.0 and 4.0.

Once you have your A, you need to sit down and determine how much of your portfolio should be invested in each asset class, such as bonds, stocks, cash, and emerging market stocks. In *A Random Walk Down Wall Street*, Burton Malkiel presents a series of pie charts with recommended asset allocations for various types of investors. Schwab has a similar series of pie charts at its Web site. From the www.schwab.com home page, click on "planning," then "general investing," and then "asset allocation" for the on-line version of the test. You can then allocate your assets for the pie chart.

After you answer the questions from Schwab's test, or any similar risk quiz, use your total score to figure out your A. The average total score for Schwab's test is about 28. If you assume that is also the average A of 2.46, you can then estimate what the A of other scores would be. Your answers will also give you a better idea of what type of investor you are. You can then use Malkiel's pie charts as a point of reference for determining your ideal asset allocations. If your risk-aversion level is average, then pick the portfolio corresponding to your age group. If you are more risk-tolerant than the average investor, you can increase the percentage of stocks in your recommended portfolio for your age group and decrease the level of bonds and cash. If you

CHARLES SCHWAB'S INVESTOR PROFILE

CharlesSchwab

Schwab Stock Screening
FREE 7 Day Trial — Click Now

Log In | Home | Open an Account | SchwabAnswers | Thursday, April 15, 1999

General Planning

Principles of
Investing

General Goal
Planner

▾ Asset Allocation

Investor Profile

Allocate Your Assets

▸ Understanding
Market Cycles

Gaining Financial
Independence

Investor Profile Questionnaire

Just answer these seven simple questions about your life stage, attitude toward risk, and other factors, then we'll show you a sample investment plan based on your profile.

1. I plan to start withdrawing money from my investments for major needs in:
(select)

2. When I begin withdrawing money, I plan to spend it in:
(select)

3. My knowledge of investments is:
(select)

4. When deciding how to invest my money, I am
○ Most concerned about the possibility of my investment losing value
○ Equally concerned about the possibility of my investment losing or gaining value
○ Most concerned about the possibility of my investment gaining value

5. Select the investments you currently own or have owned in the past (select all that apply):
☐ Money market funds/cash equivalents
☐ Bonds/bond funds
☐ Stocks/stock funds
☐ International securities/funds

6. Imagine that the stock market has dropped by 25% in value over the past three months. A stock that you own has also dropped by 25% in value. What would you do with your shares?
(select)

7. Consider the annual returns of the five hypothetical investment plans below. Based on the range of possible outcomes shown, which plan would be most acceptable to you or best suit your investment philosophy?

1 Year Return

Investment Plan	Average Annualized	Best Case Scenario	Worst Case Scenario
○ Plan A	7.2%	16.3%	-5.6%
○ Plan B	9.0%	25.0%	-12.1%
○ Plan C	10.4%	33.6%	-18.2%
○ Plan D	11.7%	42.8%	-24.0%
○ Plan E	12.5%	50.0%	-28.2%

These figures are hypothetical and do not represent the performance of any particular investment.

Cancel | Send

Site Map | Help | E-Mail

---

are more conservative than the average investor, put less in stocks and more in cash and bonds.

Malkiel recommends putting all your stock and bond investments in mutual funds. My own opinion is that part of your money should be in mutual funds, but just how much depends on your own financial goals, your tolerance for risk, and your confidence in your ability to pick winning stocks. In any case, if you decide to invest in stocks and bonds directly, you can simply substitute stocks for stock mutual funds and bonds for bond mutual funds in determining how much of your portfolio you invest in each type of asset.

SIFTING THROUGH THE ADVICE

ONCE YOU HAVE a general idea of how much of your money should be invested in each asset class, you can look at the pie charts later in this chapter to see how much of the international portion of your portfolio you should put into emerging markets, and of that, how much should go to mutual funds, ADRs, and bonds. Malkiel recommends that investors put somewhere between 30 percent and 40 percent of their stock market holdings into foreign stock funds and that a third of those be in emerging markets. Our recommendations call for an even higher percentage of emerging market investments: roughly, emerging markets should represent most of your foreign stock investments and as much as 27 percent of your total portfolio. Latin American stocks can be as much as 20 percent of your total portfolio.

The higher recommendations are in part because focusing more of your international investments on a fast-growing region like Latin America can allow you to get to know the countries and the companies more thoroughly. What's more, Latin America offers a bigger selection of heavily traded ADRs from which to choose than do other regions. Also, Malkiel tends to be conservative, and his analysis is based on a random sample of "very risky emerging markets stocks." Emerging markets stocks don't have to be very risky. Plenty of Latin American stocks are less volatile than many European or Japanese stocks but still have lower correlations with the U.S. stock market. A mix of these with some riskier, higher-returning Latin American stocks can boost your portfolio's return and lower its risk more effectively than would a comparable selection of stocks from Europe. Malkiel's recommendation that investors put all their emerging markets holdings in mutual funds also underestimates the abilities of some individual investors to beat the market.

"If you're in mutual funds for diversification, you're

probably better off purchasing a handful of ADRs," says Jim Barrineau, formerly the chief Latin American strategist for Salomon-Smith Barney. "Why pay someone else to do it for you?" Barrineau points to the high fees charged by most Latin American mutual funds.

Another reason for holding ADRs instead of mutual funds is that you don't have to sell your stocks when some financial or economic crisis causes stocks prices to plunge, whereas mutual fund managers must sell to meet redemptions from skittish shareholders.

"If you have ADRs, and you have a longer time horizon for your investments, you can ride out the volatility," Barrineau says.

Experts disagree on whether you should direct your investments toward regions, countries, or individual companies. In *Global Bargain Hunting,* Malkiel, along with coauthor J.P. Mei, says, "Look at regions, not companies. . . . Individual investors interested in active portfolio management should concentrate on country rather than on individual stock selection."

Many fund managers would take an opposing tack. "Pick stocks, not countries," says Rick Mace, who manages three international mutual funds for Fidelity. "Over time, companies with good business prospects and reasonable stock prices can have superior growth potential, no matter what country they are in or what continent they are on." Both Malkiel and Mace have good points. So the best strategy is to combine the advice of both. It's important to pick stocks in countries and regions whose growth potential is strong, such as Brazil or Argentina. But there are plenty of lemons in Brazil and Argentina. Don't pick a stock just because it's in a country that you like, and don't pick a company with a promising outlook and strong financial data if it's in a country that is poorly managed and headed for recession. Going into 1998, for example, Venezuela had some strong companies that could have done well, had it not been for the fact that the economy was ill managed.

Another strategy is to invest in countries that are moving up what the Dutch investment bank ING Barings refers to as the "convergence cone." Developing countries, according to this theory, are all in some state of convergence with the economies of the most-developed countries of North America, Europe, and Japan. True convergence is when a country reaches what we described in Chapter 1 as its "steady state" economy.

"As countries develop, they converge to the growth rates and associated volatility of their developed-world counterparts," ING strategists Shaun Roache and Matthew Merritt wrote in an October 1998 report. "Those countries that are making significant progress provide the most attractive investments. However, no country has ever moved smoothly through the convergence cone. A crisis in one emerging market (or a region) also has the capacity to knock numerous other countries off the convergence path—a theme known as *contagion*."

That's what happened in 1998 when the Asia crisis preceded the Russia crisis, which in turn led to problems in Latin America. While the 1998 crisis did not diminish the case for investing in emerging markets, it did increase the need for more active portfolio management, Roache and Merritt say.

"In this environment, country selection is paramount—having exposure to those markets in convergence mode (where large positive returns can be expected) and having minimal (or short) positions on those countries which have been temporarily shaken off the convergence path."

In an interview, Roache told me the trick is knowing when a country is moving toward true convergence and when it only appears to be converging with developed economies. "The things we have to look for are signs of unsustainability," says Roache, who is ING's chief emerging markets strategist. The three most important indications that a country's convergence is not sustainable are a high and expanding current account deficit, a large fiscal deficit, and a poorly controlled money supply that invests in unproductive areas.

Argentina and Chile, and to a lesser extent Mexico,

appear to be on paths of true convergence, while Brazil could be if it gets its fiscal deficit under control, Roache says.

In addition to the recommendations given here, and your own judgment, you should get the advice of an expert you trust, such as a stockbroker or financial adviser. More and more of them are becoming knowledgeable about investing in Latin America.

CORRELATION

IN THE 1950s, an economist named Harry Markowitz came up with what has since become known as Modern Portfolio Theory (MPT), and he won the Nobel Prize in economics for it in 1990. The theory held that a portfolio of risky (volatile) stocks could be assembled such that the overall portfolio would be less risky than any one of the individual stocks in it. Research has since proven MPT to be true, and to this day it is the main reason that Wall Street investors spend so much time making sure their own portfolios are diverse. For example, a fully diversified portfolio of U.S. stocks has only 27 percent of the volatility of the average individual U.S. stock. Already, you can see the benefits of

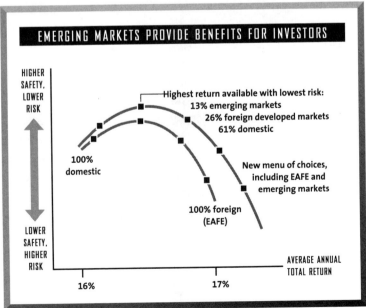

EMERGING MARKETS PROVIDE BENEFITS FOR INVESTORS

HIGHER SAFETY, LOWER RISK

Highest return available with lowest risk:
13% emerging markets
26% foreign developed markets
61% domestic

100% domestic

New menu of choices, including EAFE and emerging markets

100% foreign (EAFE)

LOWER SAFETY, HIGHER RISK

AVERAGE ANNUAL TOTAL RETURN

16%   17%

diversification. By comparison, the volatility on an internationally diversified portfolio is just 11.7 percent of that on a
typical U.S. stock. It shows two curves. The bottom curve
shows various combinations of a portfolio of domestic U.S.
stocks with a portfolio of international stocks from developed countries, represented by the Morgan Stanley EAFE
index. The top curve shows what would happen if you
added risky stocks from emerging markets to the mix.

You needn't be fully diversified to lower your risk. If you
had a portfolio representing the U.S. market and shifted
10 percent of it to the stocks making up the International
Finance Corp. emerging market index, for example, you
would lower the overall volatility of your portfolio by a full
percentage point while at the same time increasing the
expected return by half a percentage point, according to a
study by Claude Erb, Campbell Harvey, and Tadas Viskanta published in the *Journal of Portfolio Management*. Erb
and Viskanta are money managers; Harvey is a finance professor at Duke University.

This isn't true for all individual Latin America stocks
and funds, however.

"It is generally known that adding emerging markets to
a globally diversified portfolio reduces overall risk and
increases expected returns," Erb, Harvey, and Viskanta
wrote in their paper. "At the same time, little is known
about which emerging markets to choose."

Some emerging markets stocks follow the price movements of U.S. stocks so closely that they provide less diversification than would a typical U.S. stock. For example,
Micron Technology, one of the most heavily traded U.S.
stocks, has a low correlation of 0.11 with the Standard and
Poor's 500. Mexico's Cemex has a much higher 0.29 correlation. But most Latin American stocks have low correlations. To refresh your memory from Chapters 2 and 3, a
correlation is simply the degree to which the price movements of two assets—a stock, bond, mutual fund, or market indices—are related to each other. If stock A has a correlation coefficient of -1.0 with respect to stock B, then

stock A is said to have a perfectly negative correlation with stock A, meaning every time stock B moved in one direction, stock A moved in the opposite direction by the same percentage amount. A coefficient of 1.0, a perfectly positive correlation, would mean that both stocks always move in the same direction by the same percentage amount.

The best way to determine how a stock trades relative to the U.S. market is to look at its correlation coefficient with respect to the S&P 500 index. Equally useful is the square of the correlation coefficient, sometimes referred to as R squared. This number is usually easy to come by in reference materials such as Morningstar reports, and on financial Web sites. In the second half of this book, the squared correlation coefficient with respect to the S&P 500 is shown for each of the thirty-five companies profiled.

The thirty-five Latin American stocks profiled in Part Two have squared correlation coefficients that average around 0.18, with respect to the S&P 500. That's pretty good. If you can pick stocks with squared correlation coefficients below 0.20, you're doing great. If they're much higher than that, they had better be promising some extremely high returns, because as R-squared approaches 1, the stock is nearing perfect synchronization with the market and isn't giving you much diversification. Sometimes, good company fundamentals are reason enough to buy a stock, even if it doesn't contribute to reducing risk in your overall portfolio. But if you can pick some others with correlation coefficients of 0.15 or lower, you can expect to significantly reduce the overall volatility.

Correlation coefficients work just as well with mutual funds as they do with stocks. You can find the squared correlation coefficient for any fund you are considering from the mutual fund company or from Morningstar's Web site. When looking at the correlation coefficients of mutual funds, be sure to compare them to other mutual funds as a gauge, and make sure whatever sources you use have the same benchmarks, such as the S&P 500.

For most investors, the historical correlation coefficients

listed for the companies in the second half of this book are all you need to get a general idea of whether or not you're providing enough diversification in your portfolio. If you want to update these numbers, ask your broker or do some research in the sources listed in the back of this book to find the current correlation coefficients for the stocks you're considering buying, and then compare them with the historicals in this book. If you really want to get technical, you can calculate the overall correlation coefficient for the domestic part of your portfolio relative to the S&P 500, and then calculate the correlation coefficients of Latin American stocks relative to your own portfolio instead of relative to the S&P 500. This will provide you with a much more accurate picture of your overall diversification, but unless you have a computer program that does all the math for you, you would have to recalculate everything every time you buy or sell a stock.

YOUR PORTFOLIO

PORTFOLIO THEORY CONSISTS of two main steps: deciding on the assets that comprise a "risky" portfolio, and deciding on what percentage of your money to invest in each portfolio. There are various levels of portfolios into which you can categorize your investments. The first level is to divide between the *risk-free portfolio,* which consists of all the money you have invested in whatever risk-free asset you have chosen, such as Treasury bills or money market accounts; and a second portfolio that consists of all your stock and bond market investments, called the *risky portfolio.* You can further divide the risky portfolio into two separate categories: the market, or *passive,* portfolio, which consists of all your investments in index funds that track the overall performance of the stock market, and the *active* portfolio, which consists of all the other stock and bond investments that you choose by yourself. One good way to simplify your strategy is to divide your risky portfolio with a third category of several different risky portfolios. Your Latin American investments (or your emerging markets investments) can comprise one of those portfolios. By doing so, you can treat Latin America as if it were one asset, which you can overweight as a percentage of your risky portfolio during times of expected high growth, and underweight during times of crisis when you expect U.S. stocks to outperform Latin American stocks.

That brings us back to deciding which Latin American stocks to put into your risky Latin American portfolio. Constructing the optimal risky portfolio of Latin American stocks is a complicated task that involves gathering lots of statistics, such as the covariance of stocks with each other. For a detailed explanation of how to do this, look at the textbook *Investments,* by Bodie, Kane, and Marcus (Irwin, 1996). What I describe here is an easier, though less accurate way. The idea behind portfolio theory is to come up with something called your *efficient portfolio.* Each investor has an individual efficient portfolio that seeks to maximize the desired combination of expected return and risk. The formula for analyzing any asset that you add to your portfolio is the following.

$$U = E(R) - A \times S$$

Where, **U** is the "utility" of any new asset you are considering adding to your portfolio. Utility is expressed as a percentage, like expected return, that is adjusted for your risk tolerance and the variance of the asset.

E(R) is the expected return of the asset.

A is your **"A"**, or degree of risk aversity.

And **S** is the square of the standard deviation of the asset (the degree to which the price of a stock varies from the average price).

The higher the **"U"** of an asset, the better it fits into your own personal efficient portfolio.

The expected return of a stock is what you estimate the average annual return will be over the time you expect to hold onto it. You can use the formula for the CAPM, which we laid out in Chapter 3, and you can adjust that number if you believe the company's growth prospects have changed. You can also use analysts' estimates of future earnings and stock prices as a guide. The standard deviation is also somewhat subjective. You can get standard deviations for the stocks listed in this book from several financial Web sites. I found them at www.stocksmartpro.com ($12.95 a year after a thirty-day free trial) by typing in the ticker symbol and then clicking on "ticker details." But make sure the source you use tells you what period of time was used to calculate the standard deviation. If your research tells you that the stock is becoming more or less volatile over time, you may want to use the standard deviation over a smaller time period. Remember, standard deviation is the most widely used measure of volatility. It measures the degree to which the price of a stock varies from the average price. Literally, it is the square of the average variance of the stock price from the mean.

After you decide which stocks you want to buy in Latin America, you have to decide how much of each stock you should own. Again, I'll refer you to the Bodie, Kane, Marcus textbook for the precise explanation of how to do this. It involves several formulas. For most small investors, the best way is either to divide them up evenly or to use your own best judgment in allocating more money to your favorite stocks and less to the ones you're unsure about.

THE LATIN AMERICA PART

NOW YOU'RE READY to map out exactly how much Latin America should fit into your investments and how much of your Latin American investments should be in the form of ADRs and mutual funds to suit your personal profile and investment goals. Remember, these allocations should be flexible. And they're valid whether or not you combine them with the mathematical calculations we just went through. You want to keep them written down and make sure your portfolio doesn't stray too much from your desired mix, but that doesn't mean that if you discover a good stock at a bargain price you should pass it up because it exceeds your quota for that type of stock. You can trim your other investments to make room for a good one.

Following are five sample portfolios based on the recommendations of experts quoted in this book as well as the standard asset allocations recommended by Malkiel in *A Random Walk Down Wall Street* and the investor literature of Merrill Lynch and Charles Schwab. Firms such as Schwab and Merrill Lynch usually only list how much of a portfolio should be invested overseas. They do not distinguish between emerging markets and developed country stocks. Pie charts for each investor age group illustrate how much of a total stock market portfolio should be invested in each type of foreign asset, such as Latin American stocks or emerging market mutual funds. Then, examples display a typical portfolio for each age group.

All of these samples are for portfolios worth between $50,000 and $100,000. The recommended allocations don't change much with investments over $100,000. You might want to experiment with Brady Bonds (discussed in Chapter 5) or possibly delve into derivatives on a limited basis, but your mix of funds and ADRs and of stocks and bonds should remain about the same. If you have less than $50,000 in your portfolio, though, you might want to put more money in funds and less in stocks. If, for example, you are in your sixties and have only $10,000 to invest, you might want to steer clear of Latin America altogether. All of your money should be in cash and easily accessible money-market accounts and mutual funds, and most of that should be in bond funds. If you are in your mid-twenties and have $7,000, you can still buy a stock or two but should put the rest in funds.

LATE-TWENTIES TO EARLY-THIRTIES
($50,000 portfolio):

Cash: 5%

Bonds: 15% (7% U.S. bonds and bond funds; 4% international bond fund; 4% emerging market bond fund or corporate Eurobonds)

U.S. stocks and stock mutual funds: 46%

Foreign developed country stocks and stock mutual funds: 7%

(Including the portion of your international mutual funds that are invested in Europe, Japan, Canada, and Australia)
Emerging market non-Latin America stocks and stock mutual funds: 7% (Includes the portion of your international funds and your emerging markets funds that are invested in Asian, Eastern European, and African emerging markets)
Latin American stocks and stock funds: 20%

Example of Latin American portion:
$1,750 in regional Latin American mutual fund
$1,750 in closed-end country fund
$2,000 ADR of Company A
$2,000 ADR of Company B
$2,500 as the Latin American portion of your international and emerging markets mutual funds.

As your portfolio grows, and your age, you move to the following allocation for a $75,000 portfolio:

LATE-THIRTIES TO EARLY-FORTIES
($75,000 portfolio):

Cash: 5%
Bonds: 20% (U.S. bonds and bond funds 10%; international bonds and bond funds 5%; emerging markets bonds and bond funds 5%)
U.S. stocks and stock mutual funds: 44%
Foreign developed country stocks and stock mutual funds: 7%
Emerging market non-Latin America stocks and stock mutual funds: 6%
Latin American stocks and stock funds: 18%

Example of Latin American portion:
$2,500 in regional mutual fund
$2,000 in closed-end country fund
$1,750 in ADR of company A
$1,750 in ADR of company B
$1,750 in ADR of company C
$1,750 in ADR of company D

$2,000 as the Latin American portion of your international and emerging markets funds

MID-FIFTIES
($100,000 portfolio):

Cash: 10%

Bonds: 25% (15% U.S. bonds and bond funds; 5% international bonds and bond funds; 5% emerging market bonds and bond funds)

U.S. stocks and stock mutual funds: 39%

Foreign developed country stocks and stock mutual funds: 5%

Emerging market non-Latin America stocks and stock mutual funds: 6%

Latin America stocks and stock mutual funds: 15%

Example of Latin American portion:

$3,000 in a regional mutual fund

$3,000 in a second regional mutual fund or in a closed-end country fund

$2,000 in ADR of Company A

$2,000 in ADR of Company B

$2,000 in ADR of Company C

$3,000 as the Latin American portion of your international and emerging markets funds

As you move into retirement, your capacity for risk tends to be little, and investment-grade bonds are recommended for the major portion of your portfolio. Virtually all of your bonds should be invested in the United States, although owning some foreign bonds would be advisable for diversification.

LATE SIXTIES AND BEYOND
($75,000 portfolio):

Cash: 10%

Bonds: 36% (24% U.S. bonds and bond funds; 6% international bonds and bond funds; 6% emerging market bonds and bond funds)

U.S. stocks and stock mutual funds: 36%
Foreign developed country stocks and stock mutual funds: 5%
Emerging market non-Latin America stocks and stock mutual funds: 5%
Latin America stocks and stock mutual funds: 8%

Example of Latin American portion:
$2,500 in regional Latin America mutual fund
$3,500 as the Latin American portion of your international and emerging markets funds

Some investors believe they get enough international diversity simply by buying stocks of multinational companies based in the United States that have operations overseas. Procter & Gamble, Exxon, and Coca-Cola are just a few of these. There are some advantages to this theory. For one, playing the "home-team advantage" allows you to invest in companies you know, as opposed to a Mexican cement company or Peruvian bank that you may never have heard of.

However, while it is true that these multinational companies are somewhat cushioned from a downturn in the U.S. economy, it is also true that the stocks of these companies tend to move in line with the S&P 500. In other words, they are closely correlated with the U.S. stock market and therefore do not provide the risk reduction through diversification that an international stock fund or an ADR would provide. Also, large multinational companies are usually so intensely researched by analysts and investors in the United States that there is virtually no way a small U.S. investor can gain an edge.

TRADING STRATEGIES

IN ADDITION TO strategies for buying individual stocks and bonds and for dividing up your portfolio, there are a number of separate techniques designed to help you time your investments. Some of these can work well in Latin America, especially if you know the region and the issues involved well enough. More often than not, however, investors get burned by being overconfident in their ability to predict trends in the market.

INTEREST RATES

IN LATIN AMERICA, as in the United States and the rest of the world, stock markets tend to move in an inverse relationship to interest rates. Some people like to trade their stocks according to the movements in interest rates. The problem with this strategy, apart from trading costs and taxes, is that it is extremely difficult to know where rates are going, even if you happen to be the chairman of the Federal Reserve. An added problem in Latin America is that stocks react to both U.S. interest rates and local rates, which can be extremely volatile. In the early 1990s, for example, U.S. rates dropped to their lowest levels in decades (the 3-month Treasury bill dipped to below 3 percent at one point), while high inflation in Brazil pushed interest rates to as high as 100 percent.

Companies anywhere do better when rates are low and do worse when rates go up. Low rates allow them to finance new projects for less money, and corporate earnings improve. Consumers also tend to spend more when interest rates are low. When rates are high, earnings sag and companies spend less on new projects. Also, high rates usually mean higher inflation, and consumers reduce their purchases, hurting company earnings.

This is why the chapter on ADRs emphasizes the importance of finding out how much debt a company has and what percentage of that debt is in U.S. dollars. When domestic interest rates shoot up in a Latin American country and U.S. interest rates remain low, the companies that perform the best will be those that have access to foreign debt markets and consequently have a significant portion of their debt load in dollar-denominated debt instruments. Likewise, when U.S. interest rates rise and domestic interest rates fall, companies that have a significant portion of their debt denominated in their local currency will be better off. Currency devaluations can also hurt companies with high dollar-denominated debt loads. During the Mexican peso crisis, some banks and several large companies, such as Grupo Situr, were driven to bankruptcy because the interest rates companies were forced to pay on their dollar-denominated debt was suddenly twice as expensive in pesos. Many companies couldn't make the payments unless they had large export-earnings in dollars, and those loan defaults hurt the banks, too.

A company whose stock you are planning to buy should have a good mix of both debt and equity and should have a good balance of both dollar debt and debt in its local currency. The correct mix is different for each company, depending on what industry it is in and how much of its sales come from exports and other factors. I will discuss the debt levels of individual companies in the second half of this book, and more information is available through a company's annual report or a research report by one of the debt rating agencies: Moody's, Standard and Poor's, or Duff and Phelps (their Web sites are listed in the back of this book).

You should keep an eye on U.S. interest rates (Treasury bill and Fed fund rates are published in the business sections of most major newspapers) and on rates in countries in which you are heavily invested (these can be found by researching news stories from some of the Web sites listed in the appendix). Bank stocks, more than any others, depend on interest rates, especially in Latin America where periods of high inflation—which is usually accompanied by high interest rates—can double or triple a bank's earnings. But as a general rule, don't use interest rates alone as a reason to buy or not to buy a stock. It's too difficult to guess which way rates are headed and how the changes will affect your company's stock price. Instead, use interest rates as one factor in determining how fast a company's earnings will grow.

BUSINESS CYCLES

THIS BOOK HAS indicated that Latin America has entered a cycle of economic growth that could last twenty years, and that putting your money into the region now will secure you high returns if you leave it there for the long run. Inevitably, however, Latin America will pass through short-term business cycles, as does every region in the world, that affect corporate earnings. Even an occasional recession is possible. Trying to time your buy and sell decisions around these short-term cycles is a tempting but fruitless strategy because it is nearly impossible to tell when the cycles will start or end. That is why investing for the long term is so important.

It is also why diversification is so important. In Latin America, it is rare for the entire region, without exception, to be performing well simultaneously. If you are invested in several Latin American countries, you will benefit from the positive economic trends that the region as a whole is experiencing without subjecting yourself to the short-term pitfalls of any one country. Economic crises are often unexpected and can be the result of anything from political power struggles and corruption scandals to bank crises and international trade sanctions.

Having said this, there are times when predicting a business cycle can be highly profitable. On Wall Street, several big investment houses accurately predicted that the Mexican peso crisis would be followed by a period of increased consumer buying. They were right, and the consumer stocks they bought in Mexico such as Grupo Modelo SA and Fomento Económico Mexicano SA outperformed the rest of the market.

EMERGING MARKETS STRATEGIES

BOTH ACADEMICS AND investment experts have written much about how to predict stock market returns in the highly volatile atmosphere of emerging markets such as Latin America. While a detailed analysis of these studies is beyond the scope of this book, I have tried to describe below a few of the more important ones.

THE IFC INDEX, CREDIT RATINGS, AND
SURVIVORSHIP BIAS

WHEN ASSET MANAGERS of big international mutual funds sit down to decide how to split up their portfolios among individual countries, they are constantly trying to come up with ways to predict which countries' stock markets are going to do best. One popular method is by charting the IFC index of emerging markets. The IFC index is published by the International Finance Corp., a division of the World Bank. Between 1984 and 1995, the index showed average annual returns of 19.1 percent, compared with 12.5 percent for all emerging markets.

Investors who simply mimicked the index, therefore, would have done well for themselves. However, they could have done even better by taking advantage of a trend called "survivorship bias." Studies have shown that when a country first becomes a part of the IFC index, its stock market shoots up for the first three- or four-year period of its inclusion in the index. There is no certainty that this trend will continue in the future, but since the returns of new members in the IFC index were about double the index's average, it might be worth consideration as an investment strategy. To do so, you would first need to do some research into the IFC index, either by calling or writing the World Bank in Washington, D.C., or by doing a keyword search for "IFC index" in some of the Web sites listed in the back of this book. Then, once you find the names of countries that have either recently been added to the index or are next in line for inclusion, you could buy stocks in those countries. Unfortunately, most such countries don't sell ADRs, and buying stocks in them directly would be prohibitively expensive because of transaction fees and minimum investment requirements.

Other studies have been done linking stock market returns to everything from dividend yields to relative inflation growth, although most have not been able to show strong positive correlations over time and across countries and regions. Among the most convincing of these studies is the one mentioned earlier by Claude Erb, Campbell Harvey, and Tadas Viskanta. The study showed that a good way of predicting future stock market returns is by looking at a country's sovereign credit rating—the rating of the credit-worthiness of foreign debt issued by the government, as determined by one of the two biggest international rating agencies, Moody's and Standard & Poor's. The study showed that a portfolio that included 10 percent of stocks from high-credit-risk countries would have reduced the portfolio's volatility by 1 percentage point and increased its returns by 1.3 percentage points annually between 1980 and 1993. The same portfolio with 10 percent of stocks from the IFC index, by comparison, would have reduced volatility by the same 1 percentage point but increased returns by only 0.5 percentage point.

AUTO-CORRELATION

ANOTHER CHARACTERISTIC OF emerging markets is that they tend to exhibit a high degree of auto-correlation. What that means is that returns are more predictable in the short run in emerging markets than they are in developed countries. In other words, if the stock market in Peru went up today, you can be reasonably sure it will go up tomorrow. (But because of its high volatility you would be hard-pressed to guess where it will be a month hence.) The higher degree of auto-correlation can be an important tool for speculative investors who are interested in trying to earn a quick buck and then getting out, but the risk of this type of investing is far too high for the average investor and is not recommended.

PORTFOLIO MAINTENANCE

YOU'RE DONE. YOU'VE picked your stocks and your mutual funds. You've got a balanced portfolio with the right amount of risk and expected returns and diversity. You can sit back now and watch your money grow. Right? Wrong. While picking your investments is far and away the toughest task for a small investor, portfolio maintenance is equally important. An investor who shuts his eyes to the movements of his investments is an investor who can both lose good opportunities and be stuck with a portfolio that no longer meets his investment goals.

The most important thing to keep track of is price. Keep a list of your investments written down somewhere, along with the price you bought them at and the price where you would ideally like those investments to reach before you sell them. Then list next to those the reasons you bought the stock or fund in the first place. Periodically, read over those reasons to see if the company or the fund is living up to those reasons you jotted down. If not, and if you can't think of any new reasons to own stock in the company, you may want to consider selling, even if the stock hasn't reached your ideal selling price.

Another thing to keep a watch on is the asset allocations of your portfolio. If your investments in one region, or one country, or one asset class have substantially gained or lost in value, you may want to add another investment in that area or sell one of the assets you have in order to bring your portfolio back in line with your specifications. For example, if the Latin American portion of your portfolio were to double in value within two years, you would suddenly be overweighted in Latin America, and the risk of a downturn in the Latin American markets could have a serious effect on your portfolio's total returns. Thus, you would want to sell some of your Latin American assets. Most investment experts recommend rebalancing your portfolio every six months or every year. When you do, it's important to be strict about not putting too many eggs in one basket. It can be easy to get carried away with the success of a high-growth stock and to hold onto it, although the portfolio theories you've just learned in this book all advised you to sell down part of it and reinvest that money somewhere else.

Over the long term, you should also keep track of the changes in the correlation coefficients of each of your investments to make sure they have not wandered too much from what you expected of them.

Note, however, that this is not something you should worry about on a day-to-day or even a month-to-month basis. Correlation coefficients usually take a long time to change substantially. Factors that could bring about a more rapid change in the correlations between the U.S. stock market and those of Latin America could be a signing of the proposed Free Trade Zone of the Americas, or a change in a country's monetary policy that linked its currency with the dollar.

Remember that many Latin American investments may not be as liquid as the domestic investments in your portfolio. Selling them at the price you want could take a few hours, or in some cases, a few days, even if your asking price is below the most recently quoted price of the stock. Therefore, you should either make sure you sell them when you're not in a hurry for the money, or be prepared to sell at slightly below the current trading price.

As stressed earlier, this book is dedicated primarily to helping you with the Latin American portion of your portfolio. The overall portfolio strategies discussed here were meant to give you some basics. If you're serious about your portfolio, you should do some more research. The books listed in the appendix are a good place to start.

Picking the right allocation of portfolio assets in your portfolio can be difficult, but some investment experts say it is the most important thing an individual investor can do—more important even than picking the right stocks or mutual funds.

Now that you have what it takes to invest in Latin America, you can start looking at the individual countries and companies for some stocks you might like to buy. If you're just starting out, skip the next chapter and go straight to Part Two, where you will learn about thirty-five of the best Latin American companies for long-term investment opportunities. If you want to learn even more, or if you're a bold investor who wants to reach beyond the seven major Latin American countries to some smaller, lesser-known places, Chapter 5 should be of interest to you.

CHAPTER 5

Fixed Income, Newly Emerging Markets, AND OFFSHORE INVESTING

HIS CHAPTER DISCUSSES methods for investing in Latin America not normally used by individual investors. You'll find this chapter of use if you already have broader knowledge about investing in Latin America or if you have a particular interest in any of these three subjects: investing in bonds and other fixed-income instruments; investing in the "emerging emerging markets" of Panama, Costa Rica, and Cuba; or investing in offshore financial centers of Latin America and the Caribbean.

INVESTING IN FIXED-INCOME SECURITIES

THE TERM *FIXED-INCOME* refers to any type of investment that produces a guaranteed revenue stream, usually in the form of interest or coupon payments, such as corporate bonds, "sovereign" or government bonds, certificates of deposit, and money market instruments. In Latin America, the most popular form of fixed-income investing for foreigners is Brady Bonds—government debt that is traded internationally. Brady Bonds, along with most other types of fixed-income investments in Latin America, do not attract many individual investors. Still, there are plenty of ways for individuals to invest in them and other fixed-income instruments, and the payoffs can sometimes be huge.

In order to understand Brady bonds, it's useful to think first about how bonds work in general. Until about thirty years ago, the most popular types of bonds were savings bonds, war bonds, and similar debt instruments that people usually held onto for the life of the bonds. Today, savings bonds are still around, but they're not a very practical investment because there are so many other types of bonds that are just as safe and yield much higher returns. Also, investors today usually don't hold onto bonds until maturity. The least complicated type of bond is the zero-coupon bond, meaning you receive no payments until the bond matures, at which time you collect both the principal and the interest you accumulated. If you were to buy a $1,000, twenty-year, zero-coupon bond that paid 10 percent annually and held onto it until maturity, you would collect $6,727 at the end of the twenty years. But most corporate and many government bonds pay coupons, which are interest payments that you receive, usually semi-annually or annually. And there are lots of twists on this basic formula. For example, bonds can have *call options,* which give the seller of the bonds the right to "call" them back under certain circumstances. *Put options* give the buyer of the bonds the right to redeem them before maturity. And bonds can be convertible into types of equity, such as shares of the issuing company's stock. A good source if you want to know more is *The Bond Buyer,* a periodical listed in the back of this book.

If you plan to hold onto a bond until maturity, you don't need to worry much about fluctuations in the current market price and the implied yield of your bond in the meantime. You'll get what you paid for, providing the issuer of the bond doesn't default on it. But if you're like most people, you buy bonds with the expectation of selling them before they reach maturity. At the very least, the possibility of selling them before maturity—the bonds' liquidity—is important to you. That means you need to pay attention to prices and yields.

The price of the bond is what you paid for it, whether it was a new issue and you were the original purchaser, or you bought the bond from its previous owner in the secondary market. If you bought a $100 face-value bond "at par," then the price at the time you bought it was $100. Bonds typically gain or lose value depending on two things: how likely it is that the issuer of the bond will default on it before it reaches maturity, and how valuable the bond is relative to all comparable bonds currently in the marketplace. A bond issued by IBM or General Electric is likely to trade close to $100, while a bond issued by the pre-revolution Cuban government can trade at a price as low as twenty cents on the dollar.

Yields move in the opposite direction to prices. If interest rates fall, the prices of bonds that are already on the market typically go up, because those bonds now yield more relative to the benchmark bond, usually considered to be U.S. Treasury bonds. The implied yield of a bond is thus the interest rate that bond would pay if it were issued today. So, if you hold a bond that pays 10 percent annually, you could sell that bond for more than what you paid for it—minus any income you've already received—if interest rates have gone down since you bought the bond.

As we saw in Chapter 4, most investment experts advise almost everyone to make bonds a part of their portfolios. Not only do bonds provide a steady, reliable source of income, but they also provide diversification, since the prices of bonds and stocks often move in opposite directions.

WHAT ARE BRADY BONDS?

BRADY BONDS ARE named after former U.S. Treasury Secretary Nicholas Brady, who, along with former Deputy Treasury Secretary David Mulford, came up with the plan that allowed heavily indebted Third World countries to exchange billions of dollars in bank debt—much of it in default—for sovereign government bonds that could be traded on world markets. The plan was initiated in the late 1980s, but the negotiations took years and it was well into the 1990s before the new bonds were actually issued for most countries. It was a good plan for most of the parties involved. The lending banks were able to erase billions of dollars in bad debt from their balance sheets, and the new bonds were easier to sell to investors than repackaged loans. The debtor nations were able to reduce their debt levels substantially through discounts provided by the banks, which in turn lowered their yearly interest payments, while at the same time extending the maturities on the debt. Furthermore, the agreement opened up international debt markets to these countries for the first time since the debt crisis that hit Latin America in 1982. The developed nations benefited politically and financially. Countries such as the United States were able to clean up their own foreign debt balance sheets, and sell to the Third World countries billions of dollars worth of U.S. zero-coupon bonds to be held in trust as collateral for the new Brady bonds. Likewise, investors benefited by the creation of a huge new market for trading sovereign debt instruments of Third World countries, as well as by the facilitation of new issues from these countries.

Although most of the original Brady bonds are still traded, the volume of trading on them has in many cases been surpassed by new sovereign issues. Here's a brief look at the original Brady bonds, which came in six basic flavors:

◆ **Par bonds:** Bonds that were swapped for a country's debt to a foreign creditor bank. They were issued at the original face value of the loans for which they were exchanged, but at fixed coupons below the coupons of the original restructured debt. The principal and part of the interest are collateralized with U.S. Treasury strips (zero-coupon bonds), meaning if the country defaults on the payments, the U.S. Treasury strips could be used to reimburse the bondholders.

◆ **Discount bonds:** Bonds with a floating coupon tied to the coupon of the original debt but issued at a discount to the original face value of the original loan. For example, if Brazil owed Citibank $10 billion at interest rates that "floated" so that they were always 2 percentage points above Libor (the London Interbank Offered Rate), Citibank might reduce that amount to $6.5 billion, but the coupon would remain at 2 points over Libor. As in par bonds, their principal and part of their coupon payments are collateralized with U.S. zero-coupon bonds.

◆ **Debt-conversion bonds (DCBs):** Bonds issued at face value that earn a floating interest rate and are not backed by collateral. They can be used for certain debt-equity conversions.

◆ **New money bonds (NMBs):** Bonds issued with new funds (i.e., they were new loans that weren't swapped for bank debt) at short-term, floating rates, also lacking collateral.

◆ **Front loaded interest reduction bonds (FLIRBs):** Bonds carrying a fixed, low coupon which rises over the first five to seven years of the life of the bond and is then replaced by a floating coupon for the remaining life. Some of the interest payments are collateralized, but not the principal.

◆ **Capitalization bonds:** Uncollateralized, fixed-rate bonds whose initial coupons are only paid in part. The remainder of the coupon payments are *capitalized,* meaning "added on to" the value of the bond. The Brazilian capitalization bond, or C bond for short, is the most heavily traded Brady bond in the world.

Trading a bond portfolio means following the prices of the bonds and the yields, which move in opposite directions, and comparing those prices and yields to other Brady bonds of similar maturities and to other bonds that you may consider purchasing. Be careful, however, when looking at the yields of Brady bonds, because there are often two yields quoted for most Brady bonds: the blended yield and the stripped yield.

The *blended yield* is the annualized yield of the entire bond over its lifetime. Many investors argue that this yield gives you a skewed picture of what you are buying, because a big chunk of the cash flow on most Brady bonds is guaranteed by U.S. zero-coupon bonds that are purchased by the country that issued the Brady bonds and are held in trust for bondholders. For example, a typical par bond might have all of its principal payment and its first three coupon payments guaranteed by the U.S. Federal Reserve, which is a much more stable lender than the Mexican government. As a result, investors also look at the *stripped yield,* which is the yield on all of the cashflow from the part of the bond that is not guaranteed by U.S. zero-coupon bonds. Stripped yield, in other words, would be the total yield of our hypothetical par bond, minus the yield from the principal payment and the first three coupon payments.

The countries with outstanding Brady bonds on the market are: Argentina, Brazil, Bulgaria, Costa Rica, Croatia, the Dominican Republic, Ecuador, Jordan, Mexico, Morocco, Nigeria, Panama, Peru, the Philippines, Poland, Russia, Slovenia, Uruguay, Venezuela, and Vietnam. As mentioned earlier, several of these countries have since issued new sovereign debt—part of which was used to buy back Brady bonds. These new sovereign issues have taken the form of either "Yankee bonds," issued in the United States and denominated in dollars; Eurobonds, a generic term today for almost any type of bond issued on world markets and denominated in any currency other than the home country currency of the issuer; or global bonds, which are issued simultaneously worldwide.

Some countries have even been successful in launching long-term debt with maturities of as much as 30 years, something that would have been unheard of just a few years ago. Brazilian and Mexican 30-year bonds, for example, have become quite heavily traded.

CORPORATE EUROS, YANKEES, AND GLOBALS

ANOTHER TYPE OF Latin American debt instrument is the corporate bond, which, like sovereign bonds, can take the form of Eurobonds, Yankee bonds, or global bonds. As just mentioned, Eurobonds can be denominated in any currency, but they usually come in U.S. dollars, Japanese yen, or Deutsche marks. Most big companies, from Boeing to Toyota to Nestlé, issue Eurobonds at one time or another. The Latin American companies that have issued Eurobonds are usually among the strongest and biggest in the region. Many of these are sold to individual investors with minimum purchases of as little as $5,000 or $10,000. To break into the Eurobond market, a company must usually sign up one of the world's big investment banks as an underwriter, and those banks won't agree to manage a bond sale unless they determine that there is a market. Latin American companies first started selling Eurobonds in 1989, and the market for them continued to improve before drying up in mid-1998 after Russia defaulted on some of its debt and tarnished the market for everyone else. But Latin American corporate bonds will be back, if they aren't already, and investing in them can be a good way to lock in a steady stream of income over a long period of time.

The attraction of these debt instruments to investors is that the yields on these corporate bonds can sometimes be 5, 10, or even as high as 20 percentage points above the yields on comparable U.S. Treasury bonds. As one example, Bloomberg News reported that on October 16, 1998, a $10,000 bond due in 2004 from Ford Motor Co. would earn you about $550 a year, while $10,000 of bonds from Ford's unit in Brazil would earn you about $1,620 a year. To many investors, that's more than enough of a difference to compensate for any added risk.

LOCALLY ISSUED DEBT

NOT ALL LATIN American debt is issued overseas. Some Latin countries have large domestic debt markets, just as the United States does for Treasury bonds and as states and municipalities do for Muni bonds. Some of these bonds can be attractive investments because they often pay interest rates that far exceed the rates on dollar denominated debt from these countries. For example, Brazilian short-term government bonds were yielding close to 50 percent in late 1998! Of course, locally issued debt carries currency risk, which can be a huge factor, especially in countries where the currency is deemed to be overvalued. In Mexico, for example, foreign investors who bought locally issued Mexican debt got caught with losses of more than 40 percent of their investments when the peso crisis hit in late 1994. Some locally issued debt, however, is linked to the dollar, such as Argentina's Bocons and Mexico's now-extinct Tesobonos.

For foreigners, the easiest places to buy local currency debt (i.e. the countries with the least restrictions) are Mexico and Argentina. There are almost no restrictions in either of these countries. Brazil, because of its size, has one of the biggest and most liquid local debt markets, but individual foreign investors are largely kept out by requirements that foreigners set up local currency accounts in Brazil.

HOW TO BUY BONDS

UNFORTUNATELY FOR SMALL investors, Brady bonds can only be purchased in lots worth at least $250,000 face value, which depending on the going price of each Brady bond can range anywhere from about $125,000 to $230,000. As pointed out earlier, however, other types of bonds such as Yankee bonds and Global bonds and some locally issued debt such as Mexican short-term treasury bills, called *cetes,* can be purchased in smaller amounts by individual investors through a broker in the United States. Most mainstream U.S. brokerages either have their own subsidiaries in Latin American countries, or they have partnerships with local brokerage houses to facilitate trading.

The types of bonds you buy should depend in part on whether you plan to hold onto the bonds for the income from the coupon payments, or whether you're interested in selling them for capital gains.

"If you plan to collect coupons, look for high quality, illiquid corporate bonds," says Michael Pettis, a managing director at Bear Stearns in New York who manages bond issues for Latin American governments. "If you want to trade in and out, stay with the liquid stuff."

Fortunately there is a better way for the small investor to get exposure to Latin American bonds—by buying mutual funds. Brady bond expert Tulio Vera, global head of fixed income for ABN Amro Inc., a large Dutch investment bank, explains: "This is a very high-risk segment of the investment universe. For an individual, the minimum purchase requirement is too high to buy Brady bonds directly, and if you bought just one or a few, you wouldn't be getting enough diversity. If you feel you want to dedicate part of your portfolio to this asset class, it makes sense to go through mutual funds."

There are plenty of Latin American bond funds. Some invest in Brady bonds, some in Eurobonds, and some in locally issued debt. Most invest in a combination of all those types. The best fund to buy is probably a diversified emerging market bond fund or a Latin America bond fund, as opposed to one that focuses on a single country or a single type of debt. Diversification is important in fixed-income investing; spreading your holdings out minimizes the effect that the occasional default will have on your portfolio. Mutual fund managers are also likely to do some hedging to protect assets in the event of devaluations or other unforeseen events.

Pettis cautions investors "not to put too much faith in diversification. The only time you get the benefit of diversification is in stable markets. In a crisis, all emerging markets move together."

In picking a bond mutual fund, you can follow the same advice offered in Chapter 2. Buy no-load funds with low cost ratios. Look for managers with good track records. Don't be fooled by short-term high returns.

ABN Amro's Vera recommends buying a global fixed-income strategy fund, which mixes its investments across several types of bonds and several countries, both large and small; or an emerging market fixed-income fund, which does the same but limits its investments to emerging markets.

What sort of mix of bonds should you look for? "It depends on the time," Vera says. In a volatile market, "the best place to put your money is in the more liquid global Brady bonds [as opposed to corporate debt or more lightly traded government debt]. The sovereign bonds will be the first ones to come back [after a crisis]."

EMERGING MARKETS FIXED-INCOME FUNDS

EMERGING MARKET BOND FUNDS	3-YEAR AVERAGE ANNUAL RETURN
AIM Emerging Markets Debt	3.47%
Alliance Global Dollar B	4.53%
Bear Stearns Emerging Markets Debt	11.64%
Emerging Markets Income Fund	17.79%
Fidelity Advisor Emerging Markets Income	11.62%
Merrill Lynch Americas Income	-3.38%
Morgan Grenfell Emerging Markets Fixed Income Fund	0.29%
Morgan Stanley Emerging Markets Debt	9.37%
Offitbank Emerging Markets Debt	9.16%
Scudder Emerging Markets Income	2.17%
T. Rowe Price Emerging Markets Bond	7.80%
Templeton Emerging Markets Income	6.09%
Van Kampen Worldwide High Income	8.13%

SOURCE: BLOOMBERG L.P. (MICHAEL MOLINSKI)

INVESTING IN NEWLY
EMERGING MARKETS

THE LATIN AMERICA I've been referring to in previous chapters included only seven countries: Peru, Venezuela, Colombia, Brazil, Mexico, Chile, and Argentina. But there are twenty-five other countries in the region, several of which have some form of stock market and most of which offer some sort of fixed-income investment vehicles to foreign investors. These countries were excluded from the first chapters of this book for the same reasons that few institutional investors include them in their portfolios: they are riskier; their stock markets, if they exist, are smaller, and trading is less frequent; many of them are not open to foreign investors or have restrictions that make investing there unwise; and many of them simply have not been established long enough to warrant serious consideration by most individuals.

In this section, we will describe only three: Panama, Costa Rica, and Cuba. Panama and Costa Rica were chosen because they, more so than most of the other countries, are more open to outside capital and have drawn more interest recently from foreign investors. Cuba, which has no stock market, was selected because so many foreigners are interested in investing there, whether for the romanticism of investing in the last Marxist country in the Western Hemisphere or from the belief that Cuba is ripe for change. There are several other countries, from Ecuador and the Dominican Republic to Uruguay and Bolivia that would also deserve consideration, but for the sake of space, are not included here. If you're interested in those countries, you can find information on them by looking up one of the worldwide or Latin American business Web sites listed in the back of this book, such as World Business at www.bacoweb.com/worbus or Latin World at www.latinworld.com, or from a financial Web site such as Bloomberg.

Investing in countries that have not yet made the list of emerging markets involves a different strategy than investing in mainstream emerging markets like Brazil and Mexico. Risk is usually much higher, and what information you can get is usually much less detailed. But returns can sometimes be worth the extra effort and the extra risk, provided you're prepared to lose most, if not all, of the money that you invest in these markets.

PANAMA

PANAMA POSTED HIGHER RETURNS than any other stock market in Latin America in 1997, and it had the second best-performing stock market in the world in the first nine months of 1998, behind Costa Rica, although many lists don't include it because it's not yet considered an emerging market. For some investors, Panama emerged a long time ago and, after a brief setback caused by all the trouble with former dictator Manuel Noriega and the 1989 U.S. invasion, has now reemerged.

WHY INVEST IN PANAMA?

PANAMA CAN BE a good strategic investment for many reasons, besides generating high returns. First, it is so small that big institutional investors don't consider it for their portfolios. This creates opportunities for the little guy. Second, because Panama hasn't really been "discovered" yet by the international investing community, it's still possible to find some exceptional bargains. Third, the country is growing fast—about 4 percent annually—and a number of planned privatizations by the Panama government should prompt some IPOs over the next few years. That should improve the volume of trading on the stock market and attract more foreign investors. Finally, to the extent there are any safe havens against turmoil in the world's stock markets, Panama is one of them. Let's look at each of these incentives in a little more detail.

The reason that big investors such as mutual funds and pension funds shy away from Panama is because the volume of trading is too low, and they fear that if they purchased large amounts of stock in any company, they wouldn't be able to sell those shares fast enough if they needed to. This usually isn't a problem for small investors, as it is much easier to sell 100 or 200 shares than it is to sell 100,000.

"International funds do not invest in Panama," says Arturo Tapia, president of Wall Street Securities, Panama's largest stock brokerage. "It's such a small market that they really don't pay attention to it. Our stock market is dominated by local investors."

As of late 1998, the market capitalization of the stock market—the total value of all the companies' stocks traded—was about $3.8 billion. To give you an idea how small that is, a single Brazilian company, Petrobrás, has a market capitalization of $14 billion, and IBM has a market capitalization of $135 billion.

Within this micromarket hide some good values. Foreign investors usually discover emerging markets one country at a time, and then within those countries they discover stocks one stock at a time—it's a process known as *herding*, and it has happened in virtually every emerging market. Each discovery pushes the price of a stock up sharply initially, but after a while the stock price starts to level off. Panamanian companies haven't yet been discovered, although the stellar price performances of 1997 and 1998 are sure to attract the attention of a larger number of foreigners and even some institutional investors. Price-to-earnings ratios for Panama companies, on the other hand, are not low, ranging anywhere from 12 to 22 for the bluechip stocks in 1998.

The third rationale for investing in Panama is growth. The economy was expected to grow 4 percent in 1998, after seven consecutive years of economic expansion. Part of that growth has come from a return to the country of money that was pulled out during the Noriega fiasco.

"The key to our system is the banking sector," says Juan Luis Moreno, economic adviser in Panama's Ministry of Planning. "We're the only county in the world where our entire macroeconomic policy is set by the private sector."

Moreno has a point. With 28 offshore banks, 37 foreign commercial and investment banks, and 21 Panama-owned banks, growth financing is never far away for Panama companies.

Earnings have therefore grown even faster than the economy. The largest five firms increased their earnings an average 20 percent a year over the three years from 1996 to 1998, according to Wall Street Securities, a Panamanian brokerage firm. Individually, their three-year estimated growth rates were: Empresa General de Inversiones, 19.3 percent; Cervecería Nacional, 25.3 percent; Banco del Istmo, 26.2 percent; Corp. Incem, 13.6 percent; and ASSA, 7.7 percent. Trading has also increased, with an average 69 percent annual increase in stock exchange volume since 1991.

Finally, Panama has some immunity to turmoil in global stock markets, such as the 1998 crisis. The Asia crisis helped lead to the crisis in Russia, and after Russia fell there was a domino effect that stretched to all the world's major emerging markets. Panama, however, was virtually unscathed. Why? There are two main reasons. The first is that, as Artuto Tapia mentioned, the stock market is completely dominated by local investors, who account for about 95 percent of all stockholders who invest in the country. In other Latin American countries, foreign investors can account for 25 percent or better. Thus, the contagion effect that can hit other stock markets during a downturn was barely felt in Panama. A second reason is that most Panamanian companies are too small to access international debt markets, so when global liquidity dried up in 1998, Panamanian companies weren't hurt because they have such low foreign debt levels. Most of their borrowing is done in Panama, where the currency's peg to the dollar has kept domestic interest rates below those of most other Latin American countries.

This isn't to say that Panama can't be affected by events outside its borders. Indeed, Panama's economy was beginning to feel the effects of a global slowdown in growth in 1998 because Panama's economy depends heavily on trade, both through the inter-oceanic canal and through the "Colón" Free Trade Zone. Less world trade means less revenue for Panama, which in turn can depress consumer buying and hurt company earnings.

A big question mark for Panama, and one which I believe will turn out in its favor, is the scheduled return of the canal to Panama by the U.S. government in 1999. Critics have suggested that the economy will be hurt by the withdrawal of U.S. troops and canal workers from the country. But the added direct revenue that the canal will give the Panama government, along with the prestige of running it by themselves, should more than offset any ill effects from the withdrawal.

HOW TO INVEST IN PANAMA

THERE WERE TWENTY-FOUR companies traded on the Panama stock exchange in 1998. The top blue chips are

Cervecería Nacional and Empresa General, parent of Banco General. Only one of them, Cervecería, has an ADR, and it is only a level one ADR that is not listed anywhere and is available mostly in large lots through private transactions. Cervecería has nonetheless announced its desire to list the shares on the New York Stock Exchange at some point, so you should keep an eye on news of IPOs at your favorite financial Web site if you're interested in that stock.

There are no specific restrictions on foreigners buying shares directly in Panama. Most large U.S. brokers can do it for you, and Panamanian brokerages such as Wall Street Securities can as well. But don't expect the transaction to be done overnight. Panama's stock exchange is only open for an hour a day, and several sessions can often go by without any trading.

Unsurprisingly, the best way to invest in Panama is to buy a mutual fund. Here, too, you are limited. As I'm writing, there are only two mutual funds that focus on Panama specifically and whose prices are quoted on international exchanges. Both are traded in "offshore" financial centers, but are nonetheless open to U.S. investors if they buy them outside the United States. The Panama Balanced Fund invests in a combination of stocks of Panama companies, corporate debt issues of Panama companies, and sovereign debt issues from the Panama government. The other fund is the Panama Fixed Income Fund, which invests only in Panamanian corporate and government debt. Both are run by Wall Street Securities. For more information, you can call the fund managers at (011 507) 227-4577.

COSTA RICA

COSTA RICAN STOCKS dominated the world in the first nine months of 1998, gaining 100 percent in dollar terms. Costa Rica has a lot of the same advantages that Panama does—isolation from the contagion effects of world markets; strong growth rates; and good, undiscovered values. We won't repeat here all the reasons to invest. But there are some noticeable differences with Panama. First, Costa

Rica does not have a dollarized economy, which complicates trading slightly by bringing in the necessity of conversion and adds currency risk to the equation. Second, Costa Rica has a more diverse economy that depends less on trade but more on commodity prices, especially coffee.

Costa Rica's stock market is smaller than that of Panama. It is also even harder to access by foreigners than the Panama market. There are only nine frequently traded Costa Rican companies, led by Florida Ice and Farm Co., the country's largest beer brewer.

Like Panamanian companies, Costa Rican firms tend to have low foreign debt levels, and even if their dollar debt became high, paying it off wouldn't be difficult because close to 50 percent of Costa Rica's gross domestic product is earned in dollars, much of it from tourism. This provides a good level of security to investors by reducing the effects of a potential currency shock.

Costa Rica's economy was expected to grow 5 percent in 1998, one of the fastest rates in Latin America, up from 3.2 percent in 1997. The country also elected a new president, Miguel Angel Rodríguez, in 1998, who made clear his intentions to open the economy further to foreign investors.

Price-to-earnings ratios in Costa Rica are still fairly low, at 8 to 12 times earnings on average.

Costa Rica is still largely undiscovered by foreign investors, meaning bargains can still be found, especially among the smaller companies. The few foreigners who do invest in the country are usually those who have vacationed or retired there. Costa Rican real estate is a hot commodity among foreigners, who during the 1990s were snapping it up to use as vacation properties and as a place to spend their golden years.

CUBA

ONCE DURING A VISIT to Havana I interviewed a top Cuban banking official who described to me at length the reforms that were being undertaken to encourage Cubans to save more and to stop hiding dollars in their mattresses.

But after explaining the grand plans that sounded quite like those of any New York or London bank, he conceded that there was one big problem preventing the reforms from being successful: most Cubans aren't allowed to earn dollars, and their salaries in Cuban pesos amount to the equivalent of less than $20 a month.

That was 1996. Since then, some laws have been passed in Cuba that make it legal for some people to earn income in dollars with small family-run businesses that cater to the growing tourist trade. There are thousands more, however, who earn their money illegally—from prostitutes and clandestine cab drivers to black market dollar changers and roadside vegetable peddlers. Cuba may be a socialist country in name, but most of the people—especially in Havana—are ingenious capitalists. They have to be to survive. Before the Soviet Union fell apart in 1989, the Cuban government, with heavy Soviet aid, provided almost everything the average Cuban needed—clothes, food, medicine and health care, a job. Now, Cubans are lucky if they get five-pound bags of beans and rice a month. Thousands don't even have jobs. As a result, the Cuban government tolerates the dollar trade.

But the Cuban government tolerates a lot more than that these days. Out of necessity, it now permits foreign investment in many aspects of the economy. European hotel chains have sprung up all over the island, and cruise ships are making Havana a favored port of call. Canadian mining companies are digging up nickel, and European phone companies are laying down fiber optic cable. There's even a Club Med.

As a result of all this activity, opportunities have arisen for individuals to invest in Cuba as well. However, if you read the first four chapters of this book and thought Latin America sounded risky, then Cuba isn't for you. It is without a doubt one of the most uncertain investments in the region. The Cuban government is still just experimenting with capitalism. Fidel Castro is far from embracing it. In fact, there is still a powerful old guard within the government that opposes the economic openings of the past few years, and the recent crisis in Russia has only given fuel to their arguments against dealing with the West. Still, there is little else the government can do but to continue allowing greater and greater foreign investment. Tourism is now the No. 1 industry, having overtaken sugar production a few years ago. Cuban companies are simply not advanced enough in either experience or technology to provide the kind of infrastructure, hotels, entertainment complexes, and other amenities Western tourists demand. But the government has absolutely no other way of feeding its people.

While foreign investment is encouraged, it is also heavily restricted in Cuba. Foreign companies can't hire their own workers, for example. They must go through a government labor pool, which picks most of the workers and sets their wages—usually in line with the average Cuban salary of around $200 a year. This presents some obvious drawbacks to foreign managers, but it also has some benefits. There are no strikes. Education in Cuba is among the best in Latin America, so most of the workers are well-trained for their positions, and jobs with foreign companies are in such high demand in Cuba that those who are hired are likely to be dedicated and hard-working. Companies can train workers in their own processes, and are allowed to give small material gifts as incentive bonuses from time to time. Sometimes, those bonuses can exceed the value of workers' salaries.

Investing in this tropical island may sound like far too much of a headache to consider. However, there are some good reasons to believe that investments there could pay off. Cuba is the largest country in the Caribbean, with a population of 11 million people; it is the country closest to Florida; and it occupies a strategic location for trade. It's also one of the most beautiful places on earth, with miles and miles of white sand beaches dotted with palm trees and ferns, and lush mountainous terrain in the center of the island. It was also one of the world's hottest vacation spots until 1959—the bars where Ernest Hemingway hung out are still major tourist attractions.

INDIRECT INVESTMENTS IN CUBA

THERE IS NO STOCK MARKET in Cuba. Sizable companies in the country are owned by the government, and none of them sell shares on any world stock markets. Cuba has, from time to time, sold bonds on international markets, but those that are still outstanding are lightly traded, and the U.S. trade embargo, imposed in 1962, has prevented further issues because banks are hesitant to underwrite any Cuban bonds for fear of drawing penalties from the U.S. government. The Helms-Burton law, passed by Congress in 1996, was designed to prevent foreign companies from doing business in Cuba by allowing U.S. citizens and companies to file lawsuits against foreign companies that do business on properties in Cuba that were confiscated from them after the 1959 revolution.

Still, plenty of companies have ignored the U.S. embargo and dared the U.S. government to try to do anything about it. Most of these companies are Canadian, Mexican, and European, and most don't have any substantial assets in the United States. Indeed, the Spanish hotel chain Sol-Meliá found it so profitable to do business in Cuba that it sold its two U.S. hotels to avoid the risk of having them seized.

For individual investors, there are two mutual funds that are focused on Cuba. One, the Beta Gran Caribe fund, is managed by London-based Beta Funds and invests both in European companies that do business in Cuba and in some private commercial real estate ventures in Cuba. It targets companies that are not publicly traded. The fund, however, to prevent penalties under the U.S. embargo of trade with Cuba, is not available to U.S. investors.

The second fund is the Herzfeld Caribbean Basin Fund, managed by Thomas Herzfeld out of Miami. It trades under the ticker symbol "CUBA." It's a peculiar fund in that it is not designed to invest in Cuba per se but rather invests in companies that would expect to profit from a lifting of the U.S. embargo of Cuba. In the past, the fund has invested in some companies that do business in Cuba, but recently it has tried to avoid that in order not to run afoul of U.S. regulations. The companies it invests in include Florida East Coast Railroad, Panamerican Beverages, Carnival Corp., and MCI Worldcom Inc. Its returns have not been impressive, in part because by late 1998 there was no end in sight to either Fidel Castro's regime or the U.S. embargo. The fund's returns for recent years were: 5.95 percent in 1997, negative 7.15 percent in 1996, and negative 11.54 percent in 1995.

Herzfeld also filed an application with the Securities and Exchange Commission last year to start a new fund, called the Cuba Fund, Inc., whose shares would trade on the Nasdaq. This fund does plan to invest in companies that do business on the island in some form, although Herzfeld wouldn't reveal their names.

Other funds have also surfaced from time to time, such as one operated by Belize Holdings Inc. and another by Canadian Charles Villeneuve, who runs a firm called Ecomatrix out of the Bahamas. Villeneuve says he gathered some $500 million for a new fund to be called the Cuba Growth Fund, which would invest in Canadian companies, such as mining company Sherritt International, that do business in Cuba. But as of late 1998 he still hadn't invested any of the money in the fund.

"The prices of the companies we were going to invest in fell 60 percent so far this year," Villeneuve says. "We decided to wait." He says even those companies have had trouble finding ways to invest in Cuba, although they've got plenty of cash to invest.

Investing in the stock of companies that do business in Cuba is another way that individual investors can invest in Cuba, albeit indirectly. Some companies, such as Sherritt, have even sold securities—convertible bonds in Sherritt's case—that are directly tied to the company's Cuban operations.

IS IT LEGAL?

BUYING STOCK IN companies that do business in Cuba or in investment funds that buy stock in companies that do business in Cuba is, by some interpretations, against the law for U.S. residents. But there is no other country on Earth that makes it a crime to invest in Cuba. Even some U.S. investors have put money in the Beta Gran Caribe Fund, and Uncle Sam has yet to do anything about it and probably won't. Herzfeld's Caribbean Basin Fund is legal, even for U.S. investors, as long as it doesn't invest in companies that do business there. His new fund, if it is launched, is likely to be legal, too, because it will probably be issued on the Nasdaq with the SEC's seal of approval—although I don't know how he will swing that if he plans to invest in companies that do business in Cuba. And even though buying shares in non-U.S. companies that do business in Cuba is technically against the U.S. embargo, no one has ever been prosecuted for doing so, said Teo Babun, whose Cuba-Caribbean Development Co. advises companies that invest in Cuba. It is the principals of these companies that the U.S. government is seeking to punish, if anyone—not the small shareholders.

"Most foreign investments in Cuba are in joint ventures and are primarily made in two areas—the tourism sector and the mining industry," Babun told me. "Officially, U.S. law prohibits Americans from buying shares in companies in Canada and elsewhere that are involved in Cuba. Unofficially, it's a difficult thing to control."

In terms of Cuban law, there is nothing that prevents foreign fund companies from investing directly in the island or in companies that do business there. Likewise, the Cuban government is all too eager for foreign individuals to buy shares in the funds that invest in Cuba—even though Cubans themselves don't have access to these funds.

DIRECT INVESTMENTS IN CUBA

FOR THE EVEN more daring, investments in Cuba can be made directly. Again, U.S. residents are prohibited from investing there by U.S. law, but for citizens of most other countries, there is nothing illegal about it. There are, however, substantial risks.

The first major risk is the possibility that Cuban laws will change. The Cuban government has backtracked on its regulations governing foreign investors in the past. Still, it hasn't reversed itself on anything of significance in the past five years at least, and, in my opinion, laws governing foreign investment will continue to become more, not less, lenient. There are other regulatory risks, however. Any type of foreign investment in Cuba—whether it's buying a condo on the beach or opening a nickel mine—is subject to a series of lengthy regulatory processes that involve getting permission from several government agencies. The risk is that the permission process will change and you won't find out about it until you're back in London or Barcelona.

The second major peril is the possibility that the property you believe you have bought belonged to someone else before the Cuban revolution—someone who might want it back if Fidel Castro is ever removed from power. The Cuban government considers all such claims completely invalid, but it has nonetheless taken pains to document all properties with past ownership records, because the government knows that foreign investors demand to know what they might be getting into before laying down their money.

There are plenty of other risks, too, and I will summarize all of them under one category—political risk. I can't stress enough that investing in Cuba is only for the extremely adventurous. Although the Castro regime has lasted almost forty years, it is one of the few Marxist regimes left. What's more, there are more than one million Cubans in Florida, many of whom are ready to come back to the island given the slightest hint that change is in the air. Some of them have on occasion been even more itchy, provoking the Cuban government to engage in skirmishes in the seas and air around Cuba. If change does occur, no one knows what will happen to existing investments.

One area of risk that is usually high among Latin American countries does not exist in Cuba—currency risk. All foreign investments in Cuba are in dollars. The Cuban peso is not traded on international markets.

If you're considering investing in Cuban real estate, there are some new laws that make it much easier to do so and for the first time allow foreigners to actually own beachfront property. One company—a joint venture between Cuba's state-run Gran Caribe Hotel Corp. and Canada's Cuban Canadian Resorts International, offers time-share condos to non-U.S. citizens on some of Cuba's best beaches.

Most individuals who invest in Cuban real estate do so because they visited the island as a tourist and formed some sort of romantic attachment to it. Some do so simply as a snub to the U.S. government. In general, unless you plan to visit frequently, there is little reason to invest in Cuban real estate. To be sure, the prices are cheap, but they're not cheap enough to warrant the risks of putting your money there and the hassles involved with maintaining and protecting your ownership.

OFFSHORE INVESTING

THIS BOOK IS about investing in Latin America, not about investing in offshore financial centers. Nonetheless, many "offshore" centers are within Latin America and the Caribbean, and there are numerous Latin American securities that are better accessed through offshore centers than they are through your home country.

Investing offshore has come a long way since your Uncle Bob's offshore bank account fifty years ago. Trillions of dollars in assets are channeled through offshore centers each year by the world's largest corporations, allowing them to reduce their taxes and giving them the flexibility to shift their monies around as they choose and invest in the assets they want to, without facing the stiff regulations that they often encounter in their home countries. Some 25 percent of the $6 trillion invested in the world's mutual funds, for example, is invested offshore, according to London-based Micropal, a firm which tracks mutual funds.

Individuals, too, can reap benefits from investing offshore—if done correctly it can reduce the taxes you pay on your investments while increasing your returns. But you should always first consult a lawyer or a tax accountant, or both—advisers who are knowledgeable of the ins and outs of offshore finance. It's a complex business, and most U.S. tax preparers don't have the knowledge it takes to keep you out of trouble. If offshore investments are done wrong, you could lose a big chunk of your nest egg or, worse yet, end up in jail.

OFFSHORE FUNDS

LATIN AMERICANS HAVE BEEN using tax havens for years, and, more recently, big U.S. banks and fund companies have been using the offshore centers as a base for investing in Latin America. As a result, hundreds of offshore-based Latin America mutual funds have sprung up, some of them managed by big Latin American brokerages and banks, such as Brazil's Unibanco and Mexico's Bancomer, and others managed by big U.S. banks and fund companies, such as Citibank, Fidelity, and Templeton.

Offshore fund companies are prohibited by U.S. law to market their funds to U.S. citizens in the United States unless they register with the SEC, which most don't. However, Europeans, Canadians, and others can buy shares easily and legally. U.S. citizens can buy shares, too, if they do so from an account outside the United States, said Jerome Schneider, author of *The Complete Guide to Offshore Money Havens* (Prima Publishing, 1997).

"Americans have been blacked out from these products, because offshore funds can't advertise in the United States," Schneider told me in an interview.

There are other ways for U.S. citizens to invest in off-shore funds. One example is if you have foreign-earned income. The growth of the Internet has made it even easier to access offshore mutual funds. Taking a trip to the Cayman Islands just to buy a mutual fund can be much more costly than it's worth, but now investors can buy them on-line, directly from fund companies. This, of course, has made it even harder for the IRS to police everyone who buys offshore funds. But whether you invest from an onshore or an offshore account, U.S. tax rules may require that you report that income to Uncle Sam, and it might be subject to U.S. taxes. It's best to talk to an accountant before taking the risk.

There are plenty of good reasons to buy offshore funds. One is the selection.

"People who invest in offshore funds are looking to diversify," says Erwin Dikau, manager of the mutual funds department at Bank of Butterfield International in Grand Cayman. "You name an idea, and there's a mutual fund built around it. They come offshore for the returns, too. Some funds are pretty aggressive."

In the United States and most other industrialized countries, what mutual fund companies can and can't invest in is severely limited. They can't, for example, invest more than a certain percentage of the fund in any one company or any one type of asset.

Small investor groups often set up their own offshore funds to take advantage of "windows of opportunity," Dikau told me. For example, a fund might be set up with the specific goal of anticipating a devaluation of the Brazilian currency within three months. Although three years may be necessary to set up a U.S. fund and gain approval from regulatory authorities, a Cayman Islands fund can be in business in as little as two weeks.

Another advantage to offshore funds is that returns can sometimes be higher, in part because their costs are generally much lower than those of onshore funds. They have fewer disclosure requirements, shorter time frames for getting set up, and lower management fees, since the profits earned by managers are tax-free. Also, offshore funds do not pay capital gains taxes when they shift assets within a fund, and they don't pay withholding taxes. Returns can also be higher because of increased flexibility—being able to invest where and when they want to. Investing offshore offers the benefit of increased liquidity since they often list their shares for sale on several offshore exchanges, from Dublin, Luxembourg, and the Channel Islands to the Bahamas, Panama, and the Caymans.

Of course, there are reasons why the United States and other industrialized countries have so many rules and regulations governing mutual funds. Chief among them is to protect small shareholders. As you've already learned in this book, putting all your eggs in one basket increases risk substantially, and whereas some offshore funds may get high returns from doing so, there are plenty of other examples of funds that have had to shut down because their big ideas turned sour. When that happens, small investors usually have no legal recourse and seldom recover their losses, whereas in the United States shareholder lawsuits are becoming more prevalent, and more successful.

OTHER WAYS OF INVESTING OFFSHORE

ALTHOUGH BUYING OFFSHORE FUNDS is probably the simplest way to invest offshore, there are plenty of other ways to do so, from buying offshore insurance policies to setting up your own offshore investment company. In Latin America, there are a growing number of offshore centers. Small countries increasingly are seeing offshore finance as a good way to attract a new, wealthy, environmentally sound industry to their shores. Most of them are islands in the Caribbean, but there are exceptions such as Belize and Panama. Among the better-known ones are Bermuda, the Bahamas, the Cayman Islands, the British Virgin Islands, and the Turks and Caicos Islands. Even though most offshore centers offer a variety of services, each locale tends to have a specialty, and you should take a good look before choosing one. Bermuda, for example, is known for its offshore insurance industry; the Caymans for its offshore mutual funds; and the British Virgin Islands as the place to go to set up a small company quickly and cheaply.

Setting up an offshore company as a means for channeling your investment dollars may sound like a major endeavor, but it is actually a fairly simple thing to do, and there are walk-in investment shops that can help you through the process in most offshore centers. The cost of setting up a company starts at about $2,000 in the Caymans, less in the British Virgin Islands. There are thousands of individual investors who do so, both as a way to save taxes and as a way to protect their assets. The same advantages are possible through setting up offshore bank accounts, trust funds, and insurance policies, all of which cost little or nothing to set up. U.S. investors should keep in mind that they will eventually have to pay taxes on any money they make offshore if they plan to bring it back into the United States some day. But many investors never plan to bring the money back in. It sits offshore, sort of like the money in a 401(k) plan, gaining huge amounts of interest income and capital gains, all of it tax-free. Rather than spend it, they will it to their sons and daughters, avoiding inheritance taxes.

If you're just starting out, and want to test the waters, the simplest way to invest offshore is by opening a savings account in an offshore bank. The big offshore banks, such as Bank of Butterfield and the Cayman National Bank, have been around for decades and are as stable as most U.S. banks. You can set up an account by mail or even online. Later, you can talk to your institution about transferring funds into other offshore investment vehicles. Just remember, there's a question on your IRS 1040 form that asks if you have any offshore bank accounts.

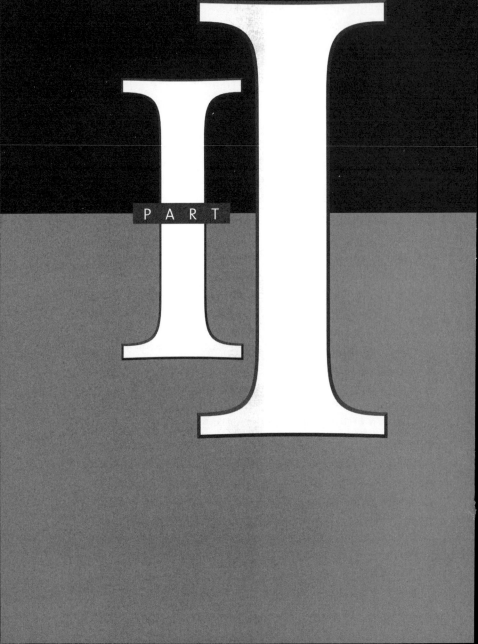

PART

I

THE FIRST HALF of this book explained why and how to invest in Latin America. The second half will discuss where to invest. In the next five chapters I will present seven countries and thirty-five companies that represent some of the best long-term investment candidates in the region. They are not the only good values in the region, but they comprise a group that experts have told me are the best of the best, a broad enough sampling from which to form a portfolio. ◆ This half of the book will be most useful to those of you who are planning on buying ADRs. But if you plan to stick with mutual funds, reading up on the companies they invest in will allow you to make much wiser decisions on which funds to buy. It will give you a better idea of how your fund money is being used and will help you chart how effectively your mutual fund assets diversify your portfolio.

KEY TO PART II COMPANY PROFILES

Cap. = market capitalization

Cia = *Companhia* or *Compania* (the Portuguese and Spanish words for "Company")

Correlation refers to R-squared

CPOs = Ordinary certificates of participation

Earnings growth = Forecasts were used where available, based on an average of analyst estimates. Otherwise, historical information was used.

Emp = *Empresa* or *Empresas* (another Spanish word for "Company")

EPS = Earnings per share, which refers to the American Depository shares

GDRs = Global depository receipts

I.B.E.S., First Call, and Zacks are all research companies that gather analyst data and forecasts on companies.

Morgan Stanley Latin America Index = Morgan Stanley EMF Latin America Index

Nasdaq = National Association of Securities Dealers Automated Quotation system

NYSE = New York Stock Exchange

Operating income = Listed only for Mexican companies because in Mexico it is a more closely watched gauge of a company's earnings than net income, which is skewed by accounting methods that take into account inflation and currency fluctuations.

OTC = Over the counter

P/BV = Price to book value

P/E = Price to earnings ratio

Preferred Shares = In the United States, preferred shares are a form of stock that pays dividends at specified rates and has preference over common stock in the liquidation of assets, but in Brazil it's another form of common shares, albeit without voting rights.

ROA = Return on assets. Used only for banks, which need different measures of analysis due to the fact that they don't really sell anything.

ROE = Return on equity: An average of the most recent periods available was used. Where ROE was unavailable, operating margin or EBITDA margin is used, in order to give some indication of the company's profitability. Operating margin is the profit a company makes through its normal operations. EBITDA is the profit margin on earnings before interest, taxes, depreciation, and amortization.

SA = *Sociedad Anónima* or *Sociedade Anônima* (the Spanish and Portuguese suffix meaning "incorporated")

S&P = Standard & Poor's

In the thirty-five company profiles that follow, the sources for data include the BLOOMBERG® service, analyst reports, and financial reports from the profiled companies.

CHAPTER

Ten
BRAZILIAN
COMPANIES

F ALL THE LATIN American countries, Brazil has the most promise in terms of economic growth potential. It has the world's sixth largest economy, by far the biggest in Latin America, and its 165 million people make up about a third of the Latin American consumer market. Brazilian stocks also tend to be cheaper than those of most other Latin American countries, at an average of about 9.5 times forecast 1998 earnings, compared with 14.5 times for Mexican companies and 13.8 for Argentina's average price-to-earnings ratio.

Brazil's modern era began in earnest in 1990, when Fernando Collor de Mello became president. Collor was the first popularly elected president after twenty-one years of military dictatorship that ended in 1985, followed by the five-year term of President José Sarney, who was appointed to rule after the military left power. The military dictatorship had ruled with an iron fist, and big business had been protected with high external tariffs that kept imports low and allowed companies to enjoy huge profit margins. That strategy worked throughout the 1970s, but because Brazil's industries were virtually shut off from the rest of the world, their products became obsolete, their manufacturing processes and equipment outdated, and their services slow and inefficient compared with the world norm. Brazil tried to borrow its way out of its problems, but foreign debt only exacerbated them, and throughout the late 1980s and early 1990s, hyperinflation further deepened the country's economic problems. Collor saw what needed to be done and started to open up the economy to competition from imports. However, he had barely started when a corruption scandal led to his impeachment. It took Brazil a while to recover from that disruption, but in July 1994 the Real Plan (the *real* is Brazil's currency and is pronounced "Hey Al") was introduced by the then finance minister, Fernando Henrique Cardoso, who was elected president later that year, and to a second term in 1998. The Real Plan was the shot in the arm that Brazil needed. It stabilized the currency, brought inflation down from 7,000 percent a year to less than 20 percent, and began to change the way investors look at the country. Until late 1994, Brazil had been the playing field of speculative investors who considered it a high risk but figured if they timed it right they could make loads of money. A lot of them did.

Among other things, the Real Plan pegged Brazil's currency to a narrow trading band that keeps it close in value to the U.S. dollar. One of the results of the plan was the establishment of a growing middle class of consumers who will help fuel company earnings in the years to come. Lower tariffs and other reduced restrictions on trade increased competition for Brazilian companies, which now must be more efficient in order to find more markets within Brazil and overseas. Huge amounts of capital have flowed into the country during the 1990s. Foreign investment—both direct and indirect—has averaged more than $12 billion a year. Even during the 1998 crisis, when some $40 billion in capital left the country, direct investment continued to flow in. Brazilian companies have borrowed hundreds of billions of dollars more on world markets. Most of that new capital is being used wisely. Average return on investments in Brazil is higher than that in most countries in Asia and Latin America.

Brazil's Real Plan finally fell apart in January 1999 as an overvalued currency, combined with high domestic interest rates and an inability to access foreign capital markets, made it impossible for Brazil to meet its financial obligations. The jury was still out at the time this book went to press as to whether the currency would continue spiraling downward, leading to higher inflation, or

whether the government would impose an austerity program that would lead the country into a deep, but stable,
recession.

There are still some other things Brazil needs to work
out, too, if its progress toward being one of the world's
economic powerhouses is to continue uninterrupted.
Corruption is still rampant in public and private life,
from the customs agent who approves a shipment of
computer parts to the traffic cop who lets you off in
exchange for a bribe. Reform of the judicial system,
which has been debated in Brazil's congress, would be
one step toward cutting down on that corruption.
Administrative reform is also important. Brazil has a
decades-old system of workers' rights that hurts both
employees and employers by making it painstakingly difficult to fire anyone. The result of those rules is that companies are often reluctant to hire, and wages suffer
because companies must fork out such huge sums for
corporate pensions and severance pay. Administrative
reform, however, is only feasible together with reform of
the social security system. In the near-term, the most
important hurdle that Brazil faces is bringing down its fiscal deficit, which in 1998 amounted to a whopping 7 percent of gross domestic product.

Solutions to all of these problems, if President Cardoso can push them through congress, will help the
economy immensely and are bound to also push stock
prices up. Conversely, if those measures fail to win
approval, the economy and companies could suffer.
However, it is unlikely that delays on any one of those or
other important economic issues will push Brazil off its
path of fast economic growth—unless they were combined with some outside economic shock such as a global recession or a severe drop in commodity prices. One
advantage of a devalued currency is that stock prices
should be cheaper in dollars.

CIA. VALE DO RIO DOCE (CVRD)

Pronounced "Volleh doh HEE-O Doh-Say"

U.S. TICKER: CVROY

1 ADR = 1 Brazilian preferred share

EXCHANGE: OTC	**SECTOR:** Mining
MARKET CAP.: $4.8 billion	**1998 EARNINGS:** $853 million

FORECAST 1999 EPS: $2.44
(3 analysts surveyed by Zacks)

EARNINGS GROWTH (5-YEAR FORECAST): 15%

1998 SALES: $4.25 billion	**P/E ON JANUARY 1, 1999:** 5.41
P/BV: 0.7	**OPERATING MARGIN:** 27.7%
BETA VS. S&P 500: 1.24	**CORRELATION WITH S&P 500:** 0.20

DIVIDENDS PER SHARE (1998): $1.93

CVRD is one of the largest companies in Latin America. It is principally an iron ore producer and is the world's largest exporter of iron ore. In recent years, though, it has been rapidly expanding its production of gold, and the potential for huge, hidden reserves of gold beneath the ground at such mines as Serra Pelada and Serra Leste in the Amazon region are part of the reason that CVRD shares could be a surprise winner in coming years. Even more important is the turnaround that is going on at the company. A 42 percent voting stake in CVRD was purchased in May 1997 for $3.13 billion by a group led by Companhia Siderúrgica Nacional, a steel company that itself was privatized by the Brazilian government in 1992. Other big players in the CVRD investment group are NationsBank Corp. and billionaire hedge fund manager George Soros. Before then, CVRD was owned and operated by the Brazilian government. Like most government-run companies in Brazil, CVRD was rife with inefficiencies, although it was probably better run than most. The CSN group has wasted no time in cutting costs and moving to increase gold exploration, and NationsBank is helping by providing low-cost loans. As the turnaround gets further along, earnings should begin to increase and lead to higher share prices.

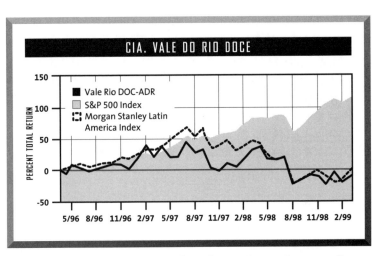

CIA. VALE DO RIO DOCE

CVRD also benefits from decades as the major supplier of iron ore to Brazil's largest steel companies, including CSN itself. The company's relations with the government are impeccable, such that it has managed to win mining rights throughout the country with little effort. It is also vertically integrated in the areas it needs to be, with interests not just in mining but in railways and trucking and shipping fleets. It also has some interests in paper and pulp. Overseas, it has powerful connections for its export markets, holdovers from the days when CVRD was one of the biggest suppliers of iron ore to the Allied Powers during World War II. It also owns stakes in nine foreign companies.

Aside from the potential of the company itself, there is another reason CVRD shares could be a good buy in the long term: The shares were basically unknown to the public until 1996, and in 1997 only some 250 shares a day of the company's ordinary stock changed hands. (By comparison, about 6,000 Telebrás shares change hands a day.) That is bound to change. The Brazilian government has long stated its intention to sell its remaining 28 percent stake in a public offering. When that happens, the number of shares traded publicly will increase by more than four times. That will give the stock more exposure, and CVRD will all of a sudden be rivaling Petrobrás and the

Telebrás subsidiaries as the most widely traded stock in Brazil. Also, the public offering will probably be conducted both in Brazil and New York, and CVRD shares will be listed on the New York Stock Exchange for the first time. All that, if it happens, is almost sure to push up the price of the stock.

CVRD's share price is dependent on the world price of iron ore and, to a lesser extent, the price of gold. This means that an increase in the price of ore would boost CVRD's share price. Historically, the share price has not been closely correlated with the price of gold, but gold is becoming a bigger portion of the company's total revenue and any sharp increases in the price of gold in the future could help the stock price. Of course, any sharp decreases in the price of either iron or gold would hurt CVRD's share price.

The ADRs listed as "CVROY" are equivalent to Brazilian preferred shares, which in Brazil is similar to common stock in the United States. They are traded over the counter. In late 1998, the U.S. shares traded at a slight premium to the Brazilian shares, meaning they were about 10 percent more expensive than if you were to buy them in Brazil. The shares are available only through brokers, and can be bought in lots of as few as 100 shares. That means the minimum investment is about $1,500, given a $15-per-ADR price of the stock. Once they're listed in New York, it will be easier to buy fewer shares at a time. Another added bonus is that devaluations of the Brazilian Real have little impact on the price of CVRD's ADRs, because CVRD has huge dollar earnings from exports.

♦ **Downside:** The price-to-book-value of the ADRs is high by Latin American standards and isn't much lower than other large, multinational mining companies.

♦ **What to Look For:** Read the company news section in any of the financial Web sites listed in the back of this book for news of the sale of new CVRD shares by the government. If the shares are sold simultaneously in Brazil and on the New York Stock Exchange, it will be listed as an IPO in the

United States. Ask your broker if you can get in on the sale at the opening price. If you can't, wait at least a few days after the sale before buying the shares because IPOs tend to push share prices up more than they should be. You can also look at CVRD's own Web site for company news and for information on the company's cost-cutting program and its gold discoveries. Watch the price of iron ore and gold, too. Both Bloomberg and Reuters have good commodity pages on their Web sites that carry news and prices. Reuters, at www.commods.reuters.com/index.html, has spot and futures prices from the London Metals Exchange. A good time to buy is when gold and ore prices are starting to climb after a long downturn.

CIA. BRASILEIRA DE DISTRIBUIÇÃO GRUPO PÃO DE AÇÚCAR

Pronounced "Pow gee Aa-SUE-car"

U.S. TICKER: CBD

1 ADR = 1,000 Brazilian preferred shares

EXCHANGE: NYSE	**SECTOR:** Retail
MARKET CAP.: $917 million	**1998 EARNINGS:** $132 million
FORECAST 1999 EPS: $1.53	
(9 analysts surveyed by I.B.E.S.)	
EARNINGS GROWTH (5-YEAR FORECAST): 20%	
1998 SALES: $3.6 billion	**P/E ON JANUARY 1, 1999:** 8.38
BOOK VALUE PER ADR: 7.24	**OPERATING MARGIN:** 3.7%
BETA VS. S&P 500: 1.46	**CORRELATION WITH S&P 500:** 0.16
DIVIDENDS PER SHARE (1998): $0.462	

Pão de Açúcar is one of Brazil's hottest comeback stories. The name of the supermarket chain, which was taken from the famous Sugarloaf Mountain in Rio de Janeiro, was a household word during the days of the military dictatorship. During the 1970s, the chain was known for having some of the fullest produce aisles in South America, and by 1989 it had 600 stores throughout the country. That all came crashing down as the country's economic crisis, combined with family problems among the chain's

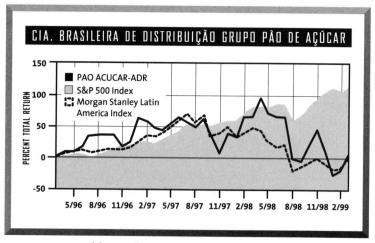

owners and heated competition from other chains, drove the company to seek bankruptcy protection in 1991. Making matters worse, Abílio Diniz, the son of the founder and now chairman of the company, was kidnapped and held for ransom.

It was Abílio Diniz who was later responsible for the company's turnaround. He shuttered some 400 stores and began focusing on quality service and efficiency rather than quantity.

"We no longer want to be the biggest. We want to be the best," Diniz told me in a telephone interview from his office in São Paulo.

Still, the company has been growing again since 1995. It had 283 stores by late 1998—an increase of 45 stores in just six months. More importantly, Diniz invested heavily in technology. He spent $1 billion in the three-year period from 1996 to 1998 and said he plans to keep spending on improving technology, expanding the chain, and acquiring other markets that fit Pão de Açúcar's business plan.

The new technology is geared mostly at using computers to better control inventory, which both cuts the company's costs and allows it to offer a better selection of the products customers want. It also allows the company to select prices and tag items faster and most cost effectively.

The company's business plan is to focus on adding to

both its regular supermarket chain and its chain of "hypermercados"—big warehouse-type stores that operate under the name "Extra" and offer more selection than the average Pão de Açúcar supermarket. The company also owns "Superboy" discount stores that are slowly being sold or converted to one of the other two types. Pão de Açúcar also owns Eletro, a chain of electronics stores that Diniz says he plans to expand.

Another company strategy has been to buy real estate, especially in its prime market in and around the city of São Paulo. It buys in areas that would be ideal locations for supermarkets, then holds onto the properties so competitors can't move in while Pão de Açúcar contemplates putting up new stores.

The company expects its total floor space to grow by about 20 percent a year over the next few years.

The family problems have evaporated, and the company is now flush with cash. It also has no dollar debt and only a small amount of debt in the local currency—a lesson Diniz apparently learned from the days when creditors were banging on the door.

Margins have also improved. The ratio of earnings before tax and interest rates to annual sales went from 3.6 percent in 1996 to 5.1 percent in 1997, and the company has a goal of hitting 7 percent by the year 2000.

◆ **Downside:** Competition. Carrefour, the French retail chain, is now the largest supermarket retailer in Brazil and keeps growing. It's a well-run company that won't be beaten easily, although Diniz says consumer-buying power is growing fast enough in Brazil for both chains to keep up rapid growth. Other new competitors, such as Wal-Mart, have begun to gain market share, too, and competition could heat up if supermarkets from Argentina and the other South American countries take advantage of newly eased trade restrictions to enter the Brazilian marketplace.

◆ **What to Look For:** You can follow same-store sales growth, a common statistic that analysts look for in any retail company, by looking at the annual report on the company's Web site. Same-store sales growth measures the percentage growth in sales among the company's existing stores, so comparing it to the same measure for other supermarkets will give you an idea of how the company is doing relative to them. If other Brazilian chains are also growing, even better, because it means the economy is doing well and people are shopping at supermarkets.

CIA. ENERGÉTICA DE MINAS GERAIS (CEMIG)

Pronounced "Say Migee"

U.S. TICKER: CEMCY

1 ADR = 1,000 Brazilian preferred shares

EXCHANGE: OTC	**SECTOR:** Utilities
MARKET CAP.: $2.7 billion	**1998 EARNINGS:** $400 million

FORECAST 1999 EPS: $1.46

(8 analysts surveyed by First Call)

EARNINGS GROWTH (5-YEAR FORECAST): 20%

1998 SALES: $1.98 billion	**P/E ON JANUARY 1, 1999:** 6.94
BOOK VALUE PER SHARE: $43	**ROE:** 5.9%
BETA VS. S&P 500: 1.59	**CORRELATION WITH S&P 500:** 0.16

DIVIDENDS PER SHARE (1998): $2.62

The electricity industry is one of the most attractive in Brazil, and Cemig is the best run of the companies that make up the national grid. Cemig is the state electric utility for Minas Gerais, the second most populated state in Brazil behind São Paulo.

Cemig was almost entirely state-owned and operated until May 1997, when the government sold a 33 percent voting stake (14.4 percent of total capital) to a group formed by two U.S. electric utilities, Southern Electric and AES. Even before the sale, Cemig was known for its efficiency. Since the sale, that reputation has increased. The Southern/AES group was allowed to appoint four board members and three of the seven executive officers of the company. The new owners have focused their input on operations, which are being modernized and brought in

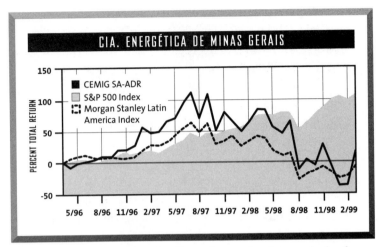

CIA. ENERGÉTICA DE MINAS GERAIS

- ■ CEMIG SA-ADR
- □ S&P 500 Index
- ┇┇ Morgan Stanley Latin America Index

PERCENT TOTAL RETURN

SOURCE: BLOOMBERG L.P.

line with world standards. Costs have also been slashed, including an agreement that came as part of the sale to cut 20 percent of the workforce, from 15,000 at the end of 1996 to about 12,000 at the end of 1998. That raised the company's consumer-to-employee ratio to more than 350 by the end of 1997.

In 1997, Cemig sold 42,397 gigawatts of electricity, about 13 percent of all the electric energy sold in Brazil. Their loss ratio (the amount of electricity produced that is lost and not sold) is about 8.3 percent, higher than that of most U.S. electric companies but on par with much of Europe and lower than any other Brazilian utility. Prospects for the future are good. Minas Gerais is home to some of the biggest mining operations in Brazil and also to some big automaking plants, including Fiat's. Fiat is currently building two more plants, and Mercedes Benz is building a plant in the city of Juiz de Fora. All of those plants will be big electricity users.

"We produce electricity for about $35 a megawatt, which is about the cheapest that anyone in Brazil can produce it," says Francisco Moreira Penna, the chief financial officer. "We keep hearing about foreign companies that are going to come into the market and produce it cheaper, but the truth is that until now, no one has shown that they can come into Brazil and generate electricity for less than that $35."

In 1997 Cemig produced about 62 percent of the energy it sold. The remainder it purchased from the Eletrobrás grid system. Its sales are directed about 40 percent to small consumers, about 42 percent to big energy users such as mines and auto manufacturers, and the remainder to other Brazilian utilities on Brazil's grid system. Generating capacity was about 390 megawatts in 1998.

The company's rate structure must be approved by the Brazilian government, but annual readjustments tied to inflation have been scheduled through 2002. That's why Cemig was one of the stocks least affected by the January 1999 devaluation. Beyond 2002, the rate structure is a question mark and will depend in part on how profitable the country's utilities are on average. To some extent, the government rebates profits that are deemed too high back to the consumer.

◆ **Downside:** The Minas Gerais state government still controls 51 percent of the company's voting stock, and thus in the end is responsible for any big corporate decisions. The chief executive officer, who was appointed by the former governor, told me flat out that profits and shareholders are second priorities, behind consumers. That's admirable, but it doesn't give much comfort to shareholders.

A proposal to sell the government's stake in Cemig in 1997 was nixed by then Governor Eduardo Azeredo, who bowed to political pressure. Now the chances of such a sale are even less: former Brazilian President Itamar Franco—a strict opponent of the sale of Cemig—was elected governor of Minas Gerais in October 1998. A sale could have enormously boosted the company's growth prospects and would most likely have led to higher share prices. Still, many analysts believe Franco will be forced to sell it before his term ends in 2003.

◆ **What to Look For:** Aside from renewed indications of a sale of the government's stake, investors should monitor news reports for progress of the Brazilian government's reforms of the electricity sector. Recent legislation has allowed for the sale of utilities into private hands and also opened up the electricity industry to competition from private generating companies. The rules that will determine how that will pan out were still being negotiated when this book went to print. Among other things, the government is expected to set up a new wholesale energy market and to establish rules about how independent operators can have access to the national grid.

CIA. CERVEJARIA BRAHMA (BRAHMA)

U.S. TICKER: BRH
1 ADR = 20 Brazilian preferred shares

EXCHANGE: NYSE	**SECTOR:** Beverages
MARKET CAP.: $2.62 billion	**1998 EARNINGS:** $272 million

FORECAST 1999 EPS: $0.63
  (11 analysts surveyed by I.B.E.S.)
EARNINGS GROWTH (3-YEAR HISTORICAL): 6%

1998 SALES: $2.6 billion	**P/E ON JANUARY 1, 1999:** 11.62
P/BV: 2.5	**OPERATING MARGIN:** 13%
BETA VS. S&P 500: 1.33	**CORRELATION WITH S&P 500:** 0.26

DIVIDENDS PER SHARE (1998): $0.30

Brahma is the largest beer company in Latin America. Most of its revenue comes from selling beer to Brazilians, who each consume a massive 13 gallons of beer a year, compared to about 1.5 gallons for the average U.S. citizen. The company has been expanding recently into other markets, especially Latin America, and is beginning to gain brand name recognition for the beers it exports to the United States and Europe. Exports, though, play a minor role in the company's revenue picture. Brahma's present and most of its future are the huge market share it has in Brazil and the growth of the beer-drinking consumer market.

Brazil's tropical climate makes beer-drinking a popular pastime. In 1998, the El Niño weather system pushed the mercury so high that even a government-imposed tax increase on beer didn't slow growth in consumption. The slow growth in the economy in 1999 was expected to

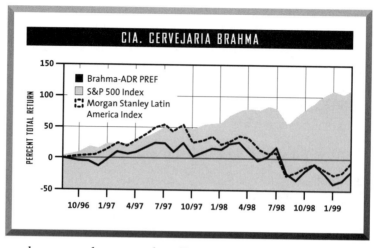

hamper sales somewhat. Even so, Brahma's sales growth was expected to be around 3 percent—more than a full percentage point above growth in gross domestic product.

Once the Brazilian economy gains steam, beer consumption will grow, too. It is unlikely Brahma will be able to increase its market share much beyond the 40 percent it now commands with its two brands, Brahma and Skol. But Brahma stands to gain from an increase in the consumption of imported beer. Since 1995, Brahma has bottled and canned Miller beer in Brazil under a joint venture with the Miller Brewing Co., and a Brazilian judge in 1998 cleared that venture of a prosecutor's contention that it violated Brazilian anti-trust laws. Brahma also increased its stake in Pepsi franchises in Brazil in 1998, attempting to strengthen its already large stake in the soft drink market.

For decades, Brahma has been locked in an intense battle for market share with Antartica, Brazil's second largest brewer. Neither company is ever likely to win the battle outright, but Brahma's ingenuity in seeking other ways to boost revenue make this company a good investment bet.

Among its diversification techniques, Brahma recently spent $50 million to expand a bottling plant in Buenos Aires, Argentina. Its marketing campaign there seeks not only to elevate the Brahma name but to increase beer consumption in Argentina, which at 9 gallons per person a year is one of the weakest beer-consuming publics in Latin America. Brahma also boosted its market share in Venezuela to 12.5 percent in 1997 from 10 percent a year earlier. Venezuela, whose populace drinks 18 gallons of beer a year per capita, is considered one of Latin America's best beverage markets.

Another good point is that Brahma ADRs trade at a low correlation with the Standard and Poor's 500. The company has been buying back its own shares, which has helped push the price of the shares up by showing investors that management believes in the company's future. The company has repurchased shares worth $300 million since 1996.

In a 1998 interview analyst Thomas Mobille of Robert Fleming Securities in New York said of the company, "We keep the 'buy' recommendation on Brahma because, despite the fact that the fundamentals for the beverage sector are not that good this year, in the long term there's no other way for the company but to grow."

◆ **Downside:** Brahma had a relatively high P/E of 17.38 in late 1998. That was still smaller than the 19.4 P/E of Anheuser Busch and well below the outrageous 39 P/E of Heineken, but it's high by Latin American standards. Also, sales growth is highly dependent on the economy and on weather.

◆ **What to Look For:** Keep an eye on El Niño. If it keeps pushing temperatures up, Brahma will do well, especially during the peak summer beer-drinking season. Also, look up the company's annual report and, if your broker has access to them, some recent analyst reports to get more up-to-date figures on Brahma's debt-to-equity ratio and its expansion plans. As of late 1998 its debt wasn't unmanageable, but it could grow as the company keeps expanding internationally and keeps diversifying within Brazil. Both of these strategies are good, however, and the company can afford to take on some more debt.

CIA. ENERGÉTICA DE SÃO PAULO (CESP)

U.S. TICKER: CESQY

1 ADR = 300 preferred shares

EXCHANGE: OTC   **SECTOR:** Utilities

MARKET CAP.: $1.6 billion   **1998 EARNINGS:** $712 million

FORECAST 1999 EPS: $1.93

(2 analysts surveyed by First Call)

EARNINGS GROWTH (5-YEAR FORECAST): NA

1998 SALES: $2.6 billion   **P/E ON JANUARY 1, 1999:** 1.44

BOOK VALUE PER ADR: $44   **ROE:** NA

BETA VS. S&P 500: 1.70   **CORRELATION WITH S&P 500:** 0.16

DIVIDENDS PER SHARE (1998): $0.85

CESP is the largest subsidiary in what was once the massive Eletrobrás government-run electricity system. Almost all the parts of Eletrobrás have since been sold to the private sector, including huge chunks of CESP itself. Texas-based Enron Corp. paid $1.27 billion in July 1998 for a 47 percent controlling stake in CESP's distribution arm, Elektro Eletricidade e Serviços SA, and a group led by BG Plc and Royal Dutch/Shell Group paid $1 billion in April 1999 for a 53 percent stake in CESP's natural gas subsidiary, Cia. de Gas de São Paulo.

What remains of CESP is its largest business, power generation, and that unit was scheduled to be sold in three parts in May and June 1999, although there was a chance the sale might be delayed. If those sales go ahead as planned, and if they fetch good prices, CESP's stock is bound to gain. But since those sales are likely to be over and done by the time you read this book, the question then becomes: where to invest?

"After the spinoff, investors should be able to buy better pieces of CESP that are being purchased by better managers," Sonia Olinto, Latin American utilities analyst at Credit Lyonnais Securities in New York, told me in an interview. "A good operator will make a huge difference."

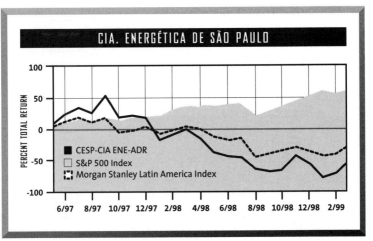

SOURCE: BLOOMBERG L.P.

There are other reasons, too, to invest in CESP: first, the stock had one of the lowest P/E ratios of Brazilian bluechips as of spring 1999, and the privatized parts will still be cheap, providing investors don't overly hype the shares after the new owners take over. CESP enjoyed a fast ride to the top as investors worldwide discovered its value in 1997, but then the price tumbled as the Brazilian government fumbled the sale of its subsidiaries and delayed them.

Electric companies, however, remain a good long-term investment in Brazil. As the country's industrial production ramps up, more energy will be required. CESP stands to gain from that in the long term, given its strategic location in the country's most populous and most productive region. São Paulo accounts for about 40 percent of the country's gross domestic product.

◆ **Downside:** The company's debt level is still high, and management needs to keep working to bring it down. The government has promised to use part of the sale of CESP assets to pay down debt, but it hasn't indicated just how much of those proceeds will be used.

◆ **What to Look For:** Search newspapers and financial Web sites for any news on the sale of CESP assets. If strong companies with lots of experience in power generation buy them, that's a plus. Partial foreign ownership would also be seen as a positive by investors, although those owners should have at least some experience in Brazil and Latin America, or a strong Brazilian partner that will educate them and help win new contracts and favorable rates from the government. However, if the sales are delayed or if the companies that buy them aren't strong, the share prices could suffer. Go back to Lindgren's list of investment selection methods in Chapter 3. Items like superior management, strong coinvestors and board, and intelligent business strategies should be applied to the companies that buy CESP as well as to CESP itself. Another important thing to watch is the government's regulation of electricity rates. The more freedom that companies are given to set their own rates, the better that will be for CESP's earnings.

UNIÃO DE BANCOS BRASILEIROS SA (UNIBANCO)

U.S. TICKER: UBB

1 GDR = 500 units of 1 preferred share of Unibanco and 1 preferred B share of Unibanco holdings

EXCHANGE: NYSE	**SECTOR:** Banking
MARKET CAP.: $1.24 billion	**1998 EARNINGS:** $376 million
FORECAST 1999 EPS: $2.72	**ROE:** 16.4%
(11 analysts surveyed by First Call)	
EARNINGS GROWTH (4-YEAR HISTORICAL): 7%	
ASSETS (END 1998): $26.3 billion	**P/E ON JANUARY 1, 1999:** 3.43
BOOK VALUE PER ADR: 24.18	**ROA:** 1.61%
BETA VS. S&P 500: 1.92	**CORRELATION WITH S&P 500:** 0.20
DIVIDENDS PER SHARE (1998): $1.51	

Unibanco is the third largest non-government-owned bank in Brazil, and quite possibly the best managed bank in the country.

The banking sector in Brazil has undergone a radical shakeup over the past four years. Banks literally had to change the way they did business overnight after President Cardoso instituted his Real Plan in July 1994. Prior to that, banks made most of their money profiting from hyperinflation. Some banks bet that the anti-inflation plan

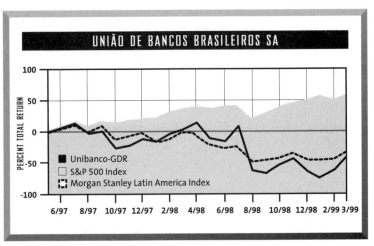

SOURCE: BLOOMBERG L.P.

wouldn't last, and they kept doing business as usual. Unibanco, on the other hand, predicted the plan would hold and quickly changed its focus toward being the kind of full-service retail bank one finds in North America or Europe.

Unibanco expanded its consumer loans division, which from 1994 to mid 1998 had been the most lucrative sector in commercial banking in Brazil. The bank also made two major purchases in the consumer loan sector. In 1996, it bought 49 percent of Banco Fininvest, and in 1998 it bought a 51 percent controlling stake in Banco Dibens, which specializes in car and truck leasing. As an example of how lucrative that type of business can be, auto loans in Brazil often come with annual interest rates of 100 percent.

The result has been that Unibanco is now rated as one of the strongest banks in the country by Atlantic Rating, a firm that specializes in comparing the balance sheets of Brazilian banks.

The bank's earnings growth has been impressive, in spite of spates of high interest rates prompted by the government's efforts to cut the federal deficit. When the Asian and Russian crises helped push Brazilian interest rates above 40 percent, Unibanco suffered along with most banks. Loans dropped, and the bank was forced to make higher-than-expected provisions for bad debt. But it was never in any danger, and as interest rates later dropped, the bank's loan portfolio improved again.

This is the only Brazilian bank that made our list, mostly because the sector as a whole is not the most promising growth story. Like Mexican banks in 1994, Brazilian banks suffered from the January 1999 devaluation, and time will tell just how much an expected increase in bad debt affects the bank's income. Still, Unibanco is well enough managed that even in such a situation, damage would likely be kept to a minimum.

"It is a very well run bank, and higher rates shouldn't hurt it too much," Brent Erensel, a Latin American banking analyst with Warburg Dillon Read in New York City, told Bloomberg News in a May 1998 interview.

The company is also diversified, with large stakes in the rapidly growing insurance industry in Brazil. It has a strong strategic partnership in the insurance sector with American International Group, the largest publicly traded U.S. financial services company.

◆ **Downside:** It's a bank. It's highly susceptible to increases in interest rates by the government. Brazilian banks went through a rough crisis in 1995 and 1996. If the economy slows and bad debts increase, the value of Unibanco shares will take a hit. Also, merger mania has seized the Brazilian banking industry. New government regulations that allow foreign banks to operate in Brazil has led to several big foreign financial companies buying up large stakes in smaller Brazilian banks. That will increase competition for Unibanco.

◆ **What to Look For:** Keep an eye on the macroeconomic scene by researching news on Brazil's efforts to cut its fiscal deficit and on any rapid increase in capital flight, both of which would lead the government to increase interest rates. If Brazil's federal deficit swells, the trade gap increases, and foreign reserves start declining, more devaluations and a return to higher inflation could also be imminent. If you think that is the situation, consider selling your shares. Also keep an eye on Unibanco's annual report for any increase in bad loans or decrease in loan reserves. And, as in any company, watch news reports and the company's own Web site for management changes. Unibanco's management team is one of its strongest assets, and if it starts losing key personnel, the company as a whole could suffer.

TELECOMUNICAÇÕES BRASILEIRAS SA (TELEBRÁS)

U.S. TICKER: TBH (formerly TBR; now TBH is the symbol representing 12 ticker symbols following the 1998 breakup)

EXCHANGE: NYSE   **SECTOR:** Telecommunications

MARKET CAP. PRIOR TO BREAKUP: $19 billion

EARNINGS GROWTH (5-YEAR FORECAST): 5%

ROE (PRIOR TO BREAKUP): 12%

Telebrás is not one stock but thirteen. Telebrás was the most highly traded ADR on the New York Stock Exchange in 1997, but the company was split into twelve separate companies (thirteen, including the small remaining assets of Telebrás itself which still trade under the TBR symbol) in the summer of 1998 when the Brazilian government sold its controlling stake in the company for about $19.5 billion. The breakup was similar to the 1980s split of AT&T in the United States. In New York trading on the twelve

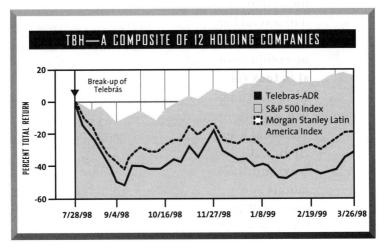

subsidiaries began in early November 1998. We use the old Telebrás name here because the twelve are viewed mostly as a group by investment professionals, and it's difficult to single out just one. Only Telesp gets its own profile, mainly because it was a blue chip stock in its own right even before the break up.

There is still a way to buy stock in the company as a whole. The ticker "TBH" is a security that trades as a piece of each of the twelve entities. That security, however, will probably just serve as a transition between the disappearance of Telebrás stock and the time it takes the subsidiaries to establish their own international investing clientele.

"The whole post-breakup Telebrás will be extremely attractive," says Jim Barrineau, former chief Latin America strategist at Salomon Smith Barney in New York. "Telecommunications companies in general in Latin America are good investments because they are plays on both local growth and on technology."

The Telebrás companies are good long-term investments not just because of the potential for economic growth in Brazil but also because they could benefit from deregulation of the phone industry and the increased competition that will bring. While some Latin American phone companies like Mexico's Telmex and Telefónica del Perú might actually be hurt by the competition, Telebrás's offspring will most likely gain. These companies are well managed. Most of them are either controlled by foreign companies or have foreign companies as minority partners who participate with seats on the boards of directors. And the government has structured the deregulation so that the "Baby Bras" companies will receive big fees for use of their lines, and it will be extremely difficult for new entrants to wrest substantial market share away from the existing companies.

Part of the optimism among Brazilian phone companies stems from the fact that the country severely lacks good phone service. Only one in 9.1 Brazilians has a phone line.

Service is so bad and so antiquated that calls routinely don't get through, and it can take two years to get a new phone line installed. Also, when it was split up, Telebrás had an average of one employee for every 186 fixed lines, as compared to one for every 300 lines among local phone companies in the United States. That means that there's lots of room for improving both revenue and profit and for reducing costs. All of that is likely to boost earnings, as well as the companies' share prices.

Among the twelve Telebrás subsidiaries are four fixed-line operators and eight cellular phone companies. Those two types in themselves can be totally different investments. Cellular phone growth has boomed over the past several years, in part because cellular lines can cost less than regular fixed-line service in many cases, and it comes without the wait. But competition is also a lot heavier among cellular companies, against both existing competitors and new entrants. The government over the past few years has sold licenses to companies to operate cellular phone systems in direct competition with the established former Telebrás subsidiaries. If Brazil enters into a long recession, however, the high cost of cellular phones might prompt customers to migrate to regular phone lines, whose prices are dropping fast.

"Over the long term we definitely prefer the fixed-line operators to the cellular operators," says Luiz Carvalho, telecommunications analyst for Morgan Stanley Dean Witter & Co. "These companies in our view will be much less affected by the recession we expect in Brazil in 1999."

The four fixed-line companies are Telesp (TSP), Tele Centro Sul (TCS), Tele Norte Leste (TNE), and Embratel (EMT).

Among the strong cellular companies are Tele Sudeste Celular (TSD); Telesp Celular (TCP), a former division of Telesp from São Paulo; and Tele Nordeste Celular (TND).

◆ **Downside:** Competition is the biggest drawback for these firms, especially the cellular companies. Keep an eye on prices to see how fast they decline in Brazil and how much that eats into profits—both for cellular and fixed-line companies. The Brazilian government was scheduled to auction off licenses in 1999 to companies that would establish fixed-line phone systems in competition with the four fixed-line Baby Bras. Renato Navarro Guerreiro, the head of the Brazilian communications commission, Anatel, told me he expects these companies to gain anywhere from 5 to 10 percent of market share in the regions they operate by the year 2003.

Another drawback is strict regulations that, even after deregulation, are making it hard going for the companies. Rates are watched closely by the government, and several of the post-breakup Telebrás companies were sold under the condition that no layoffs take place for at least six months. It's obvious that these companies need to trim their payrolls, and when the new foreign owners start doing that it could cause a backlash by the public and from government officials.

◆ **What to Look For:** All of the issues I have referred to here will determine the future profit structure of the Telebrás companies, and they can be followed by looking up news stories on each of the Telebrás subsidiaries on financial Web sites. Another important part of their earnings structure is the rates they charge local customers. Keep an eye on government legislation that could free up those restrictions or, on the negative side, impose more.

TELECOMUNICAÇÕES DE SÃO PAULO SA (TELESP)

U.S. TICKER: TSP
1 ADR = 1,000 preferred shares

EXCHANGE: NYSE	**SECTOR:** Telecommunications
MARKET CAP.: $5.52 billion	**1998 EARNINGS:** $560 million

FORECAST 1999 EPS: $1.75
  (8 analysts surveyed by I.B.E.S.)
EARNINGS GROWTH (1-YEAR): 12%

1998 SALES: $3.7 billion	**P/E ON JANUARY 1, 1999:** 18.0
BOOK VALUE PER ADR: $29	**ROE:** 21%

SOURCE: BLOOMBERG L.P.

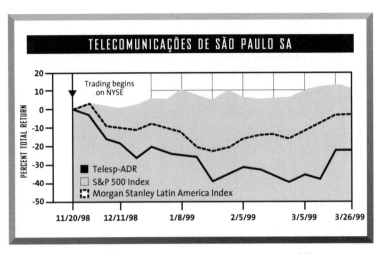

TELECOMUNICAÇÕES DE SÃO PAULO SA

Trading begins on NYSE

PERCENT TOTAL RETURN

■ Telesp-ADR
□ S&P 500 Index
╏╏ Morgan Stanley Latin America Index

11/20/98   12/11/98   1/8/99   2/5/99   3/5/99   3/26/99

BETA VS. S&P 500: 0.88   **DIVIDENDS PER SHARE:** NA

CORRELATION WITH S&P 500: 0.04

To give you an idea about the potential of Telesp, look at the price Spain's Telefónica SA paid for the company in July 1998. The price tag of almost $4.9 billion represented about a 64 percent premium over the price at which the shares were being traded at the time. Telefónica is no slouch of a phone company, and you can bet Telefónica did its homework on valuing the future of Telesp.

Telesp is the largest of the Telebrás subsidiaries sold by the government in 1998. The company sells fixed-line phone service throughout the state of São Paulo, the most populous of Brazil's states. With Telefónica's management expertise behind it, Telesp has a lot of room for both revenue growth and improved operating efficiency, producing better margins. Telefónica said it plans to spend $3.8 billion in 1999 alone to expand its telephone networks in Brazil. Most of that was destined for Telesp, although Telefónica also had investments in a fixed-line phone company in the state of Rio Grande do Sul and a cellular company in Rio de Janeiro. Juan Villalonga, president of Telefónica, says he expects Telesp to add 2 million new lines in 1999, bringing the total to 8.2 million lines.

Among the publicly traded phone companies in Brazil, Telesp has several strengths: it's well managed, in the biggest market, with shares that can be bought and sold easily and traded everywhere.

"Brazil has many areas in terms of pent-up demand for telephone lines, but Telesp's population area has a GDP per capita that is almost twice the national average," says Luiz Carvalho, telecommunications analyst at Morgan Stanley. "We expect Telesp in terms of number of lines to double in the next four or five years."

Buying shares in Telesp, however, also means that you are buying into the massive Telefónica of Spain Latin American phone network. Telefónica has spent tens of billions of dollars to buy up shares and expand phone companies across the Americas over the past several years. There is a lot to be said for the efficiencies that such a network can bring. But there's also a lot to be said for the risks. The company had to take on a lot of debt in order to make the purchases, and Standard & Poor's put some of the company's outstanding debt on credit watch soon after the Telesp purchase.

◆ **Downside:** Competition. Telesp has almost a monopoly on fixed-line phone service in São Paulo, but the government is gradually changing regulations that will allow other phone companies to compete with Telesp in a number of services. Telesp also competes with cellular phone companies, because a lot of people buy cellular phones instead of waiting for new lines from Telesp, which often cost as much if not more than cellular service. Also, as competition increases, rates will eventually start decreasing, and that could cut into Telesp's margins. Still, the growth in new client revenue and increases in operating efficiency could far outweigh any drop in earnings from lower rates.

◆ **What to Look For:** Look at the company's Web site and ask your broker for some recent analyst reports that monitor the debt-to-equity levels of both Telefónica and Telesp. Telesp will need a lot of new investment to improve its antiquated phone lines and expand service. Watch newspapers and company news on the Web for government rate changes and for changes that open up competition. Competition could be both good and bad, because it will force Telesp to invest in infrastructure, which in the long run will be good for company earnings.

ARACRUZ CELULOSE SA

U.S. TICKER: ARA
1 ADR = 10 class B preferred shares
EXCHANGE: NYSE   **SECTOR:** Paper and pulp
MARKET CAP.: $1.2 billion   **1998 EARNINGS (LOSS):** ($58.8 million)
FORECAST 1999 EPS: $0.85
   (3 analysts surveyed by Zacks)
EARNINGS GROWTH (5-YEAR AVERAGE): NA
1998 SALES: $444 million   **P/E ON JANUARY 1, 1999:** 7.8
BOOK VALUE PER ADR: 21.8   **EBITDA MARGIN:** 42.6%
BETA VS. S&P 500: 1.41   **CORRELATION WITH S&P 500:** 0.21
DIVIDENDS PER SHARE (1998): $0.21

Aracruz is a pulp and paper manufacturer with its headquarters in Rio de Janeiro. It has the distinction of being the first Brazilian ADR to be listed on the New York Stock Exchange. Perhaps for that reason and perhaps for others, Aracruz has been overlooked by most big institutional

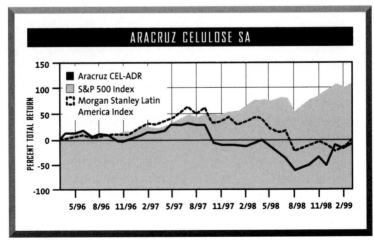

ARACRUZ CELULOSE SA

■ Aracruz CEL-ADR
□ S&P 500 Index
▥ Morgan Stanley Latin America Index

PERCENT TOTAL RETURN

150, 100, 50, 0, -50, -100

5/96 8/96 11/96 2/97 5/97 8/97 11/97 2/98 5/98 8/98 11/98 2/99

SOURCE: BLOOMBERG L.P.

investors as well as individuals. The price to earnings ratio, therefore, was low in early 1999, even by Latin American standards, and represented a good bargain considering the long-term strength of the company. That may change, however, as a rally in Aracruz's stock price in early 1999 was starting to reduce its bargain status. Aracruz was one of the ten Brazilian stocks that gained when the *real* was devalued, due to the fact that its sales are mostly in dollars, but its costs are in *reals*.

If you're interested in environment-friendly stocks, you'd be hard pressed to do better than Aracruz. The company gets all of its wood from its own eucalyptus groves, which line highways throughout the state of Espírito Santo. The company maintains strict control over the groves, cutting in a different place each year so that the other plants and animals that occupy the forest groves aren't left without a place to live.

Eucalyptus is also a very efficient tree. It grows fast, producing more pulp than any of the grove trees that North American and European growers use. As a result, Aracruz is one of the world's lowest-cost pulp producers, at just over $300 per metric ton for bleached eucalyptus pulp. And that cost has been coming down as a result of the company's investment in a larger and more efficient mill in the state of Espírito Santo. A $336 million expansion at the site was recently completed.

While Aracruz does have some paper mills, the bulk of its revenue and profit comes from making pulp and shipping it to customers in the United States, Asia, and Europe. In 1997, the company produced 1.08 million tons of pulp, 90 percent of which was exported. Of that, 37 percent went to the United States; 30 percent went to Europe, and 23 percent went to Asia. The pulp is used to make a variety of mostly high-quality paper products including tissue paper, writing paper, and specialty papers such as those used in magazines.

The company has also been well managed, although its chief executive officer, Carlos Lira Aguiar, has only been in office since April 1998 and hasn't yet had time to prove himself.

Aracruz also has one of the lowest correlation coefficients of any Brazilian ADR, and as such is a good addition to an investment portfolio because of the added diversification it would bring.

◆ **Downside:** The main drawback to the stock is the company's exposure to a slide in pulp prices on world markets. As with all forestry product companies, price dips in paper and pulp affect Aracruz heavily. It's one industry in which following the business cycle (see Chapter 4) can pay off if done correctly.

◆ **What to Look For:** When you buy Aracruz, try to buy when the price of pulp is at or near its low point. Read analyst reports to get a clearer picture of this. But when you hold it, hold it for the long run, considering its competitive advantages and the continued growth of the world paper industry.

CENTRAIS ELÉTRICAS BRASILEIRAS SA (ELECTROBRÁS)

U.S. TICKER: CAIFY

1 ADR = 500 common shares

EXCHANGE: OTC	**SECTOR:** Electricity
MARKET CAP.: $8.7 billion	**1998 EARNINGS:** $1.65 billion

FORECAST 1999 EPS: $1.93
(3 analysts surveyed by Zacks)

EARNINGS GROWTH (5-YEAR FORECAST): 5.2%

1998 SALES: $6.16 billion	**P/E ON JANUARY 1, 1999:** 5.0
BOOK VALUE PER ADR: $46	**ROE:** 3.3%
BETA VS. S&P 500: 1.53	**CORRELATION WITH S&P 500:** 0.20

DIVIDENDS PER SHARE (1998): $1.33

Eletrobrás is the holding company for Brazil's nationwide system of electrical power generation, transmission, and distribution. The Brazilian government is the principal shareholder, but over the past three years has been selling off pieces of Eletrobrás as well as building new

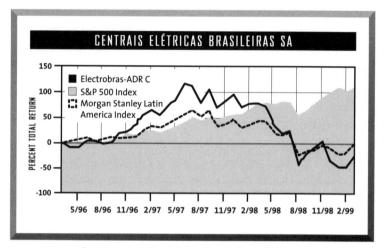

power plants to update its aging electricity system and to meet surging demand for electricity in Brazil. Eletrobrás estimates it will need to spend $14 billion in order to meet demand over the next ten years.

Eletrobrás shares were hurt in 1997 and 1998 as the Brazilian government bungled some of the privatizations of its subsidiaries. Those sales got back on track in the second half of 1998, although the stock price didn't recover due to the economic crises in Russia and Asia. Still, provided the government goes ahead with the sale in 1999 of several Eletrobrás subsidiaries, including Furnas, its biggest generation unit, Eletrobrás shares could be among the highest gainers in Brazil. Its shares did well, too, after the recent devaluation, because its rate structure allows for inflation increases and because Eletrobrás has more dollar-denominated loans among its assets than it does in its liabilities. It is one of the true bargain stocks in Latin America when one compares the price to either the company's earnings or its book value. It is also the largest and most actively traded utility stock in all of Latin America.

Studies by Lehman Brothers in August of 1998 showed the company was trading at a discount of as much as 50 percent of its net asset value.

Aside from controlling and operating several electricity

generation and transmission companies, Eletrobrás also owns shares in some 25 regional electric companies, many of which are publicly traded also.

The privatization of Eletrobrás subsidiaries is expected to be completed by 2002. In the meantime, the government is gradually opening up the electricity industry in Brazil to private competition for the first time in forty years. That opening is scheduled to be completed in 2006. Even when the new competition does come in, however, it is unlikely to substantially effect Eletrobrás's earnings because demand for electricity in Brazil is growing so rapidly that the market will be big enough for several players.

An advantage to holding Eletrobrás stock is that the company has traditionally paid high dividends to its shareholders. In 1997, the company paid a $1.24 per ADR dividend, and in 1998 raised that to $1.33.

◆ **Downside:** A recent report by Lehman Brothers sums up nicely the downside of Eletrobrás:

"The first is country risk. The second risk is sector-specific, if for some reason the privatization of Furnas does not get done during 1999. The third risk is company-specific. As an agency of the federal government, Eletrobrás does not always act in the interest of minority shareholders." A final risk that Lehman Brothers mentions is the risk that the Brazilian government will not use wisely the funds raised from the sale of Eletrobrás subsidiaries.

◆ **What to Look For:** Watching financial Web sites of newspapers for news on privatizations of Eletrobrás assets is the most important thing you can do in timing your investments in the company. Other than that, the long-term growth of the Brazilian economy and the eventual deregulation of the energy sector are issues that will effect the company's earnings down the road.

CHAPTER

Ten
MEXICAN
COMPANIES

HOOSING ONLY TEN promising Mexican companies was not easy, in part because Mexico has more
than eighty companies with American Depository
Receipts, twenty-eight of which are listed on the New
York Stock Exchange—the largest number of any of
the Latin American countries. Many of those
companies are well managed and have large, growing
markets and strong earnings potential. Many of them
are also good bargains, especially because so many
investors are still sour on Mexico from the peso crisis
of 1994–95. The ten listed here are among the best,
and span several industries to provide a diverse base
from which to choose your investments.

Mexico is no longer recovering from the peso crisis.
It recovered. The economy has more than gained back
what it lost in 1994 and 1995. The third quarter of
1998 was the eleventh consecutive quarter in which
gross domestic product grew. In 1997, the economy

grew 7 percent—the fastest annual rate in sixteen years. Growth in the second half of 1998 slowed because of the crisis that swept all emerging markets, bringing the 1998 growth rate to less than 5 percent. Growth in 1999 was expected to be 2.7 percent, among the highest in Latin America, according to a survey conducted by the central bank. These statistics are evidence that although the government might have bungled the 1994 peso devaluation in the short run, it was a necessary first step if the country was to achieve a stable path of long-term economic growth.

The growth in 1997 and the first half of 1998 was due mostly to increases in private investment, including manufacturing and construction, and growth in consumer spending. A big export surge in 1997 also helped. Retail spending has increased sharply across the board, from the more recession-proof sectors such as supermarkets to the more boomtime-dependent sectors such as department stores. The service industry more recently has grown even faster, especially restaurants, hotels, and the communications industry. Most of the increased private investment has come from U.S. companies taking advantage of the North American Free Trade Agreement (NAFTA) to set up shop in Mexico, but the contribution of foreign direct investment to GDP growth has not been great, indicating Mexican companies, too, are investing.

All of this has come in spite of weak world oil prices. Oil accounts for about 6.5 percent of Mexico's total exports and about 33 percent of the government's annual revenue—down from 38 percent in 1997. The government, meanwhile, has been cutting spending in an attempt to lessen the impact on the economy from the drop in oil prices. Still, Mexico's current account (the record of a country's purchases and sales of goods and services from and to the rest of the world) showed a ballooning deficit in 1998 and could cause problems for the economy if the government allows it to expand further. Part of the problem has been that the government is still paying off the debts it accumulated when it spent billions to bail out the banking sector in 1995. Mexico repaid the $20 billion it borrowed from the U.S. government during the crisis, but it paid it back with other debt that was borrowed in part from the domestic private sector and in part on world capital markets. One thing the government has going for it is the strong leadership of Guillermo Ortiz, Central Bank Governor. Ortiz is respected internationally, and the economic policies that he established when he was finance minister are still doctrine in Mexico.

Mexican companies, on the other hand, have paid down most of the huge piles of dollar-denominated debt they were left with after the big peso devaluation. The devaluation made it hard on business for a while, but the smart ones took advantage of the weakness of the peso to look for new export markets. The devaluation made Mexican exports suddenly cheaper and more attractive to foreign buyers. Maquiladora plants—assembly factories set up along the U.S. border—found it easier to sell their goods, and agricultural companies made inroads in marketing their produce in places where they had never been competitive before.

There are still some dangers to look out for. Aside from a growing current account deficit, interest rates rose in 1998 to more than 35 percent from about 17 percent at the beginning of the year. Higher interest rates are fine as a short-term fix for the economy, but if the government leaves them in place for too long, consumer spending will slow enough to begin to hurt earnings, and companies won't be able to invest in growth opportunities if borrowing rates are too high. Another problem that has been Mexico's downfall for decades is corruption, and there are no signs that the problem is lessening. Drug money now runs through some of Mexico's biggest banks, as well as the offices of many government officials, and those who speak out against it are either shut up with bribery money or shut down through censorship and other pressures.

The 2000 presidential elections will be a good test of the government's promises to clean things up. The ruling Revolutionary Independence Party, PRI, is no longer strong enough to sweep the elections, so the fairness of the elections will indicate the real political situation.

On the whole, though, Mexico is full of promise, especially for businesses. The firms that are investing now in the future are the ones that will see the most benefits from the growth of the economy, and the investors who buy shares in those companies will see a piece of the action.

TV AZTECA SA

U.S. TICKER: TZA
1 ADR = 16 CPOs
EXCHANGE: NYSE   **SECTOR:** Broadcasting
MARKET CAP.: $839 million   **1998 OPER. INCOME:** $164 million
FORECAST 1999 EPS: $0.42   **1998 NET INCOME:** $7.7 million
　　(9 analysts surveyed by First Call)

EARNINGS GROWTH (5-YEAR FORECAST): 6.8%

1998 SALES: $456 million   **P/E ON JANUARY 1, 1999:** 10.1

BOOK VALUE PER ADR: 1.90   **EBITDA MARGIN:** 52%

BETA VS. S&P 500: 1.51   **CORRELATION WITH S&P 500:** 0.22

DIVIDENDS PER SHARE (1998): $0.03

Mexico has two major television broadcasters, both good companies with excellent growth potential in a market that includes not just Mexico but the entire Spanish-speaking population of the world. Of the two, TV Azteca is a more exciting company and continues to surprise investors by nipping away at the domestic audience of its much larger rival, Grupo Televisa *(see page 205)*.

In 1993 a group of investors led by the current chairman, Ricardo Salinas Pliego, purchased TV Azteca from the Mexican government for $642 million. At the time of the sale, TV Azteca had just 9 percent of the country's weekday prime time television audience. That share has since shot up to 35 percent. The company's growth has come mainly on the success of self-produced prime time soap operas—"telenovelas" that are the favorite type of television show in Mexico. Azteca's popularity has come mostly at the expense of Televisa. TV Azteca operates two national television networks, Azteca 7 and Azteca 13, through more than 250 owned and operated stations.

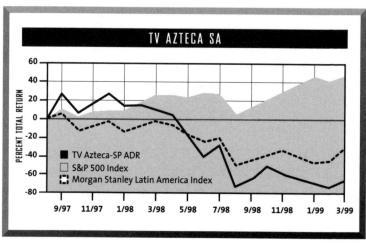

TV AZTECA SA

SOURCE: BLOOMBERG L.P.

The company's business strategy has been to continue pushing for a higher market share in Mexico while expanding internationally. Salinas's goal is to overtake Televisa and capture more than 50 percent of the market, although Televisa has responded to the competition by improving its own programming and at times winning back market share. Azteca, also, is spending more, primarily by producing about 90 percent of its prime time shows internally, up from 80 percent in 1997. The company says it's trying to concentrate more on improving its revenue stream, rather than just improving ratings.

"Ratings are important, but they aren't everything, especially when your focus is on cash flow growth," Salinas says. "The financial world has seen many examples of TV companies that are No. 1 in the ratings but still lose money." When Televisa won back some market share during one quarter in 1998, the effect on TV Azteca was a 40 percent drop in earnings for the period.

Whether or not it wins market share from Televisa, TV Azteca's advertising revenue is likely to rise on the sheer growth of the Mexican and Latin American markets. Internationally, TV Azteca owns stations in Chile and El Salvador and has been in talks at various times to buy stations in Honduras, the Dominican Republic, Costa Rica, Guatemala, and other Latin American countries. The company has said it hopes to use its own programming to boost the market shares of the stations it invests in. TV Azteca also announced in 1998 that it plans to buy minority stakes in several U.S. television stations in areas with large Spanish-speaking audiences.

Another sign of the company's growing importance in Mexico was the announcement in March 1998 that the Mexican bolsa index will include TV Azteca for the first time.

◆ **Downside:** The chairman, Salinas, is also heavily involved in other industries. He owns Elektra, a chain of small-appliance discount stores in Mexico, as well as other businesses. He has used TV Azteca to promote sales for Elektra, and he might devote more of his time to his other holdings if TV Azteca's successes diminish or if he becomes bored with television.

Moody's, the credit rating agency, cites as drawbacks Azteca's "short history as a private enterprise and increasing costs for Azteca to produce its own programming." Moody's also notes that a big portion of Azteca's debt is in dollars, while virtually all of its revenue is in pesos.

◆ **What to Look For:** TV Azteca's Mexican business is by far its largest. You can watch the Web sites of both TV Azteca and Televisa to find out if Azteca is slipping any in its market share. Look for news, too, about the company's international expansion, especially its joint ventures in the United States and any acquisitions it might make there, which could add significantly to the company's revenue stream.

CEMEX SA

U.S. TICKER: CMXBY

1 ADR = 2 Series B shares

EXCHANGE: NYSE	**SECTOR:** Building products
MARKET CAP.: $3.7 billion	**1998 OPER. INCOME:** $1.18 billion
FORECAST 1999 EPS: $1.27	**1998 NET INCOME:** $803 million
(12 analysts surveyed by I.B.E.S.)	

EARNINGS GROWTH (5-YEAR FORECAST): 10%

1998 SALES: $4.3 billion	**P/E ON JANUARY 1, 1999:** 4.44
BOOK VALUE PER ADR: $17	**OPERATING MARGIN:** 27%
BETA VS. S&P 500: 1.54	**CORRELATION WITH S&P 500:** 0.29
DIVIDENDS PER SHARE (1998): $0.22	

Cemex is the third largest cement maker in the world and one of Mexico's true multinational companies. It has operations in the United States, Spain, Venezuela, Colombia, Panama, and the Caribbean, and it exports its cement to more than sixty countries. Cemex has benefited from sharp growth in all those countries, but the fastest growth in recent years has come from its home market of Mexico. Construction in Mexico boomed between late 1996 and

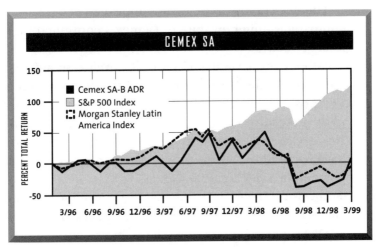

CEMEX SA

- Cemex SA-B ADR
- S&P 500 Index
- Morgan Stanley Latin America Index

PERCENT TOTAL RETURN

SOURCE: BLOOMBERG L.P.

the first half of 1998, with new government infrastructure projects and new plants being built by foreign and Mexican companies. In the first quarter of 1998, Cemex's revenue in Mexico shot up 27 percent from a year earlier. While the 1998 emerging markets crisis was expected to slow that growth somewhat, construction should resume its brisk pace in the second half of 1999 as Mexico's economy expands and trade with the United States, Canada, and other countries leads to more construction activity among Mexican firms.

The Mexican market represents about 43 percent of Cemex's total sales, followed by Spain at 19 percent. The United States accounts for 11 percent of total sales.

Cemex's business strategy has been to diversify internationally while focusing on its core cement business. In 1998, it sold two hotel properties, which were among its last remaining non-cement assets, and used the money to help pay down debt. Recently, the company has been interested in expanding into Asia, taking advantage of the weak values of Asian currencies to buy properties. It spent $91 million for a 30 percent stake in Rizal Cement Inc. of the Philippines and has been trying to find partners to buy or build cement companies in other parts of Asia.

The company had good operating margins of 28 percent in 1997 and 27 percent in 1998.

The debt rating agencies also appear to like what the company is doing, in spite of Cemex's continued high level of debt.

"Moody's believes that Cemex effectively responded to the effects of the Mexican crisis, and that the company is well positioned to benefit from future growth in many Latin American markets," the agency wrote in August 1998. "Cemex's diversification efforts outside of Mexico have resulted in a significant increase in non-peso cash flow and broader access to capital."

♦ **Downside:** Debt. The company owed $5 billion as of the end of the third quarter of 1998. That equates to a debt-to-market-capitalization ratio of about 50 percent, too high for almost any company, let alone a Mexican firm that is still feeling effects of the peso crisis. In spite of the positive ways it has refinanced its portfolio, Cemex still has "a high level of debt and a relatively short maturity profile," Moody's wrote. Cemex has been gradually reducing that debt, bringing it down by about $300 million in 1997 alone. A big portion of that debt is left over from the peso crisis, but much of it is also due to Cemex's aggressive expansion plans. As long as those projects keep paying off, the company can be assured of having enough cash to make interest payments.

♦ **What to Look For:** Watch newspapers and financial Web sites for news of new contracts, both in Mexico and throughout Cemex's other Latin American operations. For news as specific as that, you may need to go to the Web sites of a Mexican business newspaper such as *El Financiero*, listed in the back of this book. Watch also for industrial activity figures in Mexico and in Latin America as a whole. The government reports these numbers monthly, and if you can't find them on the Web you can call your broker and ask for the information from the Bloomberg system. If industrial production keeps increasing, chances are that Cemex's contracts will increase and become more lucrative. If industrial production slides, so could Cemex's share price. Watch Cemex's quarterly reports, too, to assure yourself that the company is making progress in bringing the level of debt down to at least below 50 percent of market capitalization.

CIFRA SA

U.S. TICKER: CFRVY

1 ADR = 10 series V shares

EXCHANGE: NYSE

SECTOR: Retail

MARKET CAP.: $6.1 billion

1998 OPER. INCOME: $194 million

FORECAST 1999 EPS: $0.66

1998 NET INCOME: $281 million

(11 analysts surveyed by I.B.E.S.)

EARNINGS GROWTH (5-YEAR FORECAST): 12%

1998 SALES: $5.2 billion

P/E ON JANUARY 1, 1999: 19.34

BOOK VALUE PER ADR: $5.17

ROE: 11%

BETA VS. S&P 500: 0.91

CORRELATION WITH S&P 500: 0.11

DIVIDENDS PER SHARE (1998): $0.00 (zero)

Cifra SA is Mexico's largest retailer, and it's now controlled by Wal-Mart, the world's largest retailer. Size can be good or bad in the retail industry, but in Cifra's case it can mean only positive things.

Wal-Mart, which for six years had a strategic partnership with Cifra in Mexico, paid $1.2 billion for a 51 percent controlling share in the company in 1997. The match is a good one. Wal-Mart is known for its low-cost, efficient

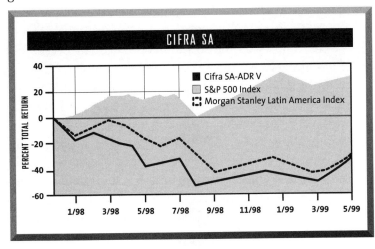

CIFRA SA

■ Cifra SA-ADR V
□ S&P 500 Index
▪▪ Morgan Stanley Latin America Index

operations, an area in which Cifra always needed improvement. Cifra's own Aurrerra grocery stores, VIP's restaurants, and Suburbia clothing outlets have strong brand-recognition, and Cifra's experience is making it easier for Wal-Mart to open its own superstores and its Sam's Club membership stores throughout Mexico.

Cifra's stock took a pounding during the first half of 1998, mostly because the cost cutting and higher sales that investors expected from the merger never came about. What many didn't realize, however, is that higher expenditures were necessary at first if the company is to realize its goal of becoming more like Wal-Mart. Better technology, for example, is being installed throughout all the chains to keep better control of inventory and costs, and that technology costs money. New stores are also being built. Cifra said it planned to invest $262 million during an eighteen-month period ending in mid-1999 to open 47 new outlets, including 19 VIP's, 6 Sam's Club stores, and 5 Aurrerra stores.

The size and growth potential of the market are another reason for investing in Cifra. Supermarket sales nationwide plunged dramatically and steadily during all of 1995 and 1996, during and after the peso crisis, but sales started climbing again in the first month of 1997. They've been mostly improving month-to-month ever since, often at a clip of more than 7 percent a month.

"Cifra is going to dominate the market for years to come," analyst Eduardo Cabrera of Merrill Lynch told Bloomberg News. "Close your eyes and buy Cifra."

Another advantage from an investor's point of view is that Cifra has no debt to speak of. That means that in the event of a devaluation, the company won't take too much of a beating. But no debt is not necessarily a good thing. Leveraging the company's strong reputation to finance new projects can be a smarter move than building only as many stores as can be financed from cash flow.

The company is also fairly insulated from downturns in the economy because its products are mostly necessities.

Milk and bread will continue to be sold during any recession, although Cifra's mix of products is evolving toward less recession-proof items that appeal to Mexico's rising middle class.

◆ **Downside:** Costs are the biggest item to watch at Cifra. Wal-Mart has spent big on revamping the operations, and it has promised many cost reductions in return. By mid-1998, those promises were far from reality. Costs company wide, in fact, rose 60 percent in the first quarter of 1998 compared with the same quarter a year earlier. There were higher sales and more stores, but revenue in the quarter rose only 49 percent.

Another drawback is that some of the talented leadership that had made Cifra the country's largest, most successful retailer have departed since Wal-Mart took over. Chief Executive Henry Davis left in March 1998, and Wal-Mart will have to work hard to prevent other defections if it wants to keep drawing on their experience—and Cifra's key connections with the Mexican government.

◆ **What to Look For:** With Cifra, as with most retailers, you should look at a key statistic called *same-store sales growth*— how fast are sales picking up (or falling) at each of the chain's existing outlets. You can find it at the company's Web site or in analyst reports, and you can also compare this statistic to that of other chains to see if Cifra is gaining or losing market share. It's a better performance measure than overall sales growth because it excludes any increase from the addition of new stores.

Monitor the company's annual and quarterly reports, too, for its cost structure and especially its operating margins, and watch for news stories about management changes. Read newspaper stories about Mexico's economy. Signs of strength will likely boost Cifra's share price.

A final note is to make sure when buying shares that you buy the right ones. Cifra has several series of ADRs on the market, and the one listed here has the highest liquidity. The others may be hard to buy and sell.

EMPRESAS ICA SOCIEDAD CONTROLADORA (ICA)

(ICA, pronounced "EEE Ka")

U.S. TICKER: ICA

1 ADR = 6 ordinary shares

EXCHANGE: NYSE   **SECTOR:** Construction

MARKET CAP.: $454 million   **1998 OPER. INCOME:** $92 million

FORECAST 1999 EPS: $0.55   **1998 NET INCOME:** $20 million
  (18 analysts surveyed by I.B.E.S.)

EARNINGS GROWTH (3-YEAR FORECAST): 19%

1998 SALES: $1.67 billion   **P/E ON JANUARY 1, 1999:** 7.5

BOOK VALUE PER ADR: $11   **ROE:** 12%

BETA VS. S&P 500: 1.07   **CORRELATION WITH S&P 500:** 0.11

DIVIDENDS PER SHARE (1998): $0.08

ICA is one of those venerable Latin American companies from the days when Mexico was still a vast desert wilderness of banditos and mule trains. In the old days, ICA's power was everywhere. It now shares that power with the new elite and the new wealth of Mexico, but it still exercises considerable influence with both government officials and the public.

ICA's main source of revenue is its heavy construction business. ICA builds everything from highways to dams to offshore oil platforms, and the government is its biggest client. But the company is diverse: It produces industrial goods and construction aggregates, such as concrete and asphalt, both for its own use and for sale domestically and internationally, but also owns and operates hotels and quarries. And it's expanding international operations—exports accounted for 32 percent of total revenue in the second quarter of 1998, up from 15 percent just a year earlier. That's a good sign for the company in the long run, allowing it to better weather those periods of downturns in the Mexican economy.

"Five years from now, ICA will be the leading engineering, procurement, and construction company in Latin

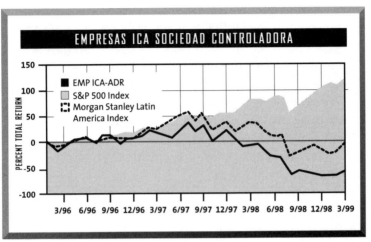

EMPRESAS ICA SOCIEDAD CONTROLADORA

Legend:
- EMP ICA-ADR
- S&P 500 Index
- Morgan Stanley Latin America Index

Y-axis: PERCENT TOTAL RETURN (150, 100, 50, 0, -50, -100)

X-axis: 3/96 6/96 9/96 12/96 3/97 6/97 9/97 12/97 3/98 6/98 9/98 12/98 3/99

America," says Bernardo Quintana, president of ICA. In Latin America, he notes, "Size does count, especially in the heavy construction field."

Quintana says the company plans to keep shifting its focus toward its core construction business, especially in infrastructure projects, by selling off non-core assets.

ICA's strategy of targeting Latin America is one of the reasons Deutsche Bank had a "buy" recommendation on the stock in late 1998, says Roberto Carillo, an analyst at Deutsche Bank securities in Mexico City. "There are roughly $31 billion in projects scheduled to be auctioned off in Latin America in the next several months alone, $5.2 billion of which are in Mexico," Carillo said at a conference in September 1998.

For example, ICA is building a road network in Colombia, a gas pipeline in Brazil, a dam in Chile, and a highway in Guatemala. For the near future, though, ICA's domestic Mexican operations will continue to be its biggest source of revenue growth. Mexico has been among the least affected countries from the emerging markets crisis of 1998. With the peso crisis over, the economy recovering, and industrial expansion booming under the auspices of NAFTA, ICA is benefiting from big government and private construction projects. The contracts aren't likely to let up anytime soon.

Giant construction conglomerates like ICA were once powerful in the United States as well, but fell out of favor as other industries such as high technology and service companies became more important to the economy. Some U.S. construction giants—take Morrison Knudsen, for example—were poorly managed and didn't adapt themselves to the changing economy. In Mexico, however, construction remains important due to the underdeveloped state of most of the country. ICA also has grown with Mexico's economy. When the oil industry boomed in the late 1970s and early 1980s, ICA quickly learned to build offshore platforms, pipelines, and petrochemical plants. Water treatment and irrigation are now among the fastest growing construction sectors in Mexico, and ICA is big in that area, too. Down the road, telecommunications and electricity are expected to see fast growth, and ICA is among the country's top bidders on installing the infrastructures for those industries.

◆ **Downside:** There are several issues important to ICA which, taken separately, don't amount to much danger, but a combination of which could cause the company some harm. First, there is the trend toward falling world oil prices, which if it continues could cause the Mexican government to spend less on new oil exploration projects. Second, there's the government's management of its own fiscal accounts. Although Mexico badly needs new construction projects, those projects won't be forthcoming if the government is fighting a rising federal deficit. Third, ICA needs to bring up its operating margins, which in recent quarters have sagged below 7 percent. Fourth, the company is heavily labor-dependent in a country whose average wage is growing quickly. Faster growth in wages could sharply increase ICA's costs and make any improvement in margins even more difficult.

A final drawback is that ICA's price-to-earnings ratio was high in 1998 relative to most Latin American companies. That's in part because of the nature of its business, but nonetheless it marks ICA as a company to buy for its growth, not its value. Finally, its management team is not highly regarded among foreign investors, when compared with the teams of similar companies, such as Cemex.

◆ **What to Look For:** Industrial activity figures for Mexico, the government's fiscal deficit, construction wages, and oil prices are all important to ICA. What you can't find in your favorite business publication or financial Web site you should be able to locate on a Mexican government site such as: www.shcp.gob.mx/ or the Mexican investment board's www.quicklink.com/mexmib/. Monitor ICA's internal financial reports and analyst reports for changes in its operating margins and progress at achieving its goal of 14 percent return on equity.

PANAMERICAN BEVERAGES INC. (PANAMCO)

U.S. TICKER: PB

NOT AN ADR: It's traded as a U.S. company

EXCHANGE: NYSE   **SECTOR:** Beverages

MARKET CAP.: $2.67 billion   **1998 OPER. INCOME:** $469 million

FORECAST 1999 EPS: $0.61   **1998 NET INCOME:** $120 million
(14 analysts surveyed by First Call)

EARNINGS GROWTH (5-YEAR FORECAST): 11.75%

1998 SALES: $2.8 billion   **P/E ON JANUARY 1, 1999:** 18.15

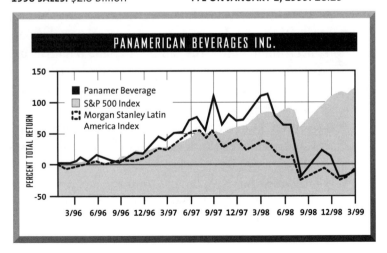

BOOK VALUE PER SHARE: $15.12   **ROE:** 13.8%

BETA VS. S&P 500: 1.48   **CORRELATION WITH S&P 500:** 0.42

DIVIDENDS PER SHARE (1998): $0.24

I've included Panamco in this list with the expectation that the price of the shares may have gone down by the time you read this book. At the price they were trading at when this book went to press, $22 a share, they were too high. A price-to-earnings ratio of 19 is high for a Latin American company and also too high for a beverage company—even if it is one of the darlings of mutual fund managers.

Having said that, Panamco is still a great company. It is truly diverse, with operations throughout Latin America and the United States, and it's well managed.

Panamco is the largest soft drink bottler in Latin America and is growing more all the time. It's also highly profitable for a beverage company, with operating margins of about 9.8 percent on annual sales of $2.5 billion.

Panamco dominates the soft drink market in Colombia and Venezuela and has recently added major acquisitions in Guatemala and Nicaragua to its list of markets. It is also a major player in Mexico, its home country, and in Costa Rica, and recently announced its intention to enter the Argentine market, most likely by acquiring a local bottler there. Panamco also has soft drink and beer interests in Brazil.

Because of its geographic diversity, Panamco's shares are unlikely to be severely hit by a downturn or a devaluation in any one country. Investing in Panamco is investing in Latin America as a whole. Economic growth in the region is likely to increase soft drink consumption and, more importantly, allow Panamco to raise its prices.

◆ **Downside:** Aside from the lofty current price of the shares, Panamco is highly leveraged with debt. It also correlates closely with U.S. stocks.

◆ **What to Look For:** Keep an eye on the price. If the price to earnings ratio falls below about 16, it's probably a good buy. And keep watching company news and the annual report for the debt level to see if it's improving. If the company's acquisition spree speeds up too fast, the company may put itself in a risky financial situation.

VITRO SA

U.S. TICKER: VTO   **1 ADR =** 3 common shares in Mexico
EXCHANGE: NYSE   **SECTOR:** Manufacturing/housewares
MARKET CAP.: $547 million
1998 OPER. INCOME (LOSS): ($430 million)
1998 NET INCOME (LOSS): ($25 million)
FORECAST 1999 EPS: $1.10
   (9 analysts surveyed by First Call)
EARNINGS GROWTH (5-YEAR FORECAST): 10%
1998 SALES: $2.5 billion   **P/E ON JANUARY 1, 1999:** 4.12
BOOK VALUE PER ADR: $9.99   **EBITDA MARGIN:** 24%
BETA VS. S&P 500: 1.30   **CORRELATION WITH S&P 500:** 0.22
DIVIDENDS PER SHARE (1998): $0.53

Vitro has not been a favorite among investors for the past few years, and I feel it's been neglected for no good reason. The company has some problems, but it's working at fixing them. And how can anyone overlook a P/E ratio of 4.26? Especially when it applies to a company that has a virtual monopoly on selling glass in all of Mexico.

Founded in 1909, Vitro is far and away the largest glass manufacturer in Mexico. It makes glass bottles, plastic bot-

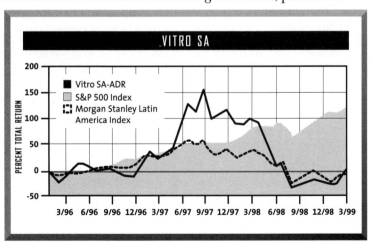

tles, crystal, flat glass for industries, automotive glass, and household appliances, as well as some chemical products and fiberglass. Until recently, it was the only flat glass-maker in Mexico, but French glassmaker Saint Gobain took a small share of the market with a plant opened in 1998. Still, demand for flat glass has been so strong that even the entry of Saint Gobain didn't dent prices.

"Vitro is a company that is not in a very good business," says Joe MacHatton, Latin America strategist at the French Banque Nationale de Paris. "Vitro was insisting for years that Mexicans would drink beer and soda out of glass bottles forever. On the other hand, it's a strong company financially. Long term, they will need to get into other kinds of businesses."

The company itself disagrees. It's expanding, but keeping to its core glass business, with ambitious plans to acquire glass manufacturing and distribution companies throughout Latin America and the United States.

"Glass containers is a mature business," Chief Executive Federico Sada González told me in an interview in November 1998. "But we're also into auto glass, flat glass, and tableware."

To be sure, glass containers accounted for only 30 percent of sales in 1998, and an impressive 44 percent of sales were in dollars rather than pesos.

For years, Vitro had lots of debt problems and operational problems. It had a rough time during the peso crisis, and some of the debt from that era still remains on its balance sheet. The company's operational efficiencies have been improving, though. The company got rid of its inefficient Anchor Glass subsidiary, which was based in Tampa, Florida. Operating margins have climbed back to a strong 26 percent.

The key to Vitro's future is the Mexican economy, which is both its guardian angel and its serpent in the garden. In a country as hot as Mexico, consumption of beer and soft drinks has always been heavy, and Vitro profits from that by selling bottles to most of the country's big beverage makers. When times are good, Vitro does well, but a slow economy can drag down its sales and prompt industries to demand lower glass prices to help boost their own margins.

◆ **Downside:** The two big drawbacks for Vitro are its large amount of debt and its refusal to expand significantly into plastics or some other fast-growth industry. Its management, while good at operations, lacks vision. Debt has been easing. At the end of the first quarter of 1998, the company had $1.623 billion in total outstanding debt, a reduction of $369 million from a year earlier. That's a big drag on the company's earnings: Vitro paid more than 1.2 billion pesos (about $160 million) in interest payments alone in the first quarter of 1997. Still, Vitro was able to reduce that 40.6 percent to 491 million pesos in the first quarter of 1998.

◆ **What to Look For:** If you're thinking of buying shares in Vitro, keep a constant eye on the stock price and be quick. When foreign institutional investors take notice that a stock is a good value, a bandwagon rush to buy it can often push prices up so fast that the "value" evaporates. Keep an eye on the company's debt level and operating margin to see if they're improving; both are best viewed at the company's own Web site or in its annual report. Industrial activity in Mexico also has a big impact on earnings.

GRUPO TELEVISA SA

U.S. TICKER: TV

1 GDR = 2 CPOs (ordinary participation certificates)

EXCHANGE: NYSE	**SECTOR:** Broadcasting
MARKET CAP.: $16 billion	**1998 OPER. INCOME:** $268 million
FORECAST 1999 EPS: $0.91	**1998 NET INCOME:** $77 million
(11 analysts surveyed by I.B.E.S.)	

EARNINGS GROWTH (5-YEAR FORECAST): 39%

1998 SALES: $1.7 billion	**P/E ON JANUARY 1, 1999:** 51.65
BOOK VALUE PER ADR: $4.05	**ROE:** 20%
BETA VS. S&P 500: 1.61	**CORRELATION WITH S&P 500:** 0.12

DIVIDENDS PER SHARE (1998): $0.00

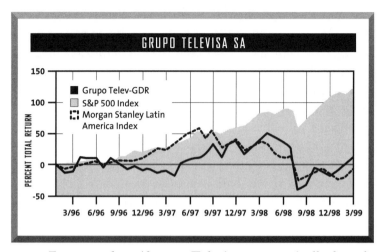

For more than 40 years, Televisa was practically the sole broadcaster in Mexico, until TV Azteca came along in 1993. The competition hurt at first, as Azteca nipped away at Televisa's market share. Televisa was slow to react, but since late 1997 has begun to respond in a positive way. If it can prevent Azteca from gaining more market share, Televisa's future is bright, as Mexico's $1.6 billion television advertising industry is expected to show fast growth in coming years.

Televisa's comeback in 1998 was in part due to its new chairman, thirty-year-old Emilio Azcárraga Jean, who took over when his father died of cancer in 1997. The young Azcárraga brought in new talent and hired firms to conduct market studies of viewers' tastes, something the network hadn't done much in the past. The result was a jump in national ratings to 78.7 percent in the third quarter of 1998, up from 74 percent in the third quarter of 1997.

One example of the changes was the hiring of new television news anchor Guillermo Ortega. After less than a year on the job, Ortega's savvy, investigative style made his newscast the most widely watched in Mexico, with an average rating of 18 points—10 points higher than either TV Azteca or the ratings of Ortega's predecessor, who had been on the job for thirty years. One of the reasons for

Ortega's success is that he hasn't been afraid to criticize the government and routinely interviews opposition political candidates. That's a big change for a network that for decades had been the voice of the government.

Televisa has also worked at bringing its costs down, trimming 4,000 workers from its workforce between late 1997 and the end of 1998.

Televisa's international operations show lots of promise. The company exports its "telenovelas" to Spanish-speaking countries worldwide, and even to countries where Spanish isn't spoken, where the programs are dubbed in the local language. Televisa also owns 10 percent of Univision, the biggest Spanish-language broadcaster in the United States.

"Televisa's efforts have been very well targeted, and they have taken advantage of them," says Rogelio Urrutia, in a November 1998 interview with Bloomberg News.

The key to winning back lost market share and advertising revenue will be not so much the success of its news and variety shows but of its "telenovelas," which are by far the most-watched programs in Mexico and among Televisa's international audience.

◆ **Downside:** Competition from TV Azteca. The management at Azteca wants to capture 50 percent of the Mexican TV audience. If it manages to do that, Televisa's earnings will be seriously affected. Even if they don't, Televisa will be forced to trim its advertising rates and spend more on better programming if it wants to hold onto market share.

◆ **What to Look For:** The independent rating agency Instituto Brasileiro de Opinião Pública, or Ibope, publishes Mexican TV ratings quarterly in news stories on financial Web sites or in analyst reports. But a good way to judge how the network is doing is by watching its shows for yourself. Even if you don't understand Spanish, it's not hard to tell a good soap opera from a bad one.

COCA-COLA FEMSA SA

U.S. TICKER: KOF
1 ADR = 10 series L shares
EXCHANGE: NYSE   **SECTOR:** Beverages
MARKET CAP.: $2.58 billion   **1998 OPER. INCOME:** $161 million
FORECAST 1999 EPS: $0.63   **1998 NET INCOME:** $65 million
(9 analysts surveyed by Zacks)
EARNINGS GROWTH (5-YEAR HISTORICAL): 16%
1998 SALES: $1.29 billion   **P/E ON JANUARY 1, 1999:** 22.69
BOOK VALUE PER ADR: $3.57   **ROE:** 15.6%
BETA VS. S&P 500: 1.42   **CORRELATION WITH S&P 500:** 0.30
DIVIDENDS PER SHARE (1998): $0.105

Mexico has one of the world's highest per capita Coca-Cola consumption rates. And, no wonder—it's hot, dry, and the water in many places isn't fit to drink. What's more, Coke is inexpensive, costing as little as twenty cents retail for a 16-ounce returnable bottle—that's less than the price of bottled water! For these reasons and plenty more, Coke Femsa is considered a good investment by those who are buying for the long term.

The company accounts for about 23 percent of all Coca-Cola sales in Mexico; about 35 percent in Argentina, although Argentines don't consume as much of it.

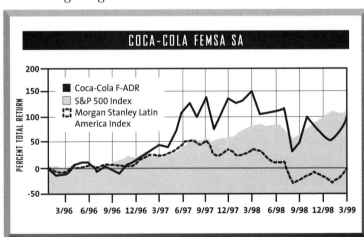

Coke Femsa is one of the so-called "anchor" bottlers of the Atlanta-based Coca-Cola Company. That designation means Coke Femsa has passed muster in terms of its financing, management, and marketing strategies. Atlanta-based Coke owns 30 percent of Coke Femsa and controls 4 of the 16 seats on its board of directors, one reason why Femsa is considered a well-managed company. Atlanta-based Coke keeps close tabs on it, and each one advises the other on marketing and operational nuances.

"We expect that the close involvement of Coca-Cola, in combination with a highly competitive position in its core markets, will enable Coca-Cola Femsa to sustain healthy cash generation on a local currency basis," says Moody's, the credit rating agency.

Coke Femsa also produces Sprite, Fanta, Fresca, Quatro, Powerade, Extra Poma, Etiqueta Azul, and Kin. Most of its distribution is in the Mexico City area, although it also controls a large swath of southeastern Mexico.

Typically, Coke Femsa raises its prices in line with inflation, which means that in dollar terms it manages to keep up with the changes in the exchange rate, although in times of economic slowdowns and big devaluations, inflation doesn't keep up with the exchange rate and a bottle of Coke ends up costing less in dollar terms. During those times, Coke Femsa's sales can suffer, not in terms of volume but in terms of lower revenue from lower prices.

Coke Femsa has been trying to shift its production away from returnable bottles, still the main way people drink Coke in Mexico, toward more profitable plastic bottles. That has been more difficult than it sounds because returnable bottles have become ingrained in the culture. In most of Mexico, if you ask for a Coke "para llevar" (to go), you won't get a plastic bottle. You get the contents of a glass bottle poured into a little plastic bag with a straw.

◆ **Downside:** Competition in the company's main Argentina market, Buenos Aires, has made it rough going for Femsa there. In some periods, revenue in Argentina has fallen even as volume grew, after the company was forced to lower prices to match price cuts from competitors. Another drawback is that as Coke Femsa has expanded into new markets, it has taken on more dollar-based debt, which has increased its interest expenses. Additionally, during times of crisis the Mexican government has been known to intervene to keep the price of Coca-Cola down. If this happens too much, Coke Femsa's earnings power will decline. A final downside is that because of its popularity among investors, the price-to-earnings ratio is fairly high.

◆ **What to Look For:** Watch news stories about the Mexican economy for signs of continued long-term growth, which will continue adding to volume growth for Femsa and allowing the company to raise prices. Also look for company news about Femsa's Buenos Aires subsidiary. If the price wars there keep going as they have been, something's bound to snap.

TELÉFONOS DE MÉXICO SA (TELMEX)

U.S. TICKER: TXM
1 ADR = 20 series L shares

EXCHANGE: NYSE	**SECTOR:** Telecommunications
MARKET CAP.: $14 billion	**1998 OPER. INCOME:** $3.0 billion
FORECAST 1999 EPS: $4.87	**1998 NET INCOME:** $1.66 billion
(6 analysts surveyed by Zacks)	

EARNINGS GROWTH (5-YEAR FORECAST): 20%

1998 SALES: $7.9 billion	**P/E ON JANUARY 1, 1999:** 11.8
BOOK VALUE PER ADR: $27.66	**ROE:** 18%
BETA VS. S&P 500: 1.04	**CORRELATION WITH S&P 500:** 0.22
DIVIDENDS PER SHARE (1998): $1.50	

Telmex is one company that almost didn't make this list, in spite of its size and reputation as the premier blue-chip stock of Mexico. There are plenty of reasons for not including it. Among them are that it has been heralded by big institutional investors for too long, and any bit of value that is left in it has already been factored into the stock prices. Also, unlike in countries like Argentina and Brazil, the 1997 deregulation of the phone industry in Mexico

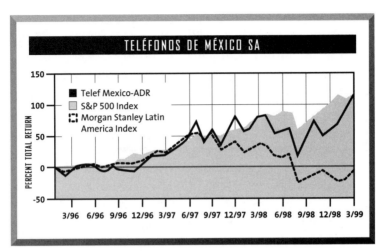

TELÉFONOS DE MÉXICO SA

- Telef Mexico-ADR
- S&P 500 Index
- Morgan Stanley Latin America Index

PERCENT TOTAL RETURN

150 100 50 0 -50

3/96 6/96 9/96 12/96 3/97 6/97 9/97 12/97 3/98 6/98 9/98 12/98 3/99

SOURCE: BLOOMBERG L.P.

could have a dampening effect on Telmex over time.

But there are three good reasons for including it:

1 It is the biggest company and one of the safest and easiest-to-buy stocks that closely follow the growth of Mexico's economy.

2 The company has been taking steps to see that deregulation will hurt as little as possible and that in some ways it might help the company's cash flow.

3 In spite of its popularity, Telmex's price-to-earnings ratio remains relatively low.

Deregulation of the Mexican phone industry was long overdue. Telecommunications in Mexico are a mess. There are only about 10 lines per 100 inhabitants, compared with about 60 per 100 in the United States. Phone connections are fuzzy at best, calls often don't get through, and the wait for a new phone line can be painfully long. Without a doubt, competition from foreign companies and foreign-backed local companies will improve infrastructure in Mexico and will quickly erode Telmex's monopolistic market share. Already, the competition has seriously cut into Telmex's long distance revenue.

However, Telmex can do and is doing a lot to help assuage that situation. It has required pretty tall fees for use of its nationwide phone line system. Also, the company has been working at improving its own technology and offering new services aimed at confronting its competitors. Nonetheless, the fees it charges competitors and the rates it charges customers are bound to keep coming down. In 1998, for example, Telmex was forced to cut the connection fees it charges for use of its equipment on long distance calls to an average of 2.7 cents a call, down from 5.7 cents. In exchange, the company's rivals agreed to help cover some costs Telmex has had in opening its network to competitors. In the first year after deregulation, Telmex collected about $875 million in call completion charges from U.S. companies, an amount which could drop substantially under the new structure.

"The key to Teléfonos de México is not the international competition," says Paul Rogers, a portfolio manager for the Scudder Kemper Latin America funds. "What Telmex has is an installed base of telephone lines, which everyone else is going to have to go through for customers."

Telmex's strategy in long distance has been twofold. It fights for the ability to charge competitors higher fees in Mexico, while at the same time it has formed an alliance with Sprint Corp. of the United States to offer long distance service from the United States to Mexico. The overwhelming majority of long distance calls made to and from Mexico is with the United States. The Sprint agreement gives Telmex a way to make revenue in the other direction, allowing it to compete on price with AT&T and other operators in calls from the United States. AT&T fought the agreement, but lost its appeal in court.

Telmex has also expanded into Internet services, buying a 20 percent stake in Prodigy Services Corp., which although losing market share in the United States, is the biggest on-line service provider in Mexico.

Telmex also has the biggest market share in cellular phone service in Mexico, through its Telcel subsidiary. That share will likely drop somewhat over the next several years, but Telmex's early presence gives it a strategic advantage over newcomers.

♦ **Downside:** The effects of deregulation are bound to cut into many parts of Telmex's revenue stream, and it's hard to tell just how much this will hurt. Telmex has been too comfortable for too long, and unless it changes its poor service record and old technology, it won't be able to meet the new price competition.

◆ **What to Look For:** Watch the effects of deregulation on small points of government regulations which will determine just how much free rein the new phone companies will get and just how much Telmex will have to cede. There are several unresolved issues that foreign long distance companies continue to argue about with Telmex, including cooperation in bill collections, shared communication ports, and accounts payable, all of which could affect Telmex's bottom line. Also keep an eye on Telmex's cellular phone business to see how fast it's growing and how much, if any, Telmex's market share can be expected to erode. And, of course, watch the Mexican economy as a barometer for Telmex's long-range growth potential. All these issues are best followed on financial Web sites or, if you read Spanish, on the Web site of Mexico's *El Financiero* newspaper, listed in the back of this book.

GRUPO IUSACELL SA

U.S. TICKER: CEL

1 ADR = 10 series L shares

EXCHANGE: NYSE	**SECTOR:** Telecommunications
MARKET CAP.: $916 million	**1998 OPER. INCOME (LOSS):** ($101 million)
ROE: −23%	**1998 NET INCOME (LOSS):** ($131 million)

FORECAST 1999 EPS: $0.06
   (6 analysts surveyed by I.B.E.S.)

EARNINGS GROWTH (3-YEAR FORECAST): 30%

1998 SALES: $285 million	**P/E ON JANUARY 1, 1999:** NA
BOOK VALUE PER ADR: $3	**CORRELATION WITH S&P 500:** 0.25
BETA VS. S&P 500: 1.74	**DIVIDENDS PER SHARE (1998):** $00

Grupo Iusacel is the second largest cellular telephone service provider in Mexico, behind Telmex, and is gaining ground on its larger rival. By mid-1998, Iusacel had

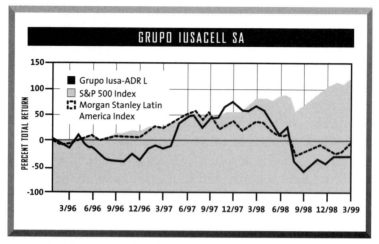

550,000 paying subscribers to its service—double the number of a year earlier.

Mexico is one of the best countries in the world for cellular phone service providers. Because the number of fixed telephone lines is so low, many Mexicans have turned to cellular phones as an alternative. Owning and using a cellular phone in Mexico has become a status symbol. A common story in Mexico is that during one recent earthquake, dozens of people were spared from a building collapse because they were standing outside on the sidewalk using their cell phones.

Iusacel has two big advantages over Telmex. First, it has better technology. In 1998, Iusacel began rolling out Code Division Multiple Access, or CDMA, technology throughout its network. Others are likely to follow, but the fact that Iusacel is the first in Mexico with the technology means it will likely gain market share. CDMA technology avoids calls being cut off when users pass from one cellular region to another, and allows clients to send written messages (and eventually images, once other parts of the technology improve).

The other advantage that Iusacel has is its management. New Jersey–based Bell Atlantic owns a 42 percent controlling equity stake in the company. Bell Atlantic is largely responsible for Iusacel's improvements in technology, which have led to the sharp growth in the customer base. The company's market share grew in 1998 to 37 percent in four regions of Mexico where it does business, up from 34 percent a year earlier.

Iusacel also had an early start over new rivals who won cellular phone licenses in 1998 government auctions. Among the companies that won new licenses were San Diego–based Qualcomm Inc. and Sistemas Profesionales de Comunicación SA, owned by Ricardo Salinas Pliego, chief executive of TV Azteca. Iusacel itself also bid on the auctions and managed to secure two potentially lucrative licenses in the northern Mexico states of Baja California and Nuevo León, which includes the fast-growing industrial city of Monterrey.

One last strong point for Iusacel is its very low correlation with the U.S. stock market, which is atypical for a Mexican company.

◆ **Downside:** Profit. For all its fast-growing customer base, new technology, and high revenue increases, the company is yet to come up with a good, steady formula for increasing its earnings. It has invested heavily in order to get the revenue growth that it has, and that investment has deflated overall earnings growth and created highly erratic earnings patterns, with heavy losses in some periods and gains in others. The other uncertainty for investors is whether or not Iusacel will lose market share once the new cellular licensees begin operating.

◆ **What to Look For:** Cellular phone growth in Mexico is bound to slow at some point, so keep an eye on the growth rates to make sure you're not getting in when the fervor is already gone. Even so, the growth of the economy, added to the fact that there are still plenty of Mexicans without cell phones, means that demand will likely be hot for some time. If you can't find stories on these issues in financial Web sites, check the Mexican government Web sites listed in the back of this book. Also monitor Iusacel's profits by getting copies of its annual report. For the stock price to keep going up, the company's costs will have to start coming down.

CHAPTER

Five

ARGENTINE COMPANIES

RGENTINA'S STORY IS unique in Latin America. It is the only country in the region— with the possible exception of Cuba—that has known true wealth and stability, and then lost it. But over the past seven or eight years it has been gaining back both its wealth and its stability, and that's what makes it a good target for foreign investment—that, and its strategic position in the fast-growing Mercosur common market.

Argentina had it all back in the 1920s, and even as late as the 1950s. But everything came crashing down in a mix of corruption, rebellions, coups, and financial disaster that spanned from the mid-1950s until the late 1980s. It wasn't until this decade that the country began to recover. A large part of that recovery was due to the economic policies of President Carlos Menem's administration. Once known for his flamboyant, playboy lifestyle, the U.S.-educated politician has since adopted a more conservative image, and his financial and economic policies have been right on. More importantly, he has stuck by those policies, even when it meant severe austerity measures that came close to costing him reelection. He remains popular among the people and as a result has been able to implement long-term growth policies with short-term pains, such as high unemployment.

The anchor of Menem's policies has been the monetary system, called a currency board, which has eliminated central bank meddling in exchange rates and has pegged the Argentine peso to the U.S. dollar since 1991. That policy created stable inflation rates and helped spark a wave of foreign investment and economic growth. One risk of the monetary system is that the peso comes under extreme pressure every now and then, as it did in 1995 during the Mexican peso crisis and again in 1997 and 1998 during the

Asian crisis and the fallout in Russia. Those crises all led to speculation that Argentina would be one of the next countries to devalue. During those periods, foreign investors pulled their money out en masse, but most of it flowed back in again once the storms passed. There is still a threat that Argentina will end the currency board and devalue its peso, but in early 1999 it remained strong enough that the government hinted it might actually go in the other direction and adopt the U.S. dollar as Argentina's official currency.

Another risk in Argentina is its high foreign debt level, which it racked up in the early 1980s and still hasn't managed to pay back in significant amounts. Argentina has a remarkably good relationship with foreign banks, which are likely to offer good refinancing conditions if the country comes under so much financial stress that it can't meet its obligations. It also was the first emerging market country in the world to be able to return to international bond markets after the Russia crisis. But that doesn't mean the debt is cheap. The interest rates that Argentina is able to capture on its new foreign debt issues shot up in 1998 and probably won't come down to the record low levels of 1997 for a while. What this means is that foreign borrowing— whether by the government or by companies—has been harder to come by, forcing borrowers to seek domestic loans with interest rates that often are double or triple those overseas. That makes it harder for companies to invest for the long term and to improve their earnings.

Nonetheless, Argentina continues to grow quickly by any standards. It was among the fastest growing countries in the world in 1997, with an 8.6 percent increase in gross domestic product. The growth rate in 1998 slid below 5 percent and was expected to fall further in 1999, possibly causing the first recession since 1995.

A big determinant of future growth will be the trend in oil prices. Argentina isn't as dependent on oil prices as Venezuela, but oil is Argentina's largest export, and the drop in crude prices last year hurt trade figures. The trade balance is important in Argentina because if it gets too far into deficit territory, it could prompt a devaluation, or a change in government policy away from the currency board to a floating exchange rate.

Trade in the long term appears strong, mostly due to Argentina's increasing role as a major supplier of everything from wheat to industrial goods and cars to Brazil and the other members of the Mercosur common market. Paraguay and Uruguay are the other formal members of the trade pact, but Chile and Peru have side agreements with Mercosur that allow Argentine goods to flow into those countries with reduced tariffs. Eventually, all of these countries are hoping that the free trade pacts will be merged with the North American Free Trade Agreement, which would make exporting to the United States, Canada, and Mexico much more cost efficient. Even without North America, though, the booming markets in Brazil and other South American countries are enough to give Argentine exporters plenty of growth in the years ahead—providing Brazil's recession doesn't last too long.

YPF SA

(Formerly Yacimientos Petrolíficos Argentinos)

U.S. TICKER: YPF

1 ADR = 1 class D share

EXCHANGE: NYSE	**SECTOR:** Oil
MARKET CAP.: $9.86 billion	**1998 EARNINGS:** $590 million
FORECAST 1999 EPS: $1.83	**ROE:** 12.8%
(8 analysts surveyed by Zacks)	

EARNINGS GROWTH (5-YEAR FORECAST): 8%

1998 SALES: $5.5 billion	**P/E ON JANUARY 1, 1999:** 11.7
BOOK VALUE PER ADR: $20	
BETA VS. S&P 500: 1.08	**CORRELATION COEFFICIENT:** 0.25

DIVIDENDS PER SHARE (1998): $0.88

YPF is an oil company, and in early 1999, as I am finishing this book, oil companies are not considered great investments. In December 1998 the price of West Texas

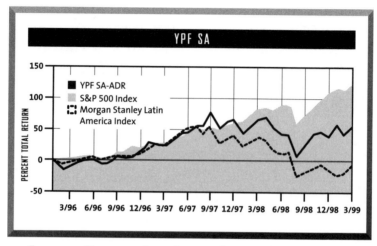

Intermediate crude—the grade of oil most similar to what YPF sells—had dropped to its lowest price in twelve years and a full 43 percent below the price of just one year earlier. The low oil prices have hurt the stocks of oil companies worldwide, and YPF is no exception. YPF shares in the summer of 1998 hit their lowest price since early 1997.

If you believe that oil prices will keep falling, then YPF is not the stock for you. However, if you're like me, and believe that oil prices are bound to go up again, then YPF is a good investment. Even if you're unsure, YPF could be a good buy. It's a solid company, and its share prices are poised to rebound once some new, long-range projects that diversify the company's revenue stream begin to kick in.

As of 1998, half of YPF's revenue came from oil and gas exploration and production, with the remaining half coming from refining of petroleum products such as gasoline and diesel fuel. While sticking to its core oil-based business, the company is investing heavily in projects throughout the region. These include seven oil exploration blocks in Brazil, a gas pipeline to Brazil, a $650 million gas pipeline and separation plant in Argentina, oil production in Bolivia, and a $600 million fertilizer plant in Argentina. Overall investment in the company continues to increase, although the weak oil prices in 1998 prompted the company to scale back somewhat on the ambitious plans it had originally.

YPF was formerly owned and operated by the Argentine government, which did a horrible job of it. YPF was one of the few money-losing oil companies in the world in the 1980s. But President Menem appointed strong new managers in the early 1990s who turned things around, and the group of investors who bought it in 1993 have improved operations even more. Despite earnings being hurt by the weak oil prices, the company managed to offset some of those declines by lowering drilling costs and improving refinery operations. The cost cuts, which have improved the company's margins, are part of a program that extends across the company's exploration and refining business.

One thing to look forward to is increased oil production. The company was producing 440,000 barrels a day in 1998. That's in line with 1997 production, although before that the company had seen six straight years of production increases. Production is likely to pick up again and to continue growing beyond 1999, especially as exports to Brazil increase as part of the reduced tariff plan of the Mercosur common market.

Another positive point is the increased earnings in YPF's refining business. Lower oil prices mean that the raw material used in the refining business is cheap, so that has improved margins on the production of gasoline and diesel fuel.

◆ **Downside:** In spite of its continued attempts to expand into other markets and other oil-based products, the company continues to be heavily dependent on the price of oil for its earnings growth. By mid-1998, it had already racked up four straight quarterly drops in earnings. The company also depends heavily on the state of the Argentine economy. That's good, providing the economy keeps growing, but if there's an extended downturn, YPF will suffer.

◆ **What to Look For:** Aside from hints about where the price of oil is headed, the one thing to look for in YPF is who, if anyone, will end up with management control. YPF is a conglomerate. As of early 1999 the biggest single shareholder was Repsol SA of Spain, with 15 percent. If they, or any of the other shareholders, were to acquire a controlling share, it could give the company more direction and possibly boost its share price. It's a big issue in Argentina, so you should be able to find news on it either on financial Web sites or on the Web site of an Argentine newspaper *(see the Resources section in the back of this book).*

TELECOM ARGENTINA SA

U.S. TICKER: TEO

1 ADR = 5 class B ordinary shares

EXCHANGE: NYSE

MARKET CAP.: $2.1 billion

FORECAST 1999 EPS: $2.27

(13 analysts surveyed by I.B.E.S.)

SECTOR: Telecommunications

1998 EARNINGS: $374 million

ROE: 13%

EARNINGS GROWTH (5-YEAR FORECAST): 12%

1998 SALES: $3.17 billion

BOOK VALUE PER ADR: $2.74

BETA VS. S&P 500: 1.29

DIVIDENDS PER SHARE (1998): $1.43

P/E ON JANUARY 1, 1999: 13.87

CORRELATION WITH S&P 500: 0.26

Telecom Argentina is the first of two Argentine telephone companies included in this list. Telecom Argenti-

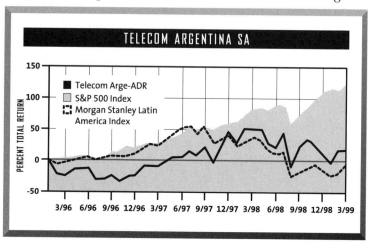

na serves the northern half of the country, which includes about half of all households. The way telecommunications work in Argentina, each of the two main telephone companies has a monopoly in its half of the country. That monopoly, however, will end in November 1999, when the industry will begin deregulating and both domestic and foreign companies will be able to compete across the spectrum of fixed-line and cellular telephone services.

Argentina's deregulation of its phone industry stands out from that of other countries such as Mexico and Peru, where it is questionable whether the existing phone companies will be able to compete over the long run with the new players. In Argentina, the deregulation has been structured so that both Telecom Argentina and Telefónica, which controls the southern half of the country, will benefit financially.

One of the big pluses shared by both companies is not only their monopoly in fixed-line service but their partial monopoly in cellular phone service. The decade-long monopoly that Telecom has enjoyed in Argentina's northern half gives it a tremendous advantage over other cellular phone companies attempting to invade its turf. Virtually all of Telecom's earnings growth in 1997 and 1998 was from its cellular phone business. The number of mobile phones in Argentina grew 200 percent in 1997 and was estimated to have grown about 130 percent in 1998.

In the fixed-line business as well, the deregulation of the industry will likely be a boon rather than a bust for Telecom. Argentina is in desperate need of more phone lines, and the number of fixed lines in the country has been growing at about 10 percent a year, a rate which would be much faster were it not that Telecom and Telefónica aren't equipped to handle the demand. Also, new entrants will be forced to pay Telecom for use of its lines, without which they won't be able to do business. Deregulation also means that Telecom will be able to steal service from Telefónica in the lucrative southern half of the country, which includes the heavily populated Buenos Aires area. Already,

Telecom has been putting down fiber-optic cables to prepare for that day.

Management is another strong point of Telecom, one which distinguishes it over the larger Telefónica. Telecom is majority-owned and managed by a partnership of France Telecom SA and Telecom Italia SpA, which together have a good start on updating the company's antiquated switching equipment and phone lines and improving overall efficiency. There's a long way to go, though, and any inroads the company makes will tend to boost earnings by helping cut the average cost of transmitting a phone call.

Argentina's rapid economic growth has been a big contributor to the demand in both fixed-line and cellular phone service. As industrial activity remains hot and more foreign companies set up shop, demand can be expected to continue booming in the business sector. In the residential sector, Argentines are consuming more and more every day, even though economic growth slowed in late 1998, and this has meant more families are able to afford telephone service.

"The fundamentals for the phone companies are great," Brad Radulovacki, who was then an analyst at Daiwa Securities America, told Bloomberg News in August 1998. "The worst is behind them in terms of collections and cleaning out bad customers."

◆ **Downside:** Telecom was hit hard in 1997 and early 1998 by writing off unpaid phone bills, most of which were incurred during a long legal battle over the legality of increases in local phone rates. The Argentine government had ruled that the increases were legal, even though they did violate Argentine regulations at the time. Consumers fought the ruling, but a Supreme Court judge upheld the government's decree in mid-1998. The judge's decision meant that Telecom doesn't have to pay about $250 million in fines for breaking the rate limits. The worst seems to be behind Telecom on this issue, but there's always the chance that such disputes could crop up again. The court challenge somewhat damaged Telecom's image with the Argentine people, which won't help when new companies come seeking clients.

◆ **What to Look For:** Keep an eye on Argentine news stories about the government's restrictions on phone rates. If unemployment and inflation start going up, the government will be forced to implement some measures aimed at pleasing the populace. Lowering phone rates could be one of those. If that happens, Telecom's earnings could suffer. If it doesn't, it will be a good sign for the future that the government will keep its promise to reduce its influence in the telephone industry and to allow free competition in the rate structures.

Also, there's no guarantee that I'm right about deregulation being a boon for Telecom. It's hard to tell exactly what will happen once new companies set up operations, and the increased competition could force both Telecom and Telefónica to cut phone rates, which would cut profit margins. Investors should keep reading news on the company to find out how it all pans out. Look at the *La Nación* and *Clarín* Web sites, two Argentine newspapers listed in the back of this book, for news about the competitive environment and phone rates. Also, call up company pages on financial Web sites to track changes in profit margins.

TELEFÓNICA ARGENTINA SA

U.S. TICKER: TAR

1 ADR = 10 class B shares

EXCHANGE: NYSE   **SECTOR:** Telecommunications

MARKET CAP.: $2.88 billion

1998 EARNINGS (FISCAL YEAR ENDING SEPTEMBER 30, 1998): $511 million

FORECAST 1999 EPS: $2.58   **ROE:** 13.5%

  (9 analysts surveyed by First Call)

EARNINGS GROWTH (5-YEAR HISTORICAL): 8%

1998 SALES: $3.43 billion   **P/E ON JANUARY 1, 1999:** 11.18

BOOK VALUE PER ADR: $14.52

BETA VS. S&P 500: 1.31   **CORRELATION WITH S&P 500:** 0.25

DIVIDENDS PER SHARE (1998): $1.40

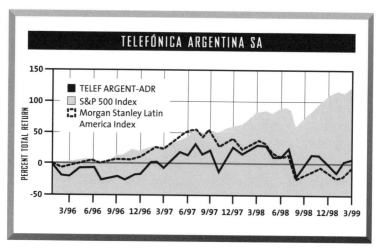

SOURCE: BLOOMBERG L.P.

Telefónica de Argentina was sold by the government in 1990 and has since streamlined its old, bloated self. There are plenty of analysts who say Telefónica won't be able to compete once the Argentine telecommunications industry is deregulated in November 1999, but there are others who say it will not only do fine but will prosper as a result of the deregulation.

Deregulation is bound to bring more competition and increasing price pressures on phone rates. Still, as in the case of Telecom, Telefónica will be able to expand nationwide once deregulation takes effect, and it can also expand its cellular phone service, thanks to a government ruling allowing it to do so.

"What you have in Argentina that is very different is two local companies basically bordering each other in the middle of a densely populated area [Buenos Aires]," says Luiz Carvalho, Latin American telecommunications analyst at Morgan Stanley Dean Witter & Co. "Therefore I am a little cautious about the long-term profitability. We will have to see how these companies deal with each other."

The company is well managed, although its chairman is fairly new. Carlos Fernández-Prida was appointed chairman in July 1998. The fifty-four-year-old Spaniard had been a member of the board of directors. The company that bought Telefónica in 1990 was Telefónica of Spain, which since then has spent more than $6.5 billion on improving and expanding service.

The result has been that in Telefónica's region, the number of lines per 100 inhabitants reached 23.5 in 1998, the highest anywhere in Latin America. The company's lines in service also increased 128 percent between 1990 and 1998, to 3.9 million. In fiscal 1998, Telefónica's number of lines in service increased a healthy 6.7 percent. Telefónica has also implemented an array of new services which have added to revenue, including conference calling, Internet access, and other features.

The company has also laid about 320,000 kilometers of fiber-optic phone lines.

◆ **Downside:** Competition. The deregulation of the telecommunications industry is going to bring competition and lower phone rates, and Telefónica's margins could be squeezed. Like Telecom, Telefónica also had problems with uncollectable debts, but by late 1998 appeared to have resolved the lion's share of them and was close to more normal levels of unpaid phone bills.

◆ **What to Look For:** Watch for news about the seemingly minor details of deregulation because they could have a big effect on Telefónica's earnings: items like how much competitors will have to pay Telefónica for the use of its lines and just how far Telefónica can move into other services before the government puts up the "anti-trust" sign. Most of all, though, watch economic growth in Argentina. If growth rates pick up, Telefónica is positioned to do well.

INVERSIONES Y REPRESENTACIONES SA (IRSA)

U.S. TICKER: IRS   **1 GDR = 10 shares**
EXCHANGE: NYSE   **SECTOR:** Real estate
MARKET CAP.: $540 million
1998 EARNINGS (FISCAL YEAR ENDING JUNE 30, 1998): $36.8 million
FORECAST 1999 EPS: $2.13   **ROE:** 9.9%
     (5 analysts surveyed by I.B.E.S.)
EARNINGS GROWTH (5-YEAR HISTORICAL): 38%

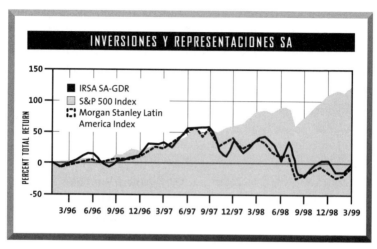

1998 SALES: $193 million   **P/E ON JANUARY 1, 1999:** 12.30

BOOK VALUE PER ADR: $46.94

BETA VS. S&P 500: 1.24   **CORRELATION WITH S&P 500:** 0.29

DIVIDENDS PER SHARE (1998): $00

There are two overriding reasons to invest in Irsa.

1 It is 17 percent owned by investment wiz George Soros, who knows what he's doing.

2 It is one of only a few Latin American ADRs in the real estate industry, and it is easily the best in terms of management, return on investment, growth, and most other measures.

Economic growth brings with it increases in the value of real estate as well as increases in the number of lucrative commercial real estate properties. That's what's happening now in Latin America, and will continue over the long term.

Irsa is well placed in the real estate industry. It is Argentina's largest real estate investor, with $800 million in assets as of mid-1998. The largest portion of that is in urban shopping malls. Irsa owns about 60 percent of Buenos Aires's shopping malls, including such prominent ones as the upscale Alto Palermo, which it acquired as part of its $183 million purchase of the property arm of Pérez Companc.

An important reason for Irsa's success is its strong

management. Irsa was founded in 1990 by Eduardo Elsztain with a $10 million check written by George Soros—an investment which has increased many times over. Elsztain, who with his brother Alejandro also controls the Cresud agriculture company, knows how to spot a good investment opportunity. Among the other jewels in the Irsa crown is the posh Liao resort near the ski resort of Bariloche.

One other strong point for Irsa is its value to investors. It's hard to find a company with a growth rate as high as Irsa's but with a price-to-book-value as low. The company's market capitalization in mid-1998 was $660 million, well below the value of its assets. That's like buying real estate on your own and getting a steep discount on the price.

◆ **Downside:** In times of economic downturns, and especially in times of major devaluations, the real estate sector is usually among the hardest hit. Mexico's real estate industry, for example, was dealt a huge blow in the 1995 peso crisis and still hasn't fully recovered. While Elsztain, with Soros's help, will do his best to withstand any devaluation, he can do only so much, and the stock is likely to suffer if the Argentine peso breaks from its dollar equivalency. A related drawback is Irsa's lack of diversification. There are no exports for a real estate company, and Irsa has no significant holdings outside Argentina, meaning it depends heavily on the strength of the Argentine economy.

◆ **What to Look For:** Keep an eye on George Soros. He knows when to buy and sell. If he sells a small portion of his share in Irsa, it probably means he is just taking in some profits from his investment. He has, for example, gradually built up his stake at times to a peak of about 25 percent, only to reduce it again in 1998 to about 17 percent. But if he sells a large share—5 percent or more—it might mean that the share price is close to its peak. By the same token, if Soros increases his investment in Irsa, you might want to take that as a sign to buy some stock yourself. Any sizable purchase or sale that Soros makes will be public record, and there are companies such as the Washington Service that keep track of insider buy and sell orders. Ask your broker to check. You may also see stories on his share sales or purchases on financial Web sites. Obviously, keep a close eye on the Argentine economy, too, and on hints that a devaluation is in the works by reading newspapers such as the *Financial Times*.

PÉREZ COMPANC SA

U.S. TICKER: CNPZY
1 ADR = 2 class B shares

EXCHANGE: OTC	**SECTOR:** Oil
MARKET CAP.: $3.37 billion	**1998 EARNINGS:** $205 million
FORECAST 1999 EPS: $0.27	**ROE:** 21.5%

(15 analysts surveyed by First Call)

EARNINGS GROWTH (5-YEAR FORECAST): 7%

1998 SALES: $1.31 billion	**P/E ON JANUARY 1, 1999:** 15.59
BOOK VALUE PER ADR: $10.72	
BETA VS. S&P 500: 1.13	**CORRELATION WITH S&P 500:** 0.22
DIVIDENDS PER SHARE (1998): $0.24	

Pérez Companc is the second largest oil producer and fourth largest natural gas producer in Argentina. It's strength is its management; in particular, the company's keen sense of when to acquire new assets, when to sell,

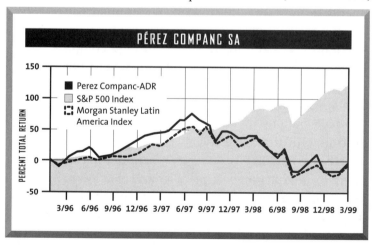

and at what price. Analyst Hernan Ladeuix of Credit Lyonnais Securities calls it "one of the best managed companies in Argentina."

Pérez Companc in 1998 was undergoing a transition in which it was gradually divesting itself from non-oil and gas assets such as forestry and telecommunications in order to focus on what it does best: exploring for and producing oil and gas. A big part of the transition involves using whatever cash it gets from the sale of non-core assets to acquire oil rights in other Latin American countries. The reasoning behind this is that the opportunities for exploration in Argentina are limited compared with those in more oil-rich countries such as Venezuela and Brazil.

In 1998 the company was producing about 100,000 barrels of oil per day. By 2002 Pérez Companc's own forecasts call for more than doubling that. Most of that increase is expected to come from its Venezuela operations, where the company has won bids on three oil fields auctioned off by the Venezuelan oil company, PDVSA. Pérez Companc has also won oil and gas exploration contracts in Peru and Bolivia, and is now targeting Brazil as its next major expansion area.

Brazil's attraction comes in two areas. First, experts predict that the Brazilian government next year will begin selling oil exploration blocks for companies that would compete directly with Brazilian oil company Petróleo Brasileiro, or Petrobrás, for the first time ever. At the same time, Petrobrás has invited foreign companies to partner with it to explore oil fields where Petrobrás already owns licenses. Pérez Companc says it plans to follow both routes into Brazil.

Although concentrating on oil might not seem to be the smartest investment plan when oil prices are at twelve-year lows, Pérez Companc is nonetheless diversified enough within the energy industry that low oil prices won't mean disaster. The company has operations in electricity, petrochemicals, and in both upstream and downstream aspects of the oil and natural gas industries, as a producer, transporter, and distributor. Its oil refining capacity amounts to about 50 percent of its oil production in Argentina.

◆ **Downside:** The price of oil. In late 1998, oil prices didn't seem to be on their way up any time soon, and if prices drop further, it will hurt Pérez Companc's earnings as it did in 1998. Another negative is the high price-to-earnings ratio, at about 20 times estimated 1999 earnings in November 1998.

◆ **What to Look For:** Watch oil prices (in the Bloomberg Web site click on "Energy" in the left-hand column). Climbing prices mean higher revenue and better earnings for Pérez Companc. Watch financial newspapers and Web sites for news of the company's plan to sell off its 25 percent stake in Nortel/Telecom, a holding company that owns 60 percent of Telecom Argentina. This sale and other asset sales are important to the company because they will raise the cash needed for making oil and gas acquisitions in other Latin American countries.

CHAPTER

Five

CHILEAN
COMPANIES

CHILE IS FAR and away the most stable country in Latin America, both in terms of its politics and economics and in terms of its stock market. Stability means Chile rarely goes through the deep plunges that markets like Mexico and Venezuela have been known to experience, and when there is a downturn it isn't as profound. But stability also means that Chile doesn't go through the big upswings in stock prices that other Latin American countries have seen in recent years. In the long term, Chile offers one of the best returns among Latin American markets. Between 1990 and 1997, Chile's selective stock index gained 1,187 percent. If you're looking for skyrocketing short-term gains, however, this isn't the place.

Chile has been the fastest growing country in Latin America over the past decade, at an average annual clip of close to 8 percent. The economy slowed to 5 percent growth in 1998 and was expected to slow further in 1999 to about 3 percent annual growth due to the leftover effects of the crises in Asia, Russia, and Latin America. Asia is a big trading partner with Chile, much more so than with any other Latin American country, and the devaluations in Asia made products from there cheaper in Chile and boosted the trade deficit.

High interest rates, implemented by the government to slow inflation, also helped cool the economy and dampen corporate earnings. But the troubles are likely to be short-lived, and most economists expect Chile's growth to resume its brisk pace in 2000.

"We have three factors that work in our favor," Finance Minister Eduardo Aninat told me in an interview in October 1998. "We have a high investment ratio—33 percent of gross domestic product is invested. We have high productivity growth, both in labor and capital. And we behave like a stable country in spite of the crises abroad. Inflation is about 4.8 percent annually."

Chilean investors dump more savings into their own stock market than other Latin Americans do, in part because of one of the world's best-run pension systems. Chilean pension funds are privately owned and operated and are allowed to invest in the stock market. This boosts the liquidity of Chilean stocks.

Chile's long-time good relationship with the United States is another plus. Economically, it means the U.S. government is willing to help bail out Chile in a crisis, and foreign banks are always there with a billion or two to loan the government. Financially, it means Chilean companies have strong ties with U.S. depository banks and the Securities and Exchange Commission. As a result, new share issues tend not to get held up with administrative red tape.

Trade is key to Chile's competitive advantage, and good relations with the United States help in that area, too. The United States is Chile's biggest trading partner, and the U.S. in turn exports many industrial goods and consumer items to Chile. Those relations suffered over the last few years as the U.S. Congress failed to give President Clinton the "fast track" negotiating ability that he needed in order to add Chile to the North American Free Trade Agreement. Still, it's only a matter of time before NAFTA extends south from Mexico, and when it does, Chile will be the first country to gain membership.

Some recent changes in Chilean law make buying ADRs less expensive and less cumbersome than it used to be for foreign investors. Until 1998 Chile was the only one of the seven major Latin American countries with significant restrictions for foreigners who buy shares in companies. To own ADRs, foreigners were required to put the equivalent of 30 percent of the value of their investment in a non-interest-bearing escrow account in the Chilean Central Bank for the first year they held the stock. What this meant to small investors was that a broker would set up this escrow account on behalf of all of his clients and would pass on the expense in the form of higher transaction costs. Those rules were thrown out in August 1998, after the Chilean government realized it was discouraging much-needed foreign investment.

Another important note is that Chile, for more than a decade the least risky country in Latin America, is finally coming to grips with its past and the memories of the 1973 coup that toppled leftist President Salvador Allende—and the brutal dictatorship of General Augusto Pinochet that followed it. Many Chileans had never been able to reconcile those events. As this book went to press, Pinochet, now 83 years old, was in England awaiting extradition to Spain to face charges for murdering numerous Spaniards during his dictatorship. But in Chile, the government wants him to return, where he remains a senator for life. In Chile most of the hard feelings seem to have been put to rest, and in a symbolic gesture in 1998, the Chilean Senate—including Pinochet—voted to eliminate a holiday marking the day of the coup and instead creating a new holiday called National Unity Day.

VIÑA CONCHA Y TORO

U.S. TICKER: VCO
1 ADR = 50 Chilean ordinary shares

EXCHANGE: NYSE	**SECTOR:** Beverages
MARKET CAP.: $372 million	**1998 EARNINGS:** $21.4 million
FORECAST 1999 EPS: $1.89	**ROE:** 9.9%
(4 analysts surveyed by I.B.E.S.)	
EARNINGS GROWTH (5-YEAR HISTORICAL): 30%	
1998 SALES: $155 million	**P/E ON JANUARY 1, 1999:** 15.30
BOOK VALUE PER ADR: $17.35	
BETA VS. S&P 500: 0.80	**CORRELATION WITH S&P 500:** 0.11
DIVIDENDS PER SHARE (1998): $0.50	

Even if you haven't heard of Concha Y Toro wine, you've probably sipped it on more than one occasion without knowing. Five years ago, Chilean wine was a newcomer in a world dominated by the French and the Californi-

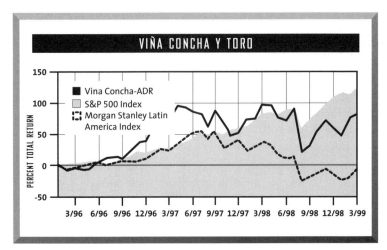

SOURCE: BLOOMBERG L.P.

ans. People would buy a bottle, perhaps for some variety, but never considered it in the same category as a Bordeaux or a Napa Valley cabernet. Now, Chile is the world's fifth largest wine exporter, due mostly to the success of Concha Y Toro and the fervor of one man, Eduardo Guilisasti.

Guilisasti bought the then small Concha Y Toro vineyard in 1961 and ran it as chairman until his death in 1998. In some cases, the death of a man like Guilisasti can wreak havoc on the management of a company, but not in the case of Concha Y Toro. Guilisasti's son, Eduardo, has been chief executive of the company since before his father died, and fills the shoes admirably.

Personally, I find Concha Y Toro's merlot and merlot/cabernet blends among the best table wines available for under $10, and its higher-priced Don Melchor wines are worthy competitors to many of France's best. Apparently, there are others who agree. The company's earnings have been driven by export growth for several years now. Concha Y Toro's revenues have been climbing at more than 25 percent a year. Chilean wine exports on the whole were estimated to top $500 million in 1998, up from $400 million in 1997 and just $182 million in 1996. Concha Y Toro has by far the biggest market share of any Chilean vineyard, both in domestic sales and exports.

Its markets include not just the United States, its biggest

market, but Europe and the astoundingly fast-growing Japanese market, where people enjoy Chilean wines as a replacement to the Italian and French wines they were previously accustomed to.

By having such a tremendous share of its revenue going to exports, Concha Y Toro has afforded itself not only immunity from downturns in the Chilean economy but also the uncommon potential of having its earnings improve when the Chilean peso slides. While the bulk of Concha Y Toro's revenue is in dollars, most of its costs are in pesos, so when the peso slid 3.5 percent in a recent quarter, the company's earnings improved, too. This relationship provides an automatic hedge to the decrease in value that the stock price might suffer from a devaluation of the peso.

Thus, when the rest of Chile's stock market might be sliding, Concha Y Toro often manages to keep its head above water. Concha Y Toro was among the few advancing stock issues on the Chilean exchange in the first half of 1998, a testimony to the company's diversity and growth.

One last plus worth noting about Concha Y Toro is the finding of a recent study by Scottish researchers that Chilean wines are higher in antioxidants than the wines of any other notable wine region in the world. Antioxidants have been shown to prevent diseases such as hardening of the arteries, lung cancer, and strokes. That might not sound like something that would have a big effect on sales at first, but a study in 1991 attributing low levels of heart disease among the French to their daily glass or two of red wine helped lift sales of French wines. Major wine purchasers have taken note.

"We will likely be looking at high levels of antioxidants when picking wines," David Matthews, director of wine control for the U.K. supermarket chain Safeway Stores Plc, told Bloomberg News in July 1998.

◆ **Downside:** As with all wine companies, Concha Y Toro is susceptible to climatic changes and disease. For example, there were two threats in 1998 that could have created big losses for the company if nature had nudged them just a little bit. The El Niño weather system caused flooding and hot weather throughout Chile, and a fungus in the south of Chile ruined up to 25 percent of the harvest in some areas. Luckily, El Niño didn't do much harm to Concha Y Toro's vineyards, and the most important vineyards were spared the fungus. Nonetheless, such environmental uncertainties add an element of risk to the stock. Another drawback is that the stock is extremely popular among foreign investors, mostly because it is seen as a sexy company. That has driven up the price to earnings ratio, although if it's under 15 it's still probably a good investment.

◆ **What to Look For:** Look for news reports that quote analysts about whether the upcoming harvest will or won't be a "good year" for Chilean vineyards. Good harvests tend to boost stock prices. Also keep an eye on the popularity of Chilean wines, and of Concha Y Toro wines specifically. Wines can go in and out of favor for no apparent reason. One danger for Concha Y Toro is that the commercialization of the company and its increasing production of commodity wines might diminish the firm's reputation. That could hurt profits by reducing the price that Concha Y Toro can capture on world markets. Still, it's important that the company take advantage of export opportunities where they exist without cheapening the brand name. The best way to research the company, though, and the most enjoyable, is to try the wine for yourself.

SOQUIMICH SA

(Formerly Sociedad Química y Minera de Chile SA)

U.S. TICKER: SQM

1 ADR = 10 B shares

EXCHANGE: NYSE	**SECTOR:** Chemicals/mining
MARKET CAP.: $406 million	**1998 EARNINGS:** $67 million
FORECAST 1999 EPS: $3.35	**ROE:** 8.2%
(9 analysts surveyed by I.B.E.S.)	

EARNINGS GROWTH (5-YEAR FORECAST): 14%

1998 SALES: $505 million	**P/E ON JANUARY 1, 1999:** 10.13
BOOK VALUE PER ADR: $30.80	

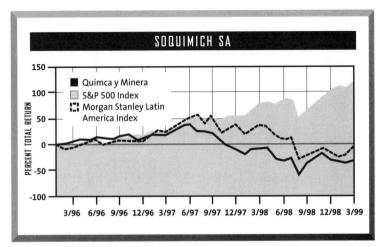

BETA VS. S&P 500: 1.04 **CORRELATION WITH S&P 500:** 0.17

DIVIDENDS PER SHARE (1998): $1.28

Buying shares in a company that specializes in fertilizer and iodine may not be as glamorous as owning stock in a winery, but it is a good investment opportunity for those looking for a solid company with a strong competitive advantage. Soquimich is one of those companies that hasn't yet been "discovered" by the international investment community. As of mid-1998, its price to earnings ratio was a low 7.63, making it a good bargain even given a recent slump in earnings brought on by the crisis in Asia.

Soquimich is the second largest landowner in Chile, behind the giant copper company Codelco (which isn't on this list because it's privately held). Soquimich owns huge swaths of the Atacama Desert, which it mines for nitrates and other minerals that are used to make fertilizers, cement, and lithium. Lithium is used in making glass, ceramics, and lithium batteries. Soquimich's land holdings include properties that are rich in copper, and the company has announced plans to seek a partner to help it develop copper mines in the Antucoya deposit in northern Chile.

Soquimich is the world's largest miner of natural nitrates and accounts for about one-third of world iodine production. Iodine is used in compounds such as germicides, antiseptics, and dyes. Soquimich's competitive advantage is its low costs. It virtually scoops up nitrates from the floor of the Atacama desert, with little separation and production costs as compared with nitrate miners in competing regions. In 1997, its low costs helped it to corner the world market for lithium carbonate, forcing Australian competitor Gwalia Consolidated Ltd. out of the business.

It's interesting to note that the mining of nitrates supported the entire Chilean economy for half a century until about 1930, when demand for the gunpowder and fertilizers, which use nitrates, dried up during the Great Depression. Copper later drove the Chilean economy and to many extents still does, but there has been a resurgence of investments in the nitrate industry by Soquimich and other companies over the past few years.

"We haven't seen this kind of investment in non-metallic minerals since the last century," said Vicente Pérez, an analyst at the government's Chilean Copper Commission, in an interview with Bloomberg News in August 1998.

Two more strong points for Soquimich: One, the diversity of its markets—the company sells its products to sixty countries. Two, its stock has a low correlation with the U.S. market, meaning the diversification benefits it adds to your portfolio are significant.

"It's undergoing a consolidation process in 1999 and 2000, and we think that will increase its operating earnings," says Guillermo Tagle, director of equity at Santander Investments.

◆ **Downside:** Like copper and most minerals, nitrates can swing wildly in both price and demand on world markets, and low prices can dig deep into Soquimich's share prices. In 1998, the crisis in Asia pushed down demand for fertilizers from China, one of the company's biggest markets, contributing to a 28 percent drop in second quarter earnings. The company's operations are also fairly capital intensive, especially when it comes to setting up production plants and expanding into related industries, like copper and cement. High investments coupled with low demand prompted the company to sell off its fledgling cement business in 1998, although it managed to secure a good price of $32 million on the sale.

◆ **What to Look For:** Watch for hints that iodine demand might pick up by watching news reports about U.S. and European industrial activity. U.S. and European industries are among the biggest clients of Soquimich products. Also monitor news reports about Soquimich's new copper operations, which could give a strong boost to earnings. Finally, watch for news and data on the company's cost structure. There were signs in 1998 that costs, which historically have been its key advantage, were increasing.

CIA. DE TELECOMUNICACIONES DE CHILE SA (CTC)

U.S. TICKER: CTC

1 ADR = 4 series A shares

EXCHANGE: NYSE   **SECTOR:** Telecommunications

MARKET CAP.: $4.52 billion   **1998 EARNINGS:** $275 million

FORECAST 1999 EPS: $1.25   **ROE:** 16.6%

(11 analysts surveyed by First Call)

EARNINGS GROWTH (5-YEAR FORECAST): 13%

1998 SALES: $1.60 billion   **P/E ON JANUARY 1, 1999:** 12.45

SOURCE: BLOOMBERG L.P.

BOOK VALUE PER ADR: $11.60

BETA VS. S&P 500: 1.24   **CORRELATION WITH S&P 500:** 0.29

DIVIDENDS PER SHARE (1998): $0.53

CTC has the distinction of being the first ADR to be issued from Latin America. That's a good sign because it's evidence of the company's commitment to foreign investors. But it also means there're very few surprises left in the stock. It's a good company, and a stable stock. It has good long-term growth potential, and as of early 1999 it was reasonably valued with a PE of about 15.

CTC is the largest phone company in Chile, with 90 percent of the overall market, although it is second in long-distance service to Entel (which has no ADR). It's also a big cellular phone service provider, with half the Chilean market through its Startel subsidiary, and it owns a 40 percent stake in Metrópolis-Intercom, a cable television company with a 50 percent share of the Chilean market.

Chile has one of Latin America's highest number of phone lines per capita, and CTC has one of the best service records in the region. That doesn't mean there's not plenty of room to grow. At 17 lines per 100 people, it still has about a fourth the rate of lines in the United States. The company's goal is to double the number of lines within the next five years.

"CTC is the strongest company in the Chilean market," says Guillermo Tagle, director of equity at Santander Investments. "It's very liquid, well organized, and can get financing when it needs it—and telecommunications still has a long way to grow in Chile."

Whereas in some Latin American companies it can take up to two years to get a phone line installed, CTC typically installs lines within forty-eight hours after they're ordered. Still, the company says there's much room for growth in services, which should boost revenue over the next few years. The company has a plan to invest $3.75 billion between 1998 and 2002 in such new technologies as caller identification and call waiting, buying equipment in bulk that will cut costs in the long run, and expanding its wireless and long-distance business. Reducing the number of workers it needs to service lines is also an important goal, according to Claudio García, president of the company. "You have to invest a lot of money in networks," García said of the company's long-term strategy in an interview with Bloomberg News in August 1998. "You have to reach the home or business of the consumer; once you're there, you can supply any service."

One of the advantages of investing in CTC rather than in other Latin American phone companies is that there's less risk of deregulation having a big negative effect on earnings. Deregulation of the phone industry in Chile happened in the 1980s. If major new players were going to steal CTC's market share, they would have done it by now. Instead, CTC has proved itself able not only to fight off competition in its core business of local service but also to enter new business segments and to gain sizable market share there as well. That's not to say there isn't competition. Foreign companies like BellSouth Corp. and SBC Communications Inc. are in Chile and working to boost their own market shares.

CTC's management is also top rate. The company is majority controlled by Telefónica SA of Spain (ADR symbol: TEF), which has shares in several phone companies in Latin America. Telefónica has its eyes set on expanding CTC, and the local management team, including García, are bent on increasing shareholder value. The company has increased the number of telephone lines per employee to 360 in 1998, from 77 in 1990. Customer service is also a strong point.

CTC hopes to develop the cellular phone business, predicting that the number of Chileans carrying mobile phones will jump to 15 percent over five years, from 3 percent now. That seems far too ambitious, but growth is nonetheless bound to be fast. The cellular phone industry should get a boost starting in 1999 after a decision by regulators that ended the billing of cellular customers for calls they receive on their mobile phones.

In the cable TV business, CTC broke even in 1998 for the first time and can look forward to making some profits going forward.

◆ **Drawbacks:** CTC is heavily dependent on the Chilean economy and on the strength of the Chilean peso. Although it is diversified inside Chile, it had as of 1998 almost no interests outside the country. That might be changing, as the company was considering taking an equity stake in a Brazilian phone company. The company is also very dependent on labor. A one-week strike of communications workers in 1998 disrupted service nationwide. A longer one could cripple operations.

Another drawback in the stock is that the shares are heavily correlated with the U.S. market.

◆ **What to Look For:** In the cellular business especially, CTC will be facing increasing competition. Watch that it doesn't get too fierce, or CTC might have trouble. Check the company news section of your favorite financial Web site or the sites of the newspaper *El Diario* or CTC itself, both listed in the back of this book. Also keep an eye on Spain's Telefónica itself which in 1998 was having its own financial troubles. If those troubles increase, the parent company's investments in its Latin American interests could slow. Growth potential is the best reason for buying CTC stock, and if there isn't money to be invested in that growth, the stock price will suffer.

GENER SA

(Formerly Chilgener)

U.S. TICKER: CHR

1 ADR = 68 ordinary Chilean shares

EXCHANGE: NYSE	**SECTOR:** Electricity generation
MARKET CAP.: $1.31 billion	**1998 EARNINGS:** $92 million
FORECAST 1999 EPS: $1.75	**ROE:** 9.5%
(9 analysts surveyed by I.B.E.S.)	
EARNINGS GROWTH (5-YEAR FORECAST): 7%	
1998 SALES: $598 million	**P/E ON JANUARY 1, 1999:** 9.75

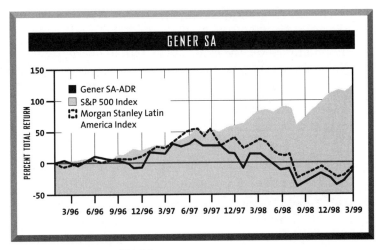

BOOK VALUE PER ADR: $51.00

BETA VS. S&P 500: 0.90   **CORRELATION WITH S&P 500:** 0.14

DIVIDENDS PER SHARE (1998): $0.78

Gener SA is the second largest electricity generating company in Chile, behind Endesa (which is controlled by Enersis, the next company on our list). Gener also has the highest costs, due to its reliance on coal for 63 percent of the energy it produces. But that doesn't mean the stock is weak. On the contrary, the fact that its energy costs more is already factored into the stock price, and any improvements in its margins will lead to improvements in the stock.

Gener is gradually reducing its production costs by moving toward natural gas production, which is cheaper than coal. It's also rapidly expanding into other countries, where it both mines coal at costs lower than in Chile and sells energy as well.

Gener operates electricity companies in Peru and Argentina and is building a transmission line across the Andes mountains that will supply energy to copper and gold mines in northern Chile. The company had planned to invest $300 million in 1998 alone, more than half of it on a power plant in Salta, Argentina, and part of the rest on buying new coal mines in Colombia and Venezuela.

The best reason for considering stock in Gener is that the country's hydroelectric power capacity is not nearly big enough to handle the expected growth in energy demand over the next decade. Increasingly, big mining firms and other industries are turning to companies like Gener to supply their energy needs, as exemplified by Gener's increasing contractual base.

Mother Nature also provides a nice surprise every now and then in the form of a drought. Droughts are a positive thing for Gener because they decrease the ability of companies like Endesa, which relies more on water power, to meet their supply contracts. Those companies have to buy energy from Gener, which charges them high prices for it. Two recent droughts, for example—one in 1997 and the other in late 1998—gave good boosts to Gener's profits.

◆ **Downside:** Standard & Poor's, the debt rating agency, believes that Gener's expansion into "riskier" countries like Colombia and Peru are a negative sign. That may be true in some ways, but the expansions have allowed Gener to produce energy at lower costs and have also reduced some of Gener's exposure to devaluations in the Chilean peso. All Chilean energy companies are susceptible to slides in the peso, which can depress earnings. Gener's diversification means its probably not as susceptible as companies like Endesa.

Another big drawback is Gener's debt level. "Debt as a percentage of capitalization has been growing and is now 46 percent of total capital, up from just 27 percent in 1995," Standard & Poor's noted in a report in July 1998. "Given that 94 percent of debt is foreign currency denominated, Gener faces significant foreign exchange risk."

◆ **What to Look For:** Get a copy of the company's annual report by calling your broker or Gener's ADR depository, listed in the back of this book. Look for Gener to reduce its debt-to-equity level, which would be a good sign and serve to reduce the risk that the stock will be hurt by a devaluation. Also look at how fast Gener is able to bring down its cost structure. Eventually, companies from other countries will supply Chile with low-cost energy that will flow across pipelines currently being built or in the planning stages. If Gener can't decrease its reliance on coal and produce energy at lower costs, it will lose market share. Also, watch the Chilean economy, especially industrial production levels, which are a strong indicator of future energy demand. The *El Diario* or Web sites should help.

ENERSIS SA

U.S. TICKER: ENI
1 ADR = 50 common shares
EXCHANGE: NYSE   **SECTOR:** Utilities
MARKET CAP.: $3.51 billion   **1998 EARNINGS:** $190 million
FORECAST 1999 EPS: $1.88
   (6 analysts surveyed by I.B.E.S.)
EARNINGS GROWTH (5-YEAR FORECAST): 14%
1998 SALES: $3.27 billion   **P/E ON JANUARY 1, 1999:** 12.30
BOOK VALUE PER ADR: $3.02   **ROE:** 17.4%
BETA VS. S&P 500: 0.98   **CORRELATION WITH S&P 500:** 0.21
DIVIDENDS PER SHARE (1998): $0.75

Enersis is one of the largest energy companies in Latin America. It holds a 25 percent stake in Chile's Endesa (ADR symbol: EOC) and also holds large stakes in electricity distribution companies in Chile and in both electri-

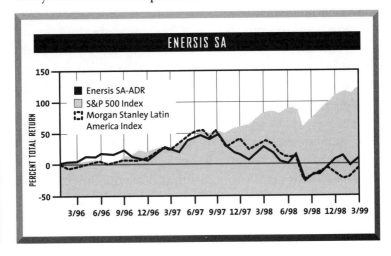

cal distribution and generation in several other countries, including Argentina, Peru, and Brazil.

Scandal plagued Enersis in 1997 and 1998, but such problems now appear to be behind the company and those involved have been fired. Some are on their way to jail. The company remains one of the biggest and best-run electric companies in Latin America with one of the best prospects for growth.

The scandal involved the $1.3 billion sale of a large stake in the company in 1997 to Endesa of Spain, which prior to the sale was not related to Endesa of Chile. The sale was carried out in a convoluted way in which Endesa of Spain bought five investment companies, called Chispas, which together owned a 29 percent stake in Enersis. It later turned out, however, that Endesa had agreed to pay huge premiums on some types of shares, which happened to be held by the then-chief executive officer of Enersis, Jose Yuraszeck, and several other Enersis officials.

Enersis still has some significant problems to resolve, not the least of which is its ownership structure. Shareholders cleared the way, in March 1999, for Endesa of Spain to pay $1.4 billion to increase its stake in Enersis to a controlling 64 percent. In the long run, that should be good for Enersis.

"In general terms, it's always good that companies have a clear and concise management control," Enersis chairman Juan Antonio Guzmán told me in early 1999.

Already, the Spanish company has added value to Enersis in many ways, and has bid together with Enersis for energy companies that come up for sale in other Latin American countries.

Even so, the scandal did lead to the firings of most of Enersis's top executives. New officers have since been hired, but the transition in management inevitably caused some short-term problems that the company has since been working out.

What's ahead for the company is the continued focus on its core generating and distribution businesses in

Chile, from which it derives most of its revenue, and probably some more expansion into other Latin American countries.

Also still to be resolved was the ownership of Endesa Chile. U.S.-based Duke Energy and Endesa of Spain were in a bidding war to gain control of Endesa Chile when this book went to print. While a purchase by either would boost Endesa Chile's share price, having Endesa Spain win the bidding war would probably be better for Enersis in the long run.

◆ **Downside:** Enersis, like Gener, is also heavily leveraged with dollar debt and is thus susceptible to devaluations in the Chilean peso. It also depends heavily on growth in the Chilean economy. Another drawback is the tarnished reputation that the scandal left in the minds of investors, who punished the company with lower share prices, and Chilean energy customers. New management will have to work hard to prove that all corruption has been weeded out of the firm. Finally, there is a downside to the stock due to susceptibility to weather patterns. In the 1996–97 drought, Enersis's earnings were hurt because the majority of its generating capacity comes from hydroelectric power plants that rely on high water levels for generating capacity. The drought forced the company to buy expensive energy from its own competitors, especially Gener.

◆ **What to Look For:** Keep watching newspapers like the *Financial Times* or *El Diario* to see if Endesa of Spain gains control of Endesa Chile. In addition, watch news reports for signs that the Chilean economy is on its way up and for signs that the mining industry, which is the biggest client of Enersis, is also on an upswing.

Note: Shares in Enersis are recommended here as opposed to shares in its Endesa subsidiary, mainly because Enersis is more diversified and less susceptible to swings in the value of the peso than is Endesa. Both types of shares are traded on the New York Stock Exchange.

CHAPTER

Five

COMPANIES

FROM THE ANDEAN COUNTRIES:

VENEZUELA, COLOMBIA, AND PERU

ENEZUELA, COLOMBIA, AND
Peru are collected in a single chapter for two reasons.
First, they offer relatively few American Depository
Receipts. At the time this book went to press, Colombia
had just two listed on the New York Stock Exchange;
Peru had three, and Venezuela had three. Second,
investing there involves a common strategy, one that
is entirely different from the way one invests in larger
countries like Brazil or Mexico, or in countries with
stable, more established stock markets like Chile.

Venezuela, Colombia, and Peru are the risk plays
among the seven major stock markets of Latin
America. The volatility of their stock markets is higher,
in part due to their much smaller size. Colombia's
entire stock market, for example, has a capitalization
of just $12 billion, smaller even than the market
capitalization of some of Brazil's largest companies,
such as Petrobrás. Higher risk is due also to their

more tenuous political and economic situations. In spite of the risks, stocks from at least one if not all of these three countries are an essential part of a truly diversified Latin American portfolio (depending, of course, on how large your portfolio is). The higher risk, in many cases, can translate over time into higher returns, and the correlations of these markets with the U.S. market are lower than the correlations of their larger Latin American neighbors, meaning shares in these countries will provide more diversity for your portfolio.

PERU

PERU HAS BEEN a surprising story of democratic stability ever since Alberto Fujimori was elected president in 1990. The word "democratic" is used lightly here, as Fujimori once dissolved the entire congress with the backing of the military and routinely censors the press and his opponents. Still, his economic policies follow most, if not all, of the modern, free-market reforms that have lifted other Latin American economies in the 1990s. Growth in Peru has been second only to Chile, at an average annual rate of 7.3 percent between 1993 and 1997.

Growth slowed in 1998 when the country was hit by two unexpected crises: the Asia financial crisis and El Niño. The Asian wave of recessions had a big effect on Peru's economy because it depressed prices for commodities, especially metals, which are Peru's biggest export. On top of that, the El Niño weather pattern that stirred up warm waters in the Pacific devastated Peru's other major industry, fishing. The result was a 0.4 percent contraction in the economy in the first half of the year and a modest recovery in the second half that brought total growth for the year to about 2 percent.

The government predicted a 3 percent growth rate in 1999, although analysts said that is a best-case scenario that assumes metals prices will rebound and El Niño won't return. Already in early 1999, both the mining and fishing industries were beginning to recover. Regardless, Peru's economic growth has been staggeringly high and is likely to continue to be reasonably high over the next ten years. Peru, more than most of the other six major countries, is still recovering from more than a decade of war with guerrillas, which wrecked the country economically. Fujimori has all but exterminated the guerrilla groups, and the country's poverty rate has been declining. That is good for companies, especially in the retail sector, because it enabled more consumers to buy their products.

For all his faults, Fujimori has the strong will necessary to see his economic reforms through.

"The tough international situation we face obliges us now, more than ever, to maintain iron-willed discipline and a prudent, responsible management of monetary policy," Finance Minister Jorge Baca told a Peruvian congressional panel in August 1998. You never would have heard top government officials talking that way ten years ago in Latin America. The difference is that today those reforms have the backing of the public, even if it means enduring tough times.

There are some gray areas, however, that could place the economy at risk. One is the trade gap. Peru's trade deficit ballooned 54 percent to $2.44 billion in 1998. That should come down in 1999 as Asian currencies strengthen.

Fujimori's health has also been a question mark at times, as has uncertainty about who, if anyone, will replace him when his second term in office expires in 2000. Fujimori might try to change the constitution to allow him to run again, or worse, implement a de facto coup that cancels presidential elections. While Fujimori is a good economic leader, either of those actions could bring turmoil to the country and lead to international trade sanctions.

CREDICORP LTD.

U.S. TICKER: BAP

NOT AN ADR: It's traded as common stock

EXCHANGE: NYSE **SECTOR:** Banking/finance/insurance

MARKET CAP.: $729 million **1998 EARNINGS:** $59 million

FORECAST 1999 EPS: $1.25 **ROE:** 5.6%

(10 analysts surveyed by I.B.E.S.)

EARNINGS GROWTH (4-YEAR FORECAST): 38%

ASSETS (END 1997): $7.8 billion **P/E ON JANUARY 1, 1999:** 9.16

P/BV: 7.15 **ROA:** 0.2%

BETA VS. S&P 500: 0.83 **CORRELATION WITH S&P 500:** 0.10

DIVIDENDS PER SHARE (1998): $0.41

Banking stocks are usually not the first ones that investors who are looking for growth would choose in Latin America, but in Peru—and also in Colombia—the future is bright for banks. Just 10 percent of Peruvians have a bank account or use bank services. That leaves more than 20 million potential customers for banks to draw from in the coming years. Given estimates that the

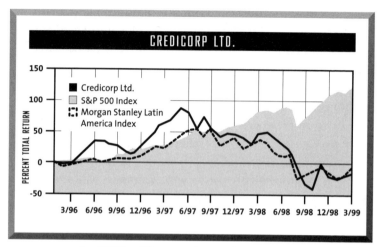

country's GDP will grow by at least 5 percent a year through 2002, the number of bank clients could double to 5.5 million by then, according to Raimundo Morales, general manager of Banco de Crédito del Perú, Credicorp's largest holding.

The United States has restrictions preventing banks and brokerages and insurance companies from joining under the same roof, but in Peru these limits don't exist. Credicorp is a big player in the insurance market with its Pacífico Peruano Suiza Insurance Company, and its Atlantic Security Holding Corp. provides a full range of brokerage and asset management services. Its 109-year-old Banco de Crédito at last count controlled 25 percent of the Peruvian banking industry in terms of deposits and loans. That share has shrunk somewhat as international banks such as Spain's Banco Santander and Banco Bilbao Vizcaya have bought their ways into the local industry, but Credicorp has responded to the competition by spending more to improve technology and to expand bank machine networks around the country. The company also is expanding its presence internationally. It already has operations in several countries including El Salvador, Bolivia, and Colombia.

Credicorp has also benefited from the growth in the Peruvian stock market and will continue to do so, providing the market resumes its rapid ascent toward higher capitalization. Savings rates in Peru should also start climbing soon, which will help all banks but mostly Credicorp because of its economies of scale.

The 1998 emerging markets crisis pushed Credicorp's earnings into negative territory in the third quarter, but analysts expected a recovery late in 1999.

"We are seeing high interest rates and credit quality deterioration across the region," Rafael Bello, a banking analyst with Morgan Stanley, told Bloomberg News in an October 1998 interview. "It's important to focus on what is going to happen going forward—Credicorp is a fine institution."

◆ **Downside:** El Niño and past-due loans. Past-due loans have been a problem for Peruvian banks, and the El Niño weather system of 1998 brought that problem to the forefront. El Niño led to torrential rain and flooding in much of Peru and badly hurt agriculture and fishing. As a result, clients couldn't repay loans, forcing banks to increase provisions for covering potential losses. By early 1998, bad loans among Peruvian banks were up 27 percent from the year earlier. Banco de Crédito's past-due loan portfolio jumped to 6.41 percent from 5.17 percent. While that problem will likely ease as El Niño recedes, bad loans are nonetheless something to watch out for, especially in a bank that draws so many of its clients from a public unaccustomed to banking services.

"The credit quality outlook is clouded by the continuation of certain negative trends in the economy," Moody's, the credit rating agency, wrote in mid-1998. "Moody's is particularly concerned about an already high and increasing level of problem loans, which could rise further as the negative effects of El Niño and the Asian crisis continue to ripple through the nation's commodity-based economy."

Those negative effects, however, are in all likelihood short-term ones, and once El Niño ends and the Asian and Russian crises ease, the bank should return to its normal profitability.

◆ **What to Look For:** As long as there's not a Mexican-style banking crisis in Peru, Credicorp will do at least reasonably well. Watch company reports on financial Web sites for signs that the company is bringing down its ratio of past-due loans to total loans, and ask your broker for recent reports from the credit rating agencies. Also read economic news in newspapers or on the Web for evidence of a devaluation of the currency and for patterns in local interest rate changes. Buy when you think interest rates are on their way down. You can also keep up with the strength of bank portfolios in Latin America by calling or looking at the Web pages of rating agencies such as Moody's and Standard and Poor's.

CIA. DE MINAS BUENAVENTURA SA

U.S. TICKER: BVN

1 ADR = 10 series B shares

EXCHANGE: NYSE	**SECTOR:** Mining
MARKET CAP.: $336 million	**1998 EARNINGS:** $31.9 million
FORECAST 1999 EPS: $0.67	**ROE:** 23%
(6 analysts surveyed by First Call)	
EARNINGS GROWTH: NA	
1998 SALES: $60.3 million	**P/E ON JANUARY 1, 1999:** 24.34
BOOK VALUE PER ADR: $11.50	
BETA VS. S&P 500: 0.58	**CORRELATION WITH S&P 500:** 0.01
DIVIDENDS PER SHARE (1998): $0.15	

Buenaventura is a company to invest in for its future, not its past. Its operating earnings have showed mostly losses in recent years as it poured capital into digging the giant Yanacocha gold mine, the largest in Latin America. But the mine is now producing gold at faster and faster rates, and Buenaventura's earnings are beginning to improve.

Buenaventura is the largest producer of silver in Latin America, but it is first and foremost a gold mining stock, as exemplified by its recent addition to the London-based FT-SE gold index, an index of the prices of gold mining stocks worldwide. Buenaventura owns a 44 percent stake

SOURCE: BLOOMBERG L.P.

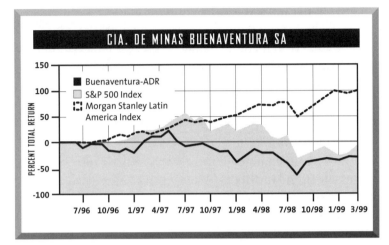

CIA. DE MINAS BUENAVENTURA SA

Legend:
- Buenaventura-ADR
- S&P 500 Index
- Morgan Stanley Latin America Index

PERCENT TOTAL RETURN (y-axis: 150, 100, 50, 0, -50, -100)

x-axis: 7/96 10/96 1/97 4/97 7/97 10/97 1/98 4/98 7/98 10/98 1/99 3/99

in Yanacocha. Denver-based Newmont Mining Corp. owns a 51 percent stake and operates the mine.

Yanacocha is a massive and highly productive mine, and in 1998 was expected to produce about 1.3 million ounces of gold, 23 percent higher than 1997 production.

Buying stock in Buenaventura is a good idea not only because of the growth potential of its gold and silver production but as a hedge against your other stocks, in both the United States and Latin America, and as a bet that the price of gold may go up. The price of gold hit its lowest point in eighteen years in 1998. Those low prices heavily affected Buenaventura's earnings and its share price, which plunged in the first half of the year. But when the crisis hit Russia and Latin America in August, investors turned to more tangible investments like gold for protection. Gold prices recovered, pushing up Buenaventura's stock from a low of 6 7/8 on August 27 to more than 12 by mid-October. The stock also has an extremely low correlation with U.S. stocks, which is good for diversification.

Looking to the future, suppose that a liquidity crisis were to spread from emerging markets to the rest of the world in 1999 or 2000, as some economists predict. It could lead to a shift of investment money out of such instruments as stocks, bonds, and currencies and into gold, real estate, and other tangibles. If that happens, mining companies like Buenaventura are likely to be spared from the brunt of the share price declines that could hit world markets. For that matter, countries like Peru that are heavily dependent on gold and other metals might also avoid some of the pain of a world economic crisis, which could help other domestic stocks such as those of retail companies and others that are dependent on domestic consumption. Mining and related activities account for as much as 15 percent of Peru's gross domestic product, and metals comprise 40 percent of Peru's exports.

◆ **Downside:** Buenaventura's upside is also its biggest downside—its heavy dependency on the price of gold. The company is also a large silver producer and recently has signed contracts for companies to explore and produce copper on its lands, but those metals don't provide much diversity since their prices tend to be highly correlated to the price of gold.

◆ **What to Look For:** The price of gold. It's hard to predict where the price of gold will move, but reading expert opinions on the matter can indicate when is the best time to buy stock in Buenaventura. And as I mentioned, even if you think there's a chance the price of gold will go up, buying Buenaventura stock could be a good hedge against a decline in your other Latin American stocks and even your U.S. stocks.

COLOMBIA

WHEN ONE HEARS the name Colombia, the first thing that usually comes to mind is drugs, or more specifically, cocaine. But investors who know better have found that some of Latin America's best-run companies are in Bogotá, Medellín, or Cali. Although the Bogotá stock market is small, it has at times posted some of the best returns in Latin America. Economic growth over the long term is also picking up, from 2 percent in 1996 to 2.8 percent in 1997.

However, 1998 was a bad year for Colombia, and should not be viewed as an indication of the country's long-term

potential. That year the country suffered first from a drop
in prices of its two main exports, oil and coffee. On top of
that, it suffered from its proximity to its closest and biggest
trading partner, Venezuela, which was undergoing its own
economic crisis. Finally, Colombia was in the midst of transition from the corruption-ridden government of President Ernesto Samper to an administration full of hope for
the future, that of President Andrés Pastrana, who took
office August 7, 1998. The result was that GDP grew by
only 0.6 percent in 1998, its slowest rate since 1943. In
1999, the government expected growth to pick up to
between 1 percent and 1.5 percent.

For the long term, there are lots of reasons to bet on
Colombia. In 1996 and 1997, vast new oil wealth was discovered in the country, and Colombia quickly and adeptly
sold off licenses and arranged joint ventures with foreign
companies to explore for and produce that oil. Oil has
now overtaken coffee as the country's principal export,
and if the crisis in oil prices ends, those contracts will be
worth billions to the economy.

Pastrana has also promised three things, which, if he is
successful and sticks to his promises, will substantially
accelerate Colombia's long-term growth. He has vowed to
eradicate corruption at all levels of government, to start
peace talks with guerrillas, and to slash the budget deficit.
The guerrilla groups are a menace to the economy
because they have blown up oil pipelines and stirred up
other trouble that can thwart investment. Reducing the
budget deficit, meanwhile, is important in both the short
and long term if Colombia is to maintain a stable currency and low inflation.

Additionally, the trend to gourmet coffee bars in the
United States and other countries looks to be a long-term
development rather than a short-term fad, and Colombia
is known as the world's premier coffee producer.

Finally, the impact of drugs on the economy shouldn't
be taken lightly. While drugs have created long-term
problems such as hampering the country's ability to nego-

tiate internationally, they have at the same time pumped billions of dollars into the economy. That money has helped to create a big middle class of spending consumers, which can lift company earnings, especially those involved in the retail sector.

BANCOLOMBIA SA (BIC)

U.S. TICKER: CIB
1 ADR = 4 Colombian preferred shares

EXCHANGE: NYSE	**SECTOR:** Banking
MARKET CAP.: $171 million	**1998 EARNINGS (LOSS):** ($6.8 million)
FORECAST 1999 EPS: $0.42	**ROE:** 5.9%
(3 analysts surveyed by First Call)	
EARNINGS GROWTH (5-YEAR FORECAST): 10.5%	
ASSETS (END 1998): $5.1 billion	**P/E ON JANUARY 1, 1999:** 4.51
BOOK VALUE PER ADR: NA	**ROA:** 0.97%
BETA VS. S&P 500: 0.58	**CORRELATION WITH S&P 500:** 0.03
DIVIDENDS PER SHARE (1998): $0.75	

Banco Industrial Colombiano, as it was known in Colombia, completed in 1998 the purchase of a 51 percent stake in Bancolombia, one of its rivals. The $418 million purchase created the largest bank in Colombia with about $5.3 billion in assets, or 16.5 percent of the Colombian banking industry. The ADR, under the name of the merged company, Bancolombia, represents shares in the joint company.

An investment in Bancolombia ADRs can be made in two ways. It can be a long-term investment based not on the bank's current performance but rather on the future of the bank and of Colombia. Loan growth at Banco Industrial Colombiano was only about 2.7 percent in early 1998, compared with about 10 percent for the whole Latin American banking industry. But the combination of the two banks seems a good fit that could boost the value of the shares once management gets rolling with consolidating branches and duplicate services and investing in client growth.

Having said that, banks in general, whether they're in

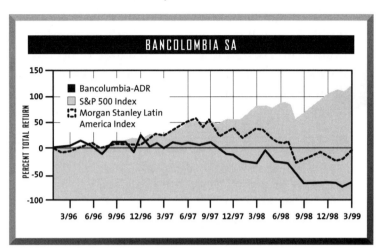

BANCOLOMBIA SA

Latin America or New York or London, are not known to be high-growth stocks. But there is another way to invest in banks: by following interest rate trends and trying to guess when rates have peaked. Bancolombia is a victim of the government's interest rate policies, which of late have called for high rates to combat fears of inflation. High rates have hurt the bank and have led to an increase in its bad-loan portfolio. When those rates start to come down, the bank's earnings should improve. That would be the time to buy. The time to sell is when rates have hit their low, but knowing when those turnabouts are coming is difficult, if not impossible. As a result, this type of business-cycle investing is not recommended for individual investors unless they're very knowledgeable about banks and have some intimate knowledge of interest rates.

Among the good long-term reasons to invest in Bancolombia is the lower costs that the merger of the two banks will bring once the transition is completed, and the overall positive long-term potential for Colombia's economy. Additionally, new Colombian President Pastrana has named a new team of banking regulators and central bankers who have been told to clean up corruption in the industry, which will be good for Bancolombia's earnings growth going forward.

◆ **Downside:** The effect of interest rates on Bancolombia

in the first half of 1998 is a good example of the bank's downside and of the dangers of trying to predict interest rate cycles. Interest rates jumped about 10 percentage points to 34 percent, prompting a sharp increase in bad debts as consumers and companies couldn't make their loan payments. Bancolombia's earnings dropped a whopping 97 percent in the period, compared with the same period in the previous year. Investors who had begun the year believing that rates would come down as the country's economy picked up steam lost heavily as Bancolombia's stock price plunged.

◆ **What to Look For:** Watch company news on a financial Web site for just how well the process of merging the two banks comes along. It should bring costs down substantially. If it doesn't, there's good reason to question the management of the bank. Also, obviously, watch interest rates. Even if you are investing for the long term, you should try to make your initial investment at a time when interest rates are on their way down, not up.

VENEZUELA

THE ONE COUNTRY among the seven that has had the most trouble getting its act together economically and financially is Venezuela. This oil-rich country could have been the fastest-growing country with the best per-capita economy in Latin America, had it not been for mismanagement by government officials, corruption, and unending riots and rebellions that, although absent in 1998, could resurface. Venezuela had 71.17 billion barrels of proved oil reserves at the end of 1997, making it the sixth most oil-rich country in the world, according to British Petroleum statistics. The government made the decision long ago that the way it would pass to the people the huge oil revenues it receives would be in the form of lower oil prices, subsidized by the government. But Venezuelans, for whatever reason, have not been able to capitalize on those lower oil prices to build low-cost industries that are competitive internationally. Imagine, for example, an airline that gets all its jet fuel at a steep discount. That airline should be highly profitable, but Venezuela's airlines posted heavy losses for years.

Venezuelan companies seem to have passed through the worst of their troubles in 1994 and 1995. Venezuela became one of the best-performing stock markets in the world in 1996 with returns of 96 percent in dollar terms, but the recovery has been volatile. The Russia crisis, along with low oil prices in the summer of 1998, put pressure again on the Venezuelan economy, prompting a rapid slide in stock prices and speculation that Venezuela's economy could collapse at any moment.

That leads one to question whether the economy is truly on a path toward steady and fast growth, as are the larger Latin American countries, or whether Venezuela will fall back into the ranks of the always emerging but never quite emerged countries. The one-third drop in oil prices in 1997 and 1998 should have been the medicine Venezuela needs to diversify away from oil and begin remolding its economy. Oil traditionally accounted for three-fourths of the country's exports. The oil price drop was devastating on the country's current account deficit—the broadest measure of a country's international flow of goods and services over the course of a year—making any defense of the country's currency extremely difficult. That would not have been the case if the country had been more diversified.

Instead, the effect on people and on companies has been a credit crunch as interest rates of more than 40 percent annually make consumers spend less and companies slice their investment plans, making it even harder to gain back ground when the crisis does lift. The big question becomes, will Venezuela close itself off from the rest of the world by enacting short-term Band-Aids such as trade restrictions, moratoriums on debt payments, and limits on foreign investment, which would make it harder to attract that investment again later? Or will the country suffer through a recession and start enacting some long-term reforms that will get the country back on the right path?

The answers will depend to a large extent on the economic policies of new President Hugo Chávez, the former leader of a military coup who was elected president in December 1998. Some of his populist policies have alarmed investors, including calls to dissolve congress and rewrite the constitution, although his first cabinet appointments and economic measures pleasantly surprised investors. Before you invest in Venezuela, educate yourself on the country through newspapers and financial Web sites and try to answer these questions for yourself. The answers will have a big effect on the long-term growth potential of the country and on the earnings potential of companies.

CIA. ANONIMA NACIONAL TELEFONOS DE VENEZUELA (CANTV)

U.S. TICKER: VNT

1 ADR = 7 class D shares

EXCHANGE: NYSE	**SECTOR:** Telecommunications
MARKET CAP.: $2.2 billion	**1998 EARNINGS:** $254 million
FORECAST 1999 EPS: $1.66	**ROE:** 18%

(9 analysts surveyed by First Call)

EARNINGS GROWTH (5-YEAR FORECAST): 10.4%

1998 SALES: $2.18 billion	**P/E ON JANUARY 1, 1999:** 4.81
BOOK VALUE PER ADR: $34.60	
BETA VS. S&P 500: 1.08	**CORRELATION WITH S&P 500:** 0.13

DIVIDENDS PER SHARE (1998): $1.56

CANTV is a company burdened by over-regulation and its reputation for poor service, but it exists in a country with an insatiable demand for more and better telecommunications, and for that reason it could be a good growth investment. Venezuela has only 13 phone lines per 100 residents.

Deregulation of the phone industry has come slower in Venezuela than in most other Latin American countries. CANTV still holds a monopoly on fixed-line service and will continue to do so until November 2000, when one government-selected company will be allowed to compete with it.

SOURCE: BLOOMBERG L.P.

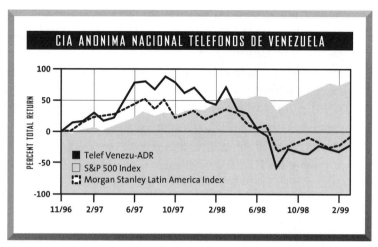

Until that time, growth in fixed-line telecommunications in Venezuela will be synonymous with growth in CANTV.

Of course, the sorry state of the Venezuelan economy in recent years hasn't left much room for optimism about economic growth. Like the country as a whole, CANTV needs to be better managed for the long term.

But CANTV has also seen growth in its other businesses, aside from fixed-line telephone service, especially in cellular phones. CANTV's cellular unit, Telecomunicaciones Movilnet SA, holds a 40 percent market share in a country that is limited by law to only two cellular phone companies, the other being TelCel Celular SA. The government passed legislation recently that would allow a third competitor to come in, and several foreign companies including British Telecom, BellSouth, Portugal Telecom, and Bell Canada International have expressed interest in bidding for the license. Even so, a market of just three companies isn't nearly as competitive as some of the others in Latin America, and CANTV should be able to hold onto a significant market share and to exploit some of the rapid growth in cellular phone demand. The government has estimated the number of cellular phone users will grow by 53 percent to at least 1.92 million by the end of 2000.

In addition, CANTV also provides paging services, public telephones, and an array of data transmission services.

Another reason for buying the stock is its low price to earnings ratio, the lowest among Latin America's major phone companies. CANTV is operated by an investment group, led by GTE Corp., which paid $1.89 billion in 1991 for a 40 percent stake in the company. Workers hold or have rights to 20 percent; 32 percent is publicly traded, and the government owns the remaining 8 percent.

◆ **Downside:** The biggest drawback is the Venezuelan economy, which until it gets some clear direction could limit CANTV's earnings and increase the risk that devaluations will hurt the price of the stock. Another drawback is over-regulation of the phone industry, which also crimps the earning power of CANTV, despite its monopoly. For example, the company continues to have trouble winning government approval for rate increases. Finally, labor is a big downside to CANTV. The company historically has had bad relations with unions, and a strike in 1996 virtually paralyzed it.

◆ **What to Look For:** Improvements in the Venezuelan economy, and economic reforms that will lead to long-term growth. Also watch for how the deregulation of the Venezuelan telecommunications industry pans out. News on all these issues is available on financial Web sites such as Bloomberg and Yahoo!.

MAVESA SA

U.S. TICKER: MAV
1 ADR = 60 ordinary shares
EXCHANGE: NYSE   **SECTOR:** Food
MARKET CAP.: $231 million
1998 EARNINGS (FISCAL YEAR ENDING OCTOBER 31, 1998): $5.4 million
FORECAST 1999 EPS: $0.26
   (4 analysts surveyed by First Call)
EARNINGS GROWTH (5-YEAR FORECAST): 20%
1998 SALES: $345 million   **P/E ON JANUARY 1, 1999:** 15.43
BOOK VALUE PER ADR: $2.66   **ROE:** 7%
BETA VS. S&P 500: 0.85   **CORRELATION WITH S&P 500:** 0.07
DIVIDENDS PER SHARE (1998): $0.086

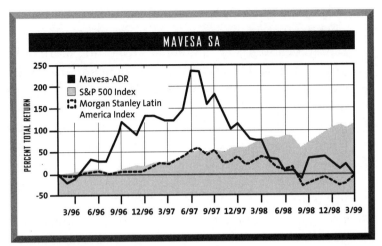

Like CANTV, Mavesa has been hurt by the Venezuelan economy. But, also like CANTV, there is little chance of Mavesa falling into bankruptcy as a result. It is one of the largest food processing companies in Venezuela, and it's doubtful that it would be allowed to go under.

Mavesa, moreover, is in the unique position of potentially benefiting rather than being hurt by a devaluation of the Venezuelan bolivar. Mavesa makes basic grocery items such as mayonnaise, margarine, cheese spreads, juice, vinegar, sauces, and soaps. It sells them under the names Mavesa, Nelly, Rikesa, La Torre Del Oro, and Las Llaves. Because its products are staples, its sales are usually not hurt during recessions. Everyone needs to eat, and everyone needs to wash clothes. On the other hand, when the value of the bolívar is high, as it was during the first half of 1998, the company's products are hurt by competition from lower-priced imports from Colombia and other countries.

One of Mavesa's key products, for example, is laundry soap. In Venezuela, most people don't own washing machines and still scrub their clothes by hand with bar soap. Mavesa's sales of bar soap declined dramatically in the first half of 1998 when the bolívar was highly valued compared with the Colombian currency, but when the reverse is true and Colombia's currency is overvalued,

Mavesa will not only have higher sales in Venezuela but will be able to sell more of its products in Colombia.

Mavesa also has been gradually exporting more of its products in an effort to reduce its dependency on the domestic economy. Between 1993 and 1997, exports tripled, although they still accounted for only about 6.3 percent of the company's sales. In 1998, the company also bought a seafood processing company, Inversiones Aledo, which exports heavily to other countries in the region.

◆ **Downside:** In addition to the added price competition that a strong bolívar brought in 1998, Mavesa saw its cost structure come under attack. The company's suppliers boosted prices for its raw materials, decreasing Mavesa's profit margins. Also, over time, imports are bound to eat away at Mavesa's market share.

◆ **What to Look For:** The most important thing to watch regarding Mavesa is the Venezuelan economy. Mavesa will do better when the economy is booming, but its earnings growth will be limited if the bolívar remains overvalued, especially relative to other currencies in the region such as that of Colombia. Watch for news of a devaluation of the currency. If the Venezuelan government enacts import controls to help fight off recession, Mavesa could gain in the short run, although in the long run it would suffer because it won't be able to import the capital goods and higher technology needed to make products that compete in price and quality with the products of other countries.

RESOURCES

ROBABLY THE KEY determinant of whether a portfolio beats or lags behind the market is the quality of the investor's information. Research is of special importance in picking Latin American stocks because reliable information is harderer to come by.

Says Fidelity Investments' investment guru Peter Lynch, "Buying what's hot without doing your research isn't investing. It's gambling."

Just ten years ago, it was nearly impossible for an individual U.S. investor to get detailed, meaningful, and timely data on Latin American companies. Now statistics and analysis are as close as your desktop computer, your mailbox, or your phone. However, the information is still not as complete as that on most Fortune 500 companies. Annual reports are not widely available through the SEC's on-line EDGAR database, as they are for U.S. companies, and many of the top financial Web sites provide information on Latin American companies only if they are listed on a U.S. exchange. Even then, the data tend to be less thorough than the data available on U.S. companies.

The following list combines favorite sources that I have used on the job as a business journalist over the past nine years with additional sites gathered from other journalistic and financial institutions.

Many sources cost something to use, even if it's only the monthly fee for on-line service and the ten-cent call to your local phone company. When you search for stocks and company information, bear in mind that a stock that costs you $101 a year in research expenses is worth $100 less than a stock that cost you a dollar to follow. For that reason, I have given preference to low-cost or free publications and Web sites. I have not included prices, because they change rapidly, but most of the Web sites I have listed charge no more than $30 a year, if they charge at all.

Some news sources are more reliable than their competitors; some rating agencies do a better job on certain types of securities; and some government agencies in some countries provide more accurate data than others. Judging what is and isn't reliable can be difficult. I've tried to exclude from the following lists the less dependable sources, but some of the sources I've included, such as on-line services with links to other sites, may route you to news or data sites that aren't tested. The best way to avoid losses from unreliable intelligence is to avoid buying or selling any asset based on information from only one source.

Also, if the information is from an analyst or someone else who is providing a personal opinion, consider whether there is any reason for that opinion to be biased. Many a Wall Street analyst will paint a rosy picture of a less-than-rosy company if the analyst's firm underwrites that company's bonds or represents it in some other way. The fine print at the end of an analyst's report will usually tell you if anything is at stake. Finally, be aware of the time span covered by the data you consider. Companies can, and often do, use data from a single quarter to illustrate what they describe as an upward trend in profits or sales, luring investors who six months later find out that that one profitable quarter was an anomaly amid a two-year decline in earnings.

ADR DEPOSITORIES

Bank of New York: One of the best sources available for information on Latin American ADRs. You can get company profiles, financial reports, and information on direct-purchase programs by calling 1-888-BNY-ADRS, or check out their Web site at www.bankofny.com/adr, which also has direct links to company sites.

Morgan Guaranty: Another of the big three depository institutions. Call 800-749-1687 for information on ADR programs and company financials, or see their Web site at www.adr.com.

Citibank: Call 877-CITI-ADR for information on ADRs deposited with Citibank, or visit their Web site at www.citibank.com/corpbank/adr.

WEB SITES

GENERAL

Yahoo!: the best gateway for information on U.S. companies, and equally good for researching most big Latin American companies and some smaller ones. Yahoo!'s own site, Yahoo! on the Money, provides a fairly good selection of news, company profiles, and stock information, and Yahoo's search engine will tell you where to look for more (www.yahoo.com).

From the main page, look for the "Business and Economy" subhead and then click on "companies." Enter a company ticker such as in the search box. The first page will list Web sites related to the company. If the company has its own Web site, you should be able to click directly to it. On the top of the page you'll see boxes for "Web pages" and "news stories," that you can click on to find more information on the company. Yahoo! also lets you customize a page of news stories on topics you are interested in, such as a specific company or region of the world. From the main Yahoo! page, click on "Personalize," then on the headlines bar, click on "Edit." Yahoo! will walk you through the rest.

America Online: The most widely used on-line service in the United States has an easy-to-use search engine for looking up company information by ticker. Look under "Personal Finance" (www.aol.com).

AltaVista: Another good search engine, known for its speed. Also good for foreign language reports, which are sometimes hard to get on Yahoo! and AOL (www.altavista.-digital.com).

Webcrawler: A simple to use, good search engine (www.webcrawler.com).

FINANCIAL

Bloomberg: A good, easy-to-use source for company news and financial information, with interactive capability that lets you run "what-if" scenarios and chart your investments over time. Better for big, NYSE-listed Latin American companies (www.bloomberg.com).

From the main Bloomberg page, type the ticker of a company in the search box on the upper left. That will take you to a page showing the current day's trading on the company. Click on the ticker symbol and you'll go to the company page, which has a description of the company, a price graph, news, and key data. All thirty-five companies listed in this book can be found on the Bloomberg Web site. For other useful information, the left-hand column of the Bloomberg Web page lists areas that you can look into for bonds, commodity futures, energy, currencies, and other topics. At the time this book went to press, Bloomberg was also experimenting with a new stock monitor function that lets you set up a list of several of your favorite stocks. Click on "portfolio tracker" in the left-and column to get to it.

Wall Street Research: Better known for its information on U.S. stocks, also includes some Latin American companies, with stock information and links to sites with news and other information (www.wsrn.com).

Hoovers: A top U.S. profiler of public and private companies now has information on many Latin American companies as well (www.hoovers.com).

Quicken: This personal finance site also has stock quotes, news, and some company information (www.quicken.com).

Wall Street Journal Interactive Edition: News and company profiles (www.wsj.com).

Business Week: Like the magazine, good for stories on the economy of Latin America and business trends (www.businessweek.com).

CNNfn: From the folks at CNN, a pretty good financial Web site for company news (www.cnnfn.com).

TheStreet.com: On-line market information is TheStreet.com's main business, and it's pretty good with company and stock information (www.thestreet.com).

Reuters: The world's largest financial news service distributes its news on several financial Web sites and also on its own sites. The main Reuters Web site is www.reuters.com, but it's big, difficult to maneuver, and designed mostly for financial professionals. For company news, it's easier to go directly to their company news site (www.moneynet.com).

Standard & Poor's and Moody's: These bond rating agencies' company reports are often as good or better than those of equity analysts (www.stockinfo.standardpoor.com).

New York Stock Exchange, American Stock Exchange, and Nasdaq: Data on the overall market and links to companies (www.nyse.com; www.amex.com; www.nasdaq.com).

Brokerages: Most major brokerage houses, including discount brokers, have their own Web sites that clients can log onto for company information, stock prices, etc. One of the best is Charles Schwab at www.schwab.com. Another good one is Merrill Lynch (www.askmerrill.com).

Morningstar: Great for mutual fund reports and much more (www.morningstar.com).

LATIN AMERICA—GENERAL AND FINANCIAL

At Americas: Information on the economy, industries, and some companies, including news (www.atamericas.com).

Latin World: A directory of resources for Latin America (www.latinworld.com).

Latin American Business Link: Information for Latin American investment buffs and anyone interested in Latin American business in general (http://LABL.com).

Inter-American Development Bank: Economic and trade data on Latin America (www.iadb.com).

World Business: News and company information, with links to other Latin American sites and to company home pages (www.bacoweb.com/worbus/).

World Bank: Economic snapshots on all the Latin American countries (www.worldbank.org/html/extdr/lac.htm).

Agenci Estado: A great site for Brazilian financila news in English (www.agestado.com/bfw/bfwire/index.htm).

Gazeta Mercantil: The top financial newspaper in Brazil has a Web site with English language news and company information in Portuguese (www.gazeta.com). **www.brazilinfo.net:** A good search engine for English language information Web sites about Brazil. **www.usbrazil.com/english/brazilinfo.html:** Another good Web site, with links to Brazilian company sites.

LATIN AMERICA: COMPANIES
Alfa: www.alfa.com.mx (English)
Aracruz: www.aracruz.com.br (English and Portuguese)
BanColombiano (BIC): www.bic.com.co (Spanish)
Brahma: www.brahma.com.br (English and Portuguese)
Buenaventura: www.buenaventura.com
Cemex: www.cemex.com (English and Spanish)
Cemig: www.cemig.com.br (English, Portuguese, and Spanish)
Cesp: www.cesp.com.br/iwelcome.htm (English, Portuguese, and Spanish)
Coke Femsa: www.femsa.com/cocacola.html
CSN: www.csn.com.br/index1.html (Portuguese)
CTC: www.ctc.cl
Disco: www.disco.com.ar (Spanish, some English)
Eletrobrás: www.eletrobras.gov.br (English and Portuguese)
Enersis: www.enersis.com
Gener: www.gener.com
ICA: www.ica.com.mx (Spanish)
IRSA: www.irsa.com (English)
Iusacell: www.iusacell.com.mx
Mavesa: www.mavesa.com.ve
Panamco: www.panamco.com (English)
Páo de Açúcar: www.grupopaodeacucar.com.br
Petrobrás: www.petrobras.com.brl (Portuguese)
Telebrás: www.telebras.gov.br (Portuguese)
Telecom (Argentina): www.telecom.com.ar (Spanish)
Telefónica de Argentina: www.telefonica.com.ar (Spanish)
Telesp: www.telesp.com.br (English and Portuguese)

Telmex: www.telmex.com.mx/telmex_n.htm (Spanish)
Unibanco: www.unibanco.com.br (English, Portuguese, and Spanish)
Vitro: www.vto.com
YPF: www.ypf.com.ar (English and Spanish)

SPANISH-LANGUAGE AND PORTUGUESE-LANGUAGE SITES

Starmedia: A good search engine for information on Latin America, with links to most top financial and company Web sites; in both Spanish and Portuguese (www.starmedia.com).

La Nación and Clarín: The two top Argentina newspapers (www.lanacion.com and www.clarin.com).

Globo: One of the top Brazilian newspapers. (www.oglobo.com.br).

El Diario and Estrategia: The main Chilean business newspapers. *El Diario*'s site is better: www.eldario.el and http://reuna.cl/estrategia/index.html.

El Espectador, El Tiempo, El Mundo and El Heraldo: The top Colombia newspapers. (www.elmundo.com; http://elespectador.com; http://eltiempo.com; http://elheraldo.com).

El Financiero: The top Mexican business daily (www.financiero.com).

El Comercio: One of Peru's top newspapers (http://elcomercioperu.com.pe).

El Nacional: One of Venezuela's top newspapers (www.elnacional.com).

BOOKS

GENERAL INVESTMENT BOOKS

The New Commonsense Guide to Mutual Funds, by Mary Rowland (Bloomberg Press, 1998; $19.95). A smart and, as the title says, commonsense look at how to invest in mutual funds. Rowland has been writing about mutual funds as a magazine columnist for years, and her point of view is right in line with that of the personal investor.

A Random Walk Down Wall Street, by Burton Malkiel (W.W. Norton & Co., 1996; $15.95). The classic book on investing in stocks and bonds, recommended by business school professors the world over. It takes the advanced theories used by Wall Street investment whizzes, throws out the useless ones, and simplifies the complicated ones. It also plays down the importance and credibility of some of the most celebrated investment theories.

The Intelligent Investor, by Benjamin Graham (Harper-Collins, 1997, $30). Another classic must-read on investing.

One Up on Wall Street, by Peter Lynch (Penguin USA, 1990, $12.95). A great look at how to beat the pros, by one of the top investment professionals of all time.

Investing in Small-Cap Stocks, Revised Edition, by Christopher Graja and Elizabeth Ungar (Bloomberg Press, 1999, $26.95). Written by two colleagues of mine at Bloomberg, this book tells you all you need to know about the art of investing in small-cap stocks. Small caps have a lot in common with Latin American stocks, and this book is both timely and easy to read.

Investment, by Zvi Bodie, Alex Kane, and Alan J. Markus (Irwin/McGraw-Hill, 1998, $95.20). Excellent textbook.

Hoover's Handbook of World Business (Hoover's, Inc., 1998). Profiles major companies around the globe, including those in several Latin American countries.

The Latino Guide to Personal Money Management, by Laura Castañeda and Laura Castellanos (Bloomberg Press, 1999, $16.95). If you're Latino, here is another book you should pick up. It's the ultimate guide to personal finance for Latinos, discussing picking a financial adviser, banking, insurance, investing, and estate planning.

EMERGING MARKET AND LATIN AMERICA BOOKS

Going Global With Equities, by Paul Melton (FT-Pitman Publishing, 1996, $50). This is one of my favorite books on emerging markets. Melton, an English journalist, writes articles pertaining to U.S. as well as European investors. He includes little on Latin America and Latin American stocks, however, and parts of the 1996 book have become dated.

Global Bargain Hunting, by Burton Malkiel and J.P. Mei (Simon & Schuster, 1998, $25). My other favorite emerging-market investment book. Malkiel and Mei largely ignore Latin America, focusing more on general emerging-market strategies, and on Asia.

On Emerging Markets, by Mark Mobius (FT-Pitman Publishing, 1996, $35). A good look into the mind of the dean of emerging-market investing.

PERIODICALS

The Wall Street Journal. The best daily newspaper for coverage of U.S. financial markets is also one of the best for news on foreign stocks, bonds, and mutual funds.

The Financial Times. Even better than the *Wall Street Journal* for covering Latin America on a daily basis, with more company news and timely economic and political news on the region. It's also the No. 1 source for news on Europe, and does a pretty good job of covering the U.S. markets.

Latin Finance. A monthly magazine devoted to everything you ever wanted to know about investing in Latin America, with good pull-out sections on the best companies.

Latin Trade. Also a monthly, with a trade and politics focus, but with an increasing amount of news on stocks and bonds.

Bloomberg Personal Finance. A monthly magazine filled with interviews with, and columns written by, top personal finance experts and investment gurus. It tackles many of the issues discussed in this book, including ADRs.

Money. The best-selling personal finance magazine in the country. It's basic and heavily focused on the United States, but almost every issue has some articles on international investing.

Morningstar Mutual Funds. More a book than a periodical, it contains up-to-date profiles on some 1,600 mutual funds. It's costly (twenty-four updates during the year cost $495 per year, U.S.; $585, Canada; $740, other countries), so look for it at your local library or ask your broker to show you the pages on the funds you're interested in.

INDEX

ABOUT BLOOMBERG

Bloomberg L.P., founded in 1981, is a global information services, news, and media company. Headquartered in New York, the company has nine sales offices, two data centers, and 80 news bureaus worldwide.

Bloomberg Financial Markets, serving customers in 100 countries around the world, holds a unique position within the financial services industry by providing an unparalleled combination of news, information, and analytic tools in a single package known as the BLOOMBERG® service.

BLOOMBERG NEWS℠, founded in 1990, offers worldwide coverage of economies, companies, industries, governments, financial markets, politics, and sports. The news service is the main content provider for Bloomberg's broadcast media, which include BLOOMBERG TELEVISION®— the 24-hour cable television network available in ten languages worldwide—and BLOOMBERG NEWS RADIO™—an international radio network anchored by flagship station BLOOMBERG NEWS RADIO AM 1130℠ in New York. BLOOMBERG NEWS has ten bureaus in Latin America, with additional editors and reporters in New York covering these key markets. Bloomberg also has a Latin America section on its Web site: **http://www.bloomberg.com/sa/sahome.html**.

In addition to the BLOOMBERG PRESS® line of books, Bloomberg publishes three magazines:

◆ *BLOOMBERG® MAGAZINE*, for market professionals subscribing to the BLOOMBERG® service
◆ *BLOOMBERG WEALTH MANAGER*™, for financial planners and advisers
◆ *BLOOMBERG PERSONAL FINANCE*™, for sophisticated individual investors. It provides information about financial markets and investment strategies with unique insights into the ways of Wall Street. Contact *BLOOMBERG PERSONAL FINANCE*™ by calling 888-432-5820; or online at www.bloomberg.com/personal.

ABOUT THE AUTHOR

Michael Molinski, emerging markets reporter at Bloomberg News in New York City, is a former Brazil bureau chief at Bloomberg L.P. and has written about Latin America for more than nine years. While he was senior Latin America correspondent, he also wrote the "Latin Markets" column, which appeared weekly in the *Miami Herald*. Fluent in both Spanish and Portuguese, he has interviewed CEOs of several Latin American blue chips for this book. Molinski holds an MBA in business economics from Columbia University and was a recipient of the prestigious Knight-Bagehot Fellowship for business journalists at Columbia.